Indebted

ISSUES OF GLOBALIZATION
Case Studies in Contemporary Anthropology
Series Editors: Carla Freeman and Li Zhang

Indebted

·······················

An Ethnography of Despair and Resilience in Greece's Second City

KATHRYN A. KOZAITIS

Georgia State University

New York   Oxford

OXFORD UNIVERSITY PRESS

Oxford University Press is a department of the University of Oxford.
It furthers the University's objective of excellence in research, scholarship,
and education by publishing worldwide. Oxford is a registered trade mark of
Oxford University Press in the UK and certain other countries.

Published in the United States of America by Oxford University Press
198 Madison Avenue, New York, NY 10016, United States of America.

For titles covered by Section 112 of the US Higher Education
Opportunity Act, please visit www.oup.com/us/he for the latest
information about pricing and alternate formats.

Library of Congress Cataloging-in-Publication Data

CIP data is on file at the Library of Congress
978-0-19-009014-2

Printing number: 9 8 7 6 5 4 3 2 1
Printed by LSC Communications, Inc., United States of America

Dedication
I dedicate this book to the memory of parents, Athanasios and Krystallo Kozaitis, and to that of my sister, Vassiliki Kozaitis Paliotheodoros.

CONTENTS

....

LIST OF ILLUSTRATIONS

....

ACKNOWLEDGMENTS

The privilege of every ethnographer is a heartfelt invitation to the field by her hosts. I am most thankful to the following friends who welcomed me to Thessaloniki, and who fostered my study through their commitment to its success: Diroui Galileas, Ioulia Kazana, Ioanna Lefaki, Aikaterini Grigoriadou, Miltiadis Zermpoulis, Loukia Hatziioannou, and Antonis Antoniadis.

For their kind reception during my year in the field, I thank my colleagues, Stelios Andreou, Georgios Agelopoulos, Aleksandra Bakalaki, and Nora Skouteri-Didhaskalou at Aristotle University of Thessaloniki, and Aigli Brouskou at the American College of Thessaloniki. I am grateful to the Center for Hellenic Studies at Georgia State University and the Fulbright US Scholar Program for partial funding of this research. My thanks also to colleagues at the Fulbright Foundation of Greece: Artemis Zenetou, Nicholas Tourides, and Tatiana Hadjiemmanuel in Athens, and Dimitrios Doutis in Thessaloniki.

I remain deeply obliged to the hundreds of Thessalonikians who shared with me their experience of the debt crisis. Their voices and activities during an era of harsh austerity illuminate the impact of a historic, global event on one urban community, and the resilience of the human spirit. I am beholden to all of them for their generosity, for facilitating my work, and for enriching my life during my time in Thessaloniki and beyond.

Sincerest appreciation for my dear colleagues and friends who read early drafts of the manuscript, and who offered invaluable feedback:

Peter Brown, Emanuela Guano, Fran Markowitz, Faidra Papavasiliou, and Louis A. Ruprecht Jr. I also thank Emmanouil Androulakis, Aikaterini Grigoriadou, Elias Lampropoulos, and Dimitri Shreckengost for their feedback and encouragement; Penelope Mavromara, for her moral support; Shelby Anderson-Badbade for her assistance with copyediting; and colleagues Marva Carter, Amanda Damarin, and Renee Schatteman, who reinforced my will to keep writing against competing demands.

I am grateful to Sherith Pankratz, Carla Freeman, and Li Zhang, who encouraged the development of this work from the outset. I also extend my appreciation to the reviewers for their critical reading of the manuscript and for their expert recommendations:

- H. Russell Bernard, Arizona State University
- Timothy P. Daniels, Hofstra University
- Michael Herzfeld, Harvard University
- Daniel M. Knight, University of St. Andrews
- Heather Levi, Temple University
- Terance L. Winemiller, Auburn University at Montgomery
- One anonymous reviewer

I give my thanks to Stanford Ullner of Stanford Ullner Fine Art Photography, Charleston, SC, for assisting with the preparation of my images for this publication, and to the editorial and production teams at Oxford University Press for turning the manuscript into a book: Olivia Clark, Patricia Berube, Anne Sanow, Stephanie Bacon, and Tony Mathias.

To my mentor, Conrad Phillip Kottak, I attribute my passion for anthropology as a way of seeing the world, and my approach to ethnography as a way of living within it. I am grateful for his integrity, his contributions to anthropology, and for his unwavering presence over the years that has inspired me and my life's work. I am also deeply indebted to him for his comprehensive editing of this book that enhances its lucidity.

To my cousin, Theodore D. Kamoutsis, I owe thanks for his companionship from afar, his empathy, and his sense of humor that tempered the isolation of writing. My beloved sons, Phillip A. K. Springer and Robert E. Springer IV, provided emotional sustenance during harried periods of this intellectual journey. I am grateful *for* them.

Global Drama, Greek Tragedy

Why Thessaloniki?

Thessaloniki chose me. I gave this answer in the summer of 2009 to all who, upon learning that I came from Atlanta to live and study Thessaloniki's changing cultural milieu, asked, "Why Thessaloniki?" Implicit in their inquiry was the question, "Why not Athens?" Local comparisons of Thessaloniki with Athens often privilege the latter, as do global market trends and political interests (Kamaras 2008). Within days of my visit to assess feasibility for long-term fieldwork in Greece's second city, I noted that my new friends there compared Thessaloniki to Athens with ever a tinge of ambivalence in their voice. The latter, after all, is the country's famous capital and the center of politics and commerce.

Dimitrios Economou, a professor of history, referred to an article by Nikolaos I. Mertzos (2009) titled "Athens: The Octopus," which likens the Greek capital to a giant, ravenous sea creature with its two eyes, hard beak, and eight far-reaching arms that collects and devours Thessaloniki's best and brightest. "Athens is a monster," Economou declared. "We lose all our intellectuals and entrepreneurs to Athens; it provides opportunities for our young people who are ambitious and talented. Here they find nothing."[1] Among Thessaloniki's enduring features Kourtesis cites its history and topography, and its sizable population of educated and professional residents who offer promise for Thessaloniki's integration into an international network of "creative" and "intelligent" cities (2008: 285–291).

1

However, Economou noted that the city lacks the institutional leadership and opportunity structures to support all those creative minds. Without catching his breath, he recalled Aristotle's notion that a great city is not to be confounded with a populous one,[2] and that Thessaloniki's reputation as Greece's "co-capital" deserves acknowledgment and pride.[3]

My new acquaintances shared with me more subjective comparisons of northern and southern Greece. Thessalonikians spoke of Athenians as "mechanically driven," and of Athens as "too large, alienating, and chaotic." Some young women compared their own "more feminine and dapper" disposition with the more "unkempt appearance" of Athenian women. Yet when they talked about visiting friends or relatives in Athens they were exhilarated about the experience, even as they complained about having to travel 502 kilometers to the city "for paperwork business." The quality of life among Thessalonikians is "the envy of Greece," explained one of my hosts, because Thessaloniki is a more

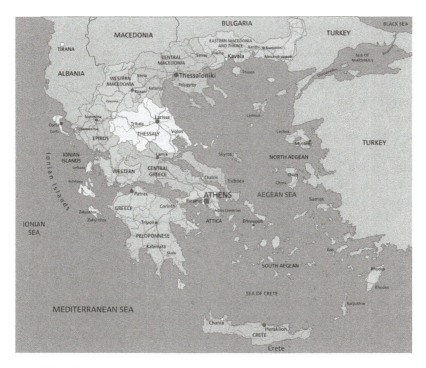

MAP 1 **Map of Greece.**
Source: Shutterstock/Bardocz Peter.

accessible city than Athens. "Thessalonikians are urbane and cosmopolitan, yet we maintain close ties with family such as those associated with life in our ancestral villages," he declared. These romantic notions of Thessaloniki stayed with me in 2011 when I chose the city to document how middle-class Greeks were coping with the worst financial crisis in the history of the grand experiment known as the European Union.

Having lived and worked in Athens in the late 1980s, two decades later I sought ethnographic knowledge of the country's cultural capital, whose history, myth, and civilizations had captured my imagination. Relatives in Athens questioned my choice to work in Thessaloniki instead of "the ancient European capital," while they referred to Thessaloniki as a Balkan, oriental region. Some Athenians mimicked what they called a "thicker" Thessalonikian dialect among a people who "are by nature more flexible," and whose temperament is "naturally more relaxed" (*halara*). Others pointed to the "more liberal" or "progressive" climate of the capital, compared with the more "eastern" or, for a few, more "backward" orientation of Thessaloniki. Indeed, as a child I learned to conflate Greece with Athens—the mecca of progressive thought, art, and politics, and the inventor of democracy to the world. Athens was also the primary destination of migrants from Thebes, including my relatives, who escaped the dire conditions of post-World War II and a dismal agrarian economy in the 1950s and 1960s.[4]

During the two months in which I identified the community that would become my ethnographic field site, my hosts boasted about the city's archaeological sites, such as Toumba, and civilizations, its ethos of valuing education (*pedhia*) above all other human endeavors, and its support of the fine arts. However, locals depicted the city's current infrastructure as problematic. Architects and engineers critiqued the spatial configuration of the city's periphery and complained about the clusters of visually offensive multistory apartment buildings in the city center. Erik Swyngedouw contrasts the city's vibrant cosmopolitan, political, economic, and cultural significance during the Ottoman Empire—when Salonica was second only to Constantinople—with the contemporary city as one bereft of economic and political elites, and "more as a pathetic spectator than an active participant, full of challenges and contradictions" (2008: 71). And yet while locals complained about the current limitations to Thessaloniki's economic viability, their collective opinion of their city was resolutely favorable.

MAP 2 **Area map of Thessaloniki.**
Source: Shutterstock/spatuletail.

The Auto-ethnography in This Ethnography

The driving force that led me to Thessaloniki as a research site was rooted in anthropological questions that guided my intellectual and personal quest. Social scientific inquiries are invariably autobiographic, and often auto-ethnographic, and my work in Thessaloniki is no exception. My earliest associations with this city come from lessons that Nikolaos I. Kozaitis, my paternal, parallel-cousin and first tutor, taught me when I was still in elementary school. He exposed me to Aristotle's ethics and poetics through dialogues that inspired me to link philosophical and aesthetic principles with my observations of village life. His teachings of Aristotle, and stories of his student, Alexander the Great, also introduced me to Thessaloniki, a part of Greece that at the time seemed distant, exotic, and mythical. Tutorials on classical Greek thought continued through my correspondence with Niko after I immigrated with my parents from Thisvi, a small village in the Boiotian region of Greece, directly to Detroit as an impressionable eleven-year-old middle school student.

While I was immersed in learning English as a second language and adapting to Detroit's public school system, I indulged nostalgically in aspects of popular Greek culture, particularly film and music. Songs that depicted Thessaloniki as *beautiful,* a *lover, beloved homeland, mother of the poor, noble woman, first heartbeat, heart's pride,* and *sorceress,* among many other sentimental and romantic references, further piqued my coming-of-age curiosity about this unfamiliar place.[5] Such images, combined with accounts of Aristotle's and Alexander's legacies, intensified for me the city's mystique, as part of what some acquaintances still call, misguidedly, "the other Greece."

My curiosity about northern Greece, and Thessaloniki in particular, increased through formal education. Reading Aristotle in my courses on Western Civilization cultivated in me a deep intellectual orientation toward empirical understanding of all things human. Studies of Aristotle in college also stirred in me a wish to visit the ancient remains of Stagira, his birthplace, and his school at Esvoria of Naoussa where he taught ethics and politics. I did so in 1985, when I finally visited Thessaloniki seeking a field site to conduct my dissertation research with Greek Roma (Gypsies). On that trip I learned a great deal more about the city—its archaeology, history, and anthropology. I noted its architecture, archaeological sites, and museum exhibits of peoples and times past. The colorful, textured, and accessible milieu of its historic city center impressed me, as did the congenial interactions I observed among its people. The sea, with its promenade on one side and Mt. Olympus in the background, left me breathless. Ultimately my doctoral research focused on the Roma of Athens, a community of sedentary, urbanized descendants of refugees from Turkey during the 1922 exchange of Christian and Muslim populations.[6] However, Thessaloniki remained a destination where I hoped that years later I would return to study and to live.

Indeed, nearly two decades later, and in anticipation of a year-long field ethnography, I returned to Thessaloniki in 2006 to present a research paper at the meetings of the International Cultural Research Network hosted by Aristotle University. During that visit I stayed at the Hotel ABC, located on Sintrivaniou (Fountain) Square (see Fig. P.1), at the junction of Ethnikis Aminis and Egnatias Avenues, a landmark structure that would accommodate me unannounced five years later when I found myself stranded upon arrival in the field. Surrounding the hotel is Aristotle University, with a view of the upper town in the distance, along with such architectural, historical, and aesthetic treasures as the Palace and Arch of Galerius, the White Tower, and the grounds of the annual Helexpo International Trade Fair. As it had nine years earlier, Thessaloniki attracted me viscerally and intellectually. I found the city

FIGURE P.1 Sintrivaniou (fountain) Square with view of upper town.
Source: Photo by Kathryn Kozaitis.

to be an extraordinary sociocultural specimen of urban life demanding the attention of ethnographic curiosity and reflection.

Its urban landscape appealed to my sensibilities for living and working in a "modern regional metropolis" where past and present, nature and culture, Greece and the world intersect to form not "another Greece," but a contemporary, globally embedded Greece (Inda and Rosaldo 2008; Hastaoglou-Martinidis 1998: 494). An affinity for the city's visible features, and those I had yet to discover through systematic research, compelled me to pursue it as an ethnographic destination. The fact that Thessaloniki was relatively foreign to me, and where neither relatives nor friends resided to distract me from my work, appealed to my ethnographic sensibilities, principally my desire to examine the unfamiliar. Meanwhile, with each visit, the demystification of the city increased. My review of popular and academic literature on the region's and the city's history accelerated this process (Vacalopoulos 1972). Predictably, while the mythical and mythologized impressions of this land diminished in importance, my intellectual curiosity rose rapidly, and my ethnographic commitment to work with its residents crystalized.

Preliminary Research

In the summer of 2009 I returned to Thessaloniki to conduct a two-month exploratory study on the socioeconomic integration (Hatziprokopiou 2006) of immigrants, specifically Albanians, and to read whatever Greek and non-Greek authors had written about this topic, including compelling historical novels that I found at the local bookstores and libraries. The primary concern among the Greeks with whom I spoke at the time was the influx of thousands of economic and undocumented immigrants who had flooded the city following the collapse of the Soviet Union in 1989 (Appadurai 2006). Locals' preoccupation with the changes that the fall of communism had imposed on the city's demographic and sociocultural profile was potent two decades later.

The increasing presence of new minorities, including undocumented immigrants and refugees from Bangladesh, China, West Africa, and Afghanistan, worried locals. Some opined that "a normal integration" into Greek society of these foreigners (*kseni*) was neither feasible nor desirable. At the time I considered that given locals' preoccupation with demographic shifts and perceived cultural decline, an ethnographic social impact assessment study would be anthropologically compelling and practically useful. My interests in ethnicity and refugee studies, and my previous work with Roma in Athens on state–minority relations, had prepared me well for a new project on questions of global-local articulations of change and transnational identities (Kozaitis 1997; 2002).

I spent the better part of each week in the summer of 2009 with colleagues and scoped out the prospects for long-term fieldwork. New acquaintances invited me to coffee and meals, and introduced me to their friends and relatives who ultimately became key cultural consultants. At the recommendation of a new friend, I studied the city's second Biennale of contemporary art, the theme of which was, as if by premonition of the fiscal disaster in the wings, "Praxis: Art in Times of Uncertainty." The organizers of the second Biennale acknowledged its artists' efforts "to question the impasse created by contemporary crisis and redefine the meaning of artistic action." Each day, with camera and audio recorder in hand, I documented visual markers of local culture, including sculptures, banners, and graffiti on the walls of public and private property, and warehouses on the port turned into venues for visual art—the Bazaar Hammam, the Bey Hammam, and the Bezesteni Market, locales now designated as sites of artistic expression.

Public spaces conducive to participant observation (e.g., parks, public squares, and markets), and sites for unobtrusive observation (e.g., churches, art exhibits, and street protests), were easily accessible (see Fig P.2). For hours I walked the city's streets and neighborhoods, visited its museums, and asked questions of locals not as a tourist this time, but as a social scientist. During this period, while I conceptualized a year-long field study and drafted a research proposal, I became more familiar with Thessaloniki's neighborhoods and its residents. The city impressed me as less inviting than it had in previous visits. I found its public spaces congested, busy, polluted, and overpopulated. Markers of a neglected cityscape, crowded neighborhoods, and an ethnically and linguistically diverse populace alerted me to global conditions that had influenced local demographic changes from my first visit twenty-four years earlier. On an evening walk at the seafront, I lost count of how many familiar and unfamiliar languages, dialects, and accents I heard my fellow strollers speak. Other markers of cultural diversity abounded, including international music, styles of dress, foods, and symbols. Phenotypes from faraway lands punctuated what might have been any promenade, in any European city.

FIGURE P.2 City Center and anti-austerity protest.
Source: Photo by Conrad Phillip Kottak.

As a prospective repatriate who romanticized a kind of a hero's return home, with wisdom I had accumulated during a forty-year sojourn abroad, I grieved the apparent loss of the Greece I longed to have waiting for me. And yet I, the anthropologist, uttered unconsciously this to a friend on the telephone: "I am in my life, and my life's work now is in Thessaloniki." My new interlocutors embraced me as a native of Greece and as a scholar from the United States. I became acquainted with several residents who integrated me into their social and professional networks, and who encouraged me to continue my work in their city. I left Thessaloniki in August 2009 convinced that a long-term ethnography on the socioeconomic integration of Albanian immigrants was feasible. I kept my promise to return in 2011, and my new friends kept theirs to host me.

Alas, by December 2009 an even more demanding problem was consuming Greeks, including Thessalonikians: the fiscal collapse of their globally linked nation-state, and the consequences of this calamity for their everyday lives. The global recession of 2007–2008 fueled Greece's fiscal crash, upended its political system, and subjected its population to harsh austerity measures that led to the loss of household income and property, and a decline in education and public health (Doxiadis and Placas 2018).[7] In early 2010 immigrants were no longer my interlocutors' primary concern, as many began to leave the country. The sharp downturn of the Greek state economy was the most compelling and urgent crisis that Greeks confronted; it merited empirical and theoretical analysis. Poised already to launch an ethnographic study in Thessaloniki, I had only to alter the focus of my research. The new topic would be an emergent fiscal "disaster" that had shifted locals' attention away from the displaced "foreigners" in their midst, to their own vulnerability as Greece's new "refugees from the middle class" (Newman 1999), and the potential of becoming economic emigrants themselves.

"Middle-class," as an analytical category, encompasses *economic indicators*, such as household income and material resources, and *sociocultural factors*, including ideologies, tastes, practices, and aspirations (Bourdieu 1984). At the height of the debt crisis, material wealth was declining across the structural hierarchy of these middle-class urbanites. Yet all study participants referenced "middle-class" as a more nuanced defining attribute of self, meaning, and community (Patico 2008; Heiman, Liechty, and Freeman 2012; Freeman 2014; Guano 2017). While they acknowledged a universal decline in material wealth, they situated themselves in a spectrum of middle-class status by emphasizing their educational level, professional credentials, values, and precrash styles and tastes of consumption and leisure (Marsh and Li 2016). Indeed, and as we will see, articulation and promotion of immaterial middle-class sensibilities and actions, including moral responsibility, civic duty, respectability, self-sufficiency, and humanistic pursuits among all participants, rose even as a near fiscal collapse threatened their household (Freeman 2007).

Technological revolutions, wars, economic depressions, and po-litical upheavals destabilize societies and fuel sociocultural crises. Such historical and political–economic antecedents in turn invite the atten-tion of scholars, and give rise to theories of social change as a process that generates emotions, deliberations, and actions by elite and ordinary citizens, who often become agents of recovery and renewal. This concep-tual framework informs my analysis of daily life among a community of self-identified middle-class Thessalonikians in the aftermath of the eu-rozone debt crisis. In this work I examine the intersections of the global recession, the national economy, and local citizens' lived experience—the ideational, emotional, cultural, and structural changes—that con-stitute the so called Greek crisis. Thessaloniki, for all the reasons I have outlined here, and as a city that scholars have depicted as "a series of changes," remained a salient site for the study of local sociocultural transformations linked, as they are, to global financial markets and structures of power (Kafkalas, Labrianidis, and Papamihos 2008).

The Makings of a Real Greek Tragedy

Since the onset of the eurozone crash, journalists, Greek officials, my friends and relatives, and prospective study participants spoke of the "tragedy" that had befallen Greece, and the "tragic circumstances" (*traghikes katastasis*) in which Greeks unexpectedly found themselves. Tragedy as trope for crisis brought to my mind Aristotle's theorization of tragedy as more philosophical and as a form of literary art. The tragedy occasioned by the debt crisis was neither art nor an imitation of reality, but human life in turmoil and in real time. As I prepared for anticipated fieldwork in Thessaloniki in the following year, I wondered: Within this Greek tragedy, might there be a plot to look for, characters to under-stand, narratives to record, a rhythm to private struggles and public per-formances, a spectacle to be observed, and a transformation to witness?

I knew that a study of Thessaloniki in crisis could not mirror the structure of a play, with a clear beginning, middle, and end. I would be observing and participating in a historical human drama whose denouement was neither written nor preordained. Nevertheless, temporality (antecedents, multilateral processes, and consequences) would have to inform my conceptual understanding of the crisis and my empirical investigation of local life in times of austerity (Knight and Stewart 2016). To that end, I examined factors that preceded the onset of the debt crisis, as well as its possible outcomes. Still an ocean away from Thessaloniki, I began to examine the Greek crisis not as the event by popular discourses and media accounts, but as a process of sociocultural changes and continuities following an unanticipated political–economic shock. Might the crisis be understood as an "uncanny present," an in-between phase of temporal experiences that fuel sociocultural transformation (Bryant 2016)? As such, Greece in crisis was no longer the Greece that had preceded the eurozone collapse, nor could the current state precisely foretell the country that might one day recover from it.

Analysis of real-world tragedies demands consideration of antecedents—conditions and characters that preceded and influenced the cataclysmic development. I could trace the onset of this economic downturn to events that followed the collapse of the ruling military junta in 1974, and the restoration of democracy by exiled center-right Prime Minister Constantinos Karmalis. In 1981, Andreas Papandreou's Socialist Party (PASOK) won elections, and Greece gained membership in the European Economic Community (EEC), a free common market that preceded the establishment of the European Union. The signing of the Treaty of Maastricht by leaders from Germany, France, Portugal, and the Netherlands affirmed a shared foreign policy and judicial cooperation between these European countries. Central to the subsequent construction of the Economic and Monetary Union (EMU) was fiscal convergence and the birth of the euro as a single currency for eleven EU countries in 1999.

Greece—with inflation below 1.5 percent, a budget deficit below 3 percent, and a debt-to-GDP ratio below 60 percent at the time—did not meet the criteria of state membership in the eurozone. However, its leaders, with the support of Goldman Sachs investment bankers and complicity on the part of EU elites, concealed the country's financial status, and in 2001 ensured Greece's inclusion in the eurozone. Proud of its global visibility as a eurozone member and host of the 2004 Olympic Games, Greece relied on loans to fund the events. This strategy exposed

MAP 3 **Map of the European Union.**
Source: Shutterstock/Paul Stringer.

the vulnerability of the Greek state economy, and a rising deficit (6.1 percent) and debt-to-GDP ratio (110.6 percent) subjected Greece to fiscal monitoring by the European Commission in 2005.

Greece's financial troubles were not unique. As factors implicated in the Greek economic collapse, I considered the market crash of the housing bubble in the United States (2007–2008), the worldwide recession that ensued, and the global credit crisis that engulfed the historically marginalized Mediterranean nation-states, including Portugal, Italy, Ireland, Greece, and Spain (derisively known as the PIIGS) (Matsaganis and Leventi 2014). A global banking crisis, marked by the collapse of Lehman Brothers and prompting government bailouts of international banks, crushed millions of American families and households across southern Europe, and catapulted a fragile Greek state economy to the brink of disaster. These conditions, I pondered, certainly led to Greece's predicament.

Aristotle's tragic plot structure features a hero of considerable magnitude, whose fatal flaw precipitates his inevitable, but unanticipated, reversal of fortune. Greece's real-world tragedy exposes its government as the flawed character that led the nation into decline. From a distance I perceived the Greek state as a kind of tragic hero in crisis, whose *hamartia* (sin) precipitated its fiscal and moral fall. As global financing ceased, Greece's financial debt grew, inviting the privatization of assets, including the Port of Piraeus in 2008. Elections in 2009 put into office George Papandreou, the son of Andreas Papandreou, reinstituting the socialist PASOK administration. Papandreou's public admission of prior corruption (*dhiaphthora*), coupled with the one-year anniversary of the killing of a teenager in Athens by police, which fueled the 2008 Greek riots, marked the onset of the Greek economic crisis. Greece's historical subjugation by external powers, its inequitable partnership with stronger European core economies, progressively deeper integration into world markets, and the 2008 recession helped me understand the vulnerability of the Greek state economy to a series of events that invited its near fiscal and moral collapse.

Evidence that Greek officials, in their determination to join the eurozone, had been misrepresenting the state's debt levels and budget deficits since 2001, and questions by Eurostat resources about the Greek state's accountability in the years preceding the crash, alerted me to the fact that the Greek state's financial downturn was inevitable. A year into the debt crisis, Greece's state officials and eurozone leaders were negotiating bailouts from the European Commission (EC), the International Monetary Fund (IMF), and the European Central Bank (ECB), known as "the troika." Credit-rating agencies downgraded Greece's debt to junk bond status, threatening a sovereign default, while creditors agreed to a 53.5 percent reduction of their debt. Thirty years of unprecedented prosperity among Greeks ended, seemingly overnight, and an era of acute adversity descended upon the Greek masses.

Greece instantly became the butt of international—albeit uncritical—ridicule and blame. Negative stereotypes, including the erroneous labeling of Greeks as greedy, lazy, and undisciplined, proliferated. Such moral accusations by Northern European elites of Greeks today reflect the West's reverence of ancient Greece and its exploitative relationship with an economically and politically dependent nation-state since its inception as a republic in 1832. For their part, Greeks floundered in a sea of confusion, rage, and guilt. Greece's precarious position provoked emotional responses the world over, including pity for the country's misfortune, and fear that the Greek state's downward spiral would not only destroy Greek society, but that it threatened the future of the euro and the stability of the entire eurozone.

In his depiction of tragedy Aristotle highlights the middle, a peak or climax in the work during which a reversal of fortune occurs, either from bad to good or from good to bad. Barely two years into the crisis Greeks declared the fiscal meltdown a tragedy from which they might not recover. Journalists' accounts of a nation in despair, and individuals' private testimonials that Greece was at risk of obliteration, prompted its citizens to question social institutions and cultural patterns that may have contributed to its decline. Throughout 2010, friends and relatives in Greece called me with updates on the crisis, determined to prepare me for my study of a society that the recession was damaging and whose moral fabric was in shreds. My contacts in Thessaloniki warned me that families, including their own, were facing the "the bottom of the barrel," and that an anticipated destruction of the nation was paralyzing them with anxiety and panic attacks.

The message from prospective study participants who phoned and wrote to me while I was still in Atlanta was that despair among them was escalating, and that a rapid downward plunge scared some to the point of mental and physical illness or suicide, propelled several to flee Greece, and left others to contemplate collective, constructive actions toward recovery. The stories about citizens' experience of the fiscal meltdown did indeed signal a reversal of fortune: a shift in the nation's economic course from prosperity to precarity that brought the country to its knees. A key question for my research became: Might such an economic crash generate a new critical consciousness and a call to resourceful action among a people devastated by loss?

From the onset, Greeks referred to their lived experience of sudden downward mobility as an economic and a moral crisis. In the popular imagination, their fall from grace signified not only loss of social security, but also a loss of national dignity. I hypothesized that the unsettling events that followed in the aftermath of the 2009 fiscal collapse would likely advance a process of transitions that might alter Greece's destiny from what at the time appeared to be bleak at best, to one of sustainability. If the crisis proved to be the catalyst for Greece's reversal of destiny, I pondered, indicators of resolution would emerge. The societal disorganization and chaos in which Greeks found themselves would likely stir in them an inclination to purge themselves of previous policies and patterns of behavior that led them to the near collapse of their society. They would adopt instead alternative, adaptive ways of life to increase the likelihood of survival. Moreover, recalling Aristotle's plot of tragedy, a shift away from a chaotic present to a brighter future might coincide with a collective *catharsis*—conscious and unconscious cleansing of debilitating emotional and cognitive states. After a financial decline and moral crisis, could healing emerge? Might sentiments such as hope, courage, and determination replace regret, guilt, and shame? Through the crisis, might a community of self-conscious and resourceful social reformers emerge?

Aristotle's concept of tragedy ends with the tragic hero's discovery of his own flaw: acknowledgment of accountability for the misfortune, denouement, and catharsis. Of course a real-life tragedy, actual or imagined, invariably leads to intended and unintended outcomes for all those who survive it. If their common drama raises participants' sense of self and nation, and if awareness of a crisis leads to catharsis, then human agency and civic engagement directed at sociocultural renewal and revitalization may be inevitable. Anthropological theories of social change and continuity, and my previous research among local communities subjected to geopolitical disruptions, had taught me as much. To be sure, Aristotle's structural plot of tragedy, as a form of literary and performing art, served only as a tentative lens through which I, still months away from onsite research, sought to make sense of the so-called tragedy in which Greeks claimed to have found themselves in 2009, and which continues to affect them in 2019. The extent to which my from-a-distance provisional conceptualization might prove valid would depend on a year-long systematic field study in Thessaloniki in 2011–2012, and follow-up ethnographic documentations of a Greece in transition.

Notes

1. Even before the economic downturn, few educated Thessalonikians were able to secure a position in their field strictly on merit. They typically found employment through political, economic, and social connections.
2. My interlocutors often quoted ancient Greek thinkers to emphasize their stance on a current issue or problem.
3. See Kafkalas, Labrianides, and Papamihos (2008) for a comprehensive analysis of contemporary Thessaloniki. It is known as the "co-capital"

(*symprotevousa*) of Greece. During the Eastern Roman Byzantine Empire, it held the title "co-reigning city" (*symvasilevousa*), along with Constantinople (present-day Istanbul, in Turkey).

4. Thebes (*Thiva*), of archaeological, historical, and mythical significance, is a small city in Boeotia, central Greece, and the closest urban center to a number of villages, including Thisvi.

5. I am grateful to Vassiliki Katsanikou for her research on songs about Thessaloniki that depict the city as metaphor for various forms of love, attachment, longing, and commitment.

6. The Roma (Gypsies) of Athens, with whom I worked in 1987–1989, were descendants of refugees from Turkey to Greece, following the Turkish War of Independence (1919–1922) and the Treaty and Convention of Lausanne (1923). Some of the Greeks in Thessaloniki who participated in the current ethnography are also descendants of the same "Greek catastrophe." See Hirschon (1998).

7. See Goldstein (2017) for an account of the 2008 Great Recession and its impact on the daily life of middle-class workers following the closure of a General Motors plant in Wisconsin.

CHAPTER 1

Crisis of Debt and Dignity

By 2011 austerity measures, structural reforms, and privatization of state-owned assets had catapulted Greece to the epicenter of a global financial calamity. The situation in which I found my hosts three years into the Great Recession of 2008 impressed me as a period of *societal liminality*—a nation-state in transition at a time and place during which a pastiche of oscillating emotions, stimulating calculations, and revitalizing actions characterized citizens whose lives were in limbo. I argue that societal crises must be understood as abrupt, often unanticipated changes in relatively stable socioeconomic conditions, and shifts in people's internalized and unquestioned dispositions regarding their social reality. The disruption may lead to diminished function of defined structures, malaise among individuals, loss of customs and, tragically, life itself. However, a societal crisis may also be a catalyst to abandon destructive elements in social structures, revitalize social institutions, and create more sustainable living conditions and cultural patterns. In this chapter I outline a theory of crisis as a period and a process of sociocultural changes, and describe the ethnographic research design on which I base my interpretations. My context of analysis acknowledges the intersections of national, regional, and global structures of power within which the study community is embedded. A brief account of Thessaloniki's transitions since its annexation into Greece in 1912 sets the tone for locals' response to the city's current changes, embedded in a nation-state vulnerable to the privileges and constraints that European integration, eurozone membership, and global markets reinforce.

Thessaloniki's New Battle

Emblematic of a people in crisis were the sights and sounds that welcomed me to Thessaloniki in the summer of 2011, this time for a year-long stay. After thirty-two hours en route from Atlanta through Rome, I landed in Thessaloniki on August 20, 2011, at 1:00 a.m., without my four pieces of luggage. They arrived intact the following day, after a detour to Venizelos Airport in Athens. Due to delays in Rome, I landed hours after the staff at Aristotle University's hostel had expected me; they had left and locked the building behind them. I was alone, and no one else was waiting for me. The exception, I decided, might be a desk clerk at a hotel with which I was familiar from previous visits. "Kendro— Hotel ABC," I directed my cab driver, who fled the airport as if he were a suspect in a car chase. Whether or not I intended to study the crisis, from the moment I arrived in Thessaloniki in 2011, this local concern engulfed me in every conversation. Fieldwork began instantaneously.

The fifty-three-year-old irritable cabbie began his litany on the country's economic collapse. "We are going from bad to worse. There is no light . . . we can't see where we are going." He lamented the drastic reduction in the demand for cabs and pointed to the empty streets and barred windows as indicators of a devastating recession. He condemned the Troika as a corrupt triumvirate. He labeled then-Prime Minister George Papandreou an unpatriotic ass and a criminal. Likening the Greek state to an irresponsible father, he complained about austerity policies and the swindlers in parliament who enforce them. He said: "I have two children, a daughter, seventeen, and a son, twelve. I tell my daughter, 'Leave, my child, leave and go abroad to be rescued. Here you will die [*Phighe sto eksoteriko na ghlitosis. Edho tha pethanis*].'" Assuming I was a native, he continued,

> You may be old enough to remember how we grew up—the times when parents told their children, "Stay here next to me so that you can give me a glass of water [care for me] when I am old." Those days are long gone. I hope my children can leave me . . . to survive. We are Greek. Do we want our children to be away from us? Of course not! But for her own good, I tell my daughter to leave us so that she may be saved. Here she will go hungry [*etho tha pinasi*].[1]

This father of two teenagers worried more about the safety of his children and the security of his livelihood than the predicament of his country. Without warning, as he saw it, Greeks had become victims of a state in fiscal collapse, and yet another foreign occupation was holding Greece hostage. "Let this misfortune become a lesson to us," he added. This man's complex and poignant perspective on the effects of the recession on families foreshadowed the opinions of hundreds of middle-class Thessalonikians I came to know in the months that followed. Their concerns reflected their former financial security as Greeks as well as the qualitative nuances of their identity as upwardly mobile urbanites dependent on the city's economy.[2]

In fact, the metropolitan centers of southern Europe suffered the most acute effects of the debt crisis. Urbanites and government employees are particularly vulnerable to global political and economic shifts (Ranci 2014). Thessaloniki's professional class is no exception. Yet urbanites also have been the constituents of—and often accomplices to—laissez-faire policymakers and demands of landers and administrators. City-dwellers have been prime beneficiaries of EU policies aimed at urban development, service-sector employment, and the tourism, construction, and real estate industries. Like their European counterparts, Thessalonikians rely on urban institutions for their livelihood, social security, and quality of life (Eckardt and Sanchez 2015). Following the eurozone collapse, villagers across Mediterranean Europe turned to the land and sea for survival, and islanders attempted to get by on a weakened tourist industry to endure their revenue losses. Loss of jobs linked to health, education, and welfare, and decreased demand for private industries and low-skilled services, subjected urbanites to an abrupt decline in their living standards.

The city that on October 26, 1912 was incorporated as a territory of the modern Greek state has a 2,300-year history as a cosmopolis under various regimes, occupations, and reconstructions.[3] Today, Thessaloniki is distinguished from other Greek cities by the following historical and geopolitical features: it has been a multinational, multireligious, and multilinguistic milieu since its founding in 315 B.C. During the Roman, Byzantine, and Ottoman Empires, it was a prominent center standing at the crossroads of East and West (Vacalopoulos 1972). The city's historical, ethno-national profile that precedes its Hellenization at the turn of the twentieth century, and its geographic location in the Balkans, inform locals' identity as one steeped in cultural trauma and

conquest (Alexander, Eyerman, Giesen et al. 2004). Strategic constructions of heterogeneous and multicultural identities are as evident in the
city's architectural styles and cuisine, as in the narratives that Thessalonikians share with one another, and those they perform for tourists
and global consumers of the city's heritage (Tzanelli 2011; 2012).

Thessaloniki celebrates its independence from the Ottomans every
autumn during the annual Dimitria, a festival of the fine arts and other
cultural events.[4] No crisis interferes with this set of rituals and ceremo-
nies. As my hosts demonstrated, even while they struggled financially,
autumn 2011 was no exception. The city abounded with visual and performing arts that lifted the spirits of an otherwise anxious people determined to celebrate even as threats of a fiscally difficult winter loomed
large. With a metropolitan population of 1,104,460 people at the time,
including 790,824 in its urban center, Thessaloniki may be "a city of
ghosts" (Mazower 2006), but it is also one bustling with life. It is better
seen as "a city on the edge," constructed through a series of catastrophes
and recoveries that, as depicted in figure 1.1, 2012 marked its centennial

FIGURE 1.1 Thessaloniki 1912–2012 Centennial, "We Celebrate We Participate We Look
Forward."
Source: Photo by Kathryn Kozaitis.

as the co-capital of Greece (*sibrotevousa*) (Kafkalas, Lambrianithis, and Papamihos 2008).

During its one hundred-plus years as part of modern Greece, Thessaloniki has confronted a series of critical junctures that have shaped its trajectory and fueled its development. These include five wars and one further tragedy in the span of thirty-seven years. World War I (1914–1918) disrupted early efforts to rebuild a Greek Thessaloniki on the ashes of the Balkan Wars (1912–1913). The Greco-Turkish War (1919–1922) led to the exodus of 500,000 Muslims from the Macedonian region to Turkey and the arrival of 1.5 million Greek Christian refugees, thousands of whom settled on the periphery of Thessaloniki (Hirschon 1998). Most potent in locals' historical consciousness and social memory (Knight 2015a; 2012a) is the 1923 compulsory exchange of Christian and Muslim populations between Greece and Turkey that most of my research participants recalled as a historical milestone in the making of modern Greece. Others spoke of it as a momentous, course-altering event that has shaped Thessaloniki ever sense. For some, it was a catastrophe that remains part of family lore and an expression of a common past and identity. This exchange forever altered the face of Thessaloniki and its coastal region where hundreds of thousands of desperate refugees settled.

World War II (1939–1945) destroyed the city's economic foundation and again altered its sociocultural composition through the extermination of nearly 51,000 of Thessaloniki's Jews, the most tragic population loss ever to strike the city.[5] The Greek Civil War (1946–1949), which pitted the Greek government army against the military of the Greek Communist Party (KKE), polarized the country politically and further weakened it demographically (Panourgia 2009). Thessalonikians referenced these wars as catastrophes that destroyed their city and annihilated its population, but from which they eventually recovered.

Between these wars, another tragedy in the city's past was the Great Fire of 1917, which destroyed the city center, including its architectural masterpieces and its commercial and residential district of Greek Jews, then the city's most prosperous urban community, along with the Armenians. This disaster left hundreds of thousands homeless, jobless, and desperate. Churches, synagogues, and mosques were destroyed, as were large industries and small neighborhood shops. Many residents migrated abroad to rebuild their lives. Most stayed on to reconstruct their city, but only after the government enlisted the work of European architects led by Ernest Hébrard to design and implement a new urban plan of spacious squares and diagonal avenues. Thessalonikians spoke of the great fire as another catastrophe that left its mark on their collective psyche as survivors and conquerors of adversity. Many pointed to how the recovery strategies that followed the 1917 conflagration had improved the city's infrastructure, albeit at a high cost in human life.

Infrastructural development in the form of multistory condominiums boomed in the 1950s to the 1970s to accommodate increasing numbers of migrants from the regional hinterlands. This demographic shift diversified the city's cultural composition and local economy that reportedly alienated local elites. New residential structures replaced some historical monuments and architectural landmarks, much to the dismay of architects today. This wave of change brought jobs in the building industry and increased population density in the city center. Urban population increase and the availability of easy bank loans in the "deregulation era" of the 1980s and 1990s increased rates of conspicuous consumption, and fueled the rise of the rentiers, a new economic category of individuals and families who supplemented their wages, salaries, and pensions with profits from rental properties (Placas 2018: 324–326). Intellectuals and artists critiqued the changes in the city's built environment—the spread of unremarkable apartment blocks that some considered "concrete monstrosities." An exception is the strip of stunning architecture that begins at Aristotle Square, continuing onward toward upper town—the district that escaped the Great Fire of 1917, and which is now a UNESCO World Heritage Site. Locals' assessments of their built environment varied, as most acknowledged the practical housing for the growing migrant laborers from the city's hinterlands, and the value of its architectural treasures that affirm their cosmopolitan identity.

My interlocutors were ambivalent about the influx of new settlers who occupied Thessaloniki and its surrounding territory following the collapse of the Soviet Union. The fall of communism in Eastern Europe changed the global landscape, including Greece. After 1989, thousands of immigrants from the Soviet bloc crossed the border to start a new life in Thessaloniki as the city's new labor force (Hart 2008). The city's demographic and sociocultural profile diversified further and rapidly with the arrival of Bulgarians, Romanians, Moldovans, Ukrainians, Georgians, and Pontic Greeks from the former Soviet Union. These newcomers brought with them different languages, dialects, practices, and beliefs. The integration of Balkan immigrants during the 1990s and beyond stood as a symptom of what locals in 2011–2012 described as "the fake boom" or "the bubble," a seemingly expanding economy that led to a rise in low-skilled service workers who earned a living by easing the lives of Greeks.

Reflections of the city's past and its people's capacity to overcome calamities often turned to the fiscal disaster of the moment and its threatening, unpredictable outcomes. In discussing possible aftermaths to the financial downturn, some respondents pondered that "we will lose people . . . many will not survive this catastrophe either," yet recalling the rebirth of the city following the fire, a resolutely materialistic downturn, most were optimistic that recovery was likely. Most theorized that in time the collective trauma would subside, and perhaps a healthier Greece is inevitable, particularly if Greeks "get some sense" (*ahn i Ellines valoun mialo*). As we will see in the chapters that follow, in their narratives of the current fiscal and moral crisis, locals referenced past events that altered the personal and communal life to make sense of a precarious present and to contemplate an uncertain future (Knight 2012b).

The *niki* in the city's name is Greek for "victory." Thessalonikians often invoked this meaning in conversations about historical and recent societal calamities and the reconstructions that followed them. It was common among participants, particularly elders, to frame the debt crisis as "another catastrophe that we must endure." Others theorized that perhaps the debt crisis was inevitable, or necessary, a "good of sorts," so that Greece might develop a competitive global economy as a sustaining member of the eurozone and so that Greeks might learn to live as meritorious citizens of the West. To be sure, an appreciation of one community's perceptions, agonies, and hopes related to surviving the recession, calls for an understanding of the Greek state, and its integral role in the debt crisis.

A Vulnerable Greek State Economy

Symptomatic of Greece's crypto-colonial status and paradoxical identity as "at once the collective spiritual ancestor and a political pariah" of Europe (Herzfeld 2002: 903) is its current position as a people historically, economically, and politically *indebted* (*ipokhreomeni*) and *in debt* (*khreomeni*) to European structures of power. Implicit in this political–economic relationship between modern Greece and the West is a mythicized, cultural alliance of mutual, "classical debt" (Hanink 2017; Gallant 2016). The promotion by nineteenth-century European intellectuals and Philhellines of ancient Athens as the cradle of Western civilization signifies Westerners' *symbolic debt* to modern Greece and Greeks' *literal debt* to the West (Ruprecht 2018: 169). Indeed, accounts of ancient Greece as the birthplace of Western intellectual and aesthetic heritage fueled the Greek rhetoric of the 2004 Olympics as rightful national heritage (Tzanelli 2004), a global event veiled in notions of indebtedness, and one perched on a mountain of debt. This "triangular relationship among the West, classical antiquity, and modern Greece" figures prominently in the Greek state's current "agonizing inclusion" in Europe, and the country's regional identity as *European* (Ruprecht 2018: 168; 2016).

The Greek state's current fiscal collapse must be considered within its historical economic dependency on global capital markets, a fraudulent, poorly managed financial system prone to defaults on foreign debt obligations for most of its existence as the Hellenic Republic, and a party patronage democracy (Mazower 2008).[6] Greece's development into a sovereign state in 1832, following the War of Independence from the Ottoman Empire (1821–1829), implied economic and political dependence on Europe (Doxiadis 2018). The first Hellenic Republic was established in 1828 by Ioannis Kapodistrias, only to crumble from inept governance in 1832 following his assassination and the failure of his brother, Augustinos Kapodistrias, to stabilize a nation in economic and political unrest. Another intervention by the Great Powers—Russia, Great Britain, and France—resulted in their appointment of Prince Otto of Bavaria as the first king of modern Greece (1832–1862), whose charge was to stabilize the developing new nation-state. Contemporary Greeks' indebtedness and debt to the Anglophone West reflects their embrace of Greece's integration in the EEC, the European Union, and to its now ambivalent, controversial, and costly inclusion in the eurozone.

The Greek state has consistently relied on inflows of international capital, and its trade deficits averaged 6.7 percent of GDP between 1974 and 2016 (Floros and Chatziantoniou 2017).[7] The following timeline reveals the conditions that led to a corrupt Greek state economy. As the 2008 global financial downturn unfolded, and weeks into his administration in November 2009, then-Prime Minister George Papandreou announced that the government faced default on its massive external debt. He revised that year's budget deficit from 3.7 percent to an astounding

12.5 percent of GDP, and announced to the world that the Greek state was bankrupt. Greece's budget deficit reached 12.9 percent of its GDP, as the world's rating agencies downgraded its credit ratings.

Prospects for repaying debts and lowering the deficit to the 3 percent limit consistent with EU requirements within one year remained dismal, subjecting the country by 2010 to yet another default on foreign aid. By 2011, the center-right supported negotiations of another joint bailout agreement from the European Union and International Monetary Fund (IMF), while Papandreou called for a national referendum before he resigned, and economist Lucas Papademos assumed the leadership of a provisional government (2011–2012). A second EU-IMF bailout worth 130 billion euros ($172 billion) was confirmed on the condition that Greece must reduce its debt-to-GDP ratio from 160 percent to 120.5 percent by 2020. This agreement included a 53.5 percent reduction or "haircut" for private Greek bondholders.

In the spring of 2012, twenty-five EU member states signed a fiscal compact treaty to reinforce stricter budget criteria in European fiscal integration. This agreement requires that each member state maintain a balanced budget and keep deficits below 0.5 percent of GDP. During this period Greeks rejected the two mainstream political parties, the conservative New Democracy and the socialist PASOK, and turned to fringe political parties who opposed EU-IMF interventions in the form of bailout packages and austerities. Yet elections in June 2012 put into power the center-right leader Antonis Samaras, with 30 percent of the vote, to form a coalition and to implement the bailout plan. In fall of that year, eurozone finance ministers and representatives of the IMF lowered interest rates on Greek bailout loans and a debt-buyback program. This strategy would allow Greece to cut its debt-to-GDP ratio to 124 (rather than 120 percent) by 2020, and to bring its debt levels below 110 by 2022.

In the summer of 2013 Greek parliamentarians agreed to a new bailout package worth 7 billion euros ($9 billion) and approved austerity measures, while protests and strikes from labor unions in opposition to increased rates of layoffs, wage cuts, tax reforms, and other budget cuts multiplied. By April 2014 eurozone financiers released more funds to the Greek government and raised 4 billion euros in five-year bonds, renewing investor confidence and returning Greece to global markets. In January 2015 Alexis Tsipras of the left-wing, anti-austerity party, Coalition of the Radical Left [Synaspismos Rizospastikis Aristeras]

(SYRIZA) won a snap general election ending forty years of a two-party rule. He promised to renegotiate the terms of the bailouts with international creditors to prevent Greece's exit from the eurozone. By June 2015, the European Central Bank (ECB) ended emergency funding and the Greek government missed its 1.6 billion euro ($1.7 billion) payment to the IMF. Greek banks closed, and Tsipras imposed capital controls on citizens.

Tsipras proposed a referendum on the EU proposal, which a majority rejected with a resounding *oxi* (no). Threatened by the possibility of a Grexit, in July 2015 Tsipras secured a third bailout for 86 billion euros and imposed further austerity measures and cuts in public spending, while promising to reform tax laws and to privatize more state assets. In 2016 Greek banks continued to lose money, while the state failed to meet the criteria of the last bailout. By 2017 eurozone financiers offered short-term debt relief and agreed to more lenient budget cuts. The bailout program ended in August 2018, and poverty plagued a large segment of the Greek population. Greece remains under "enhanced surveillance" by EU financial institutions, austerity measures continue, and the unemployment in 2019 is at 18 percent—the highest in the European Union.

The government's boundless spending, unaccompanied by increasing revenue, created deficits in the state budget and left a population vulnerable to financial embarrassment and social disintegration. The crash required 246 billion euros in emergency funding from the European Union and the IMF, increasing the country's debt. Meanwhile, severe austerity bewildered private citizens who faced rising rates of unemployment, devastating losses of income, and a widespread increase in precarious circumstances (Spyridakis 2013). While officials negotiated with foreign lenders for billions of euros in bailout funds to ostensibly protect Greece from further collapse, ordinary citizens wondered about the logic of "borrowing money to pay back borrowed money." Indeed. Meanwhile, demands resurfaced for reparations from Germany for the World War II crimes in place of austerity measures that the state's creditors imposed.

The European Union relies on each of its member states to manage its own fiscal policies, including taxation, public sector wages, and pension benefits. EU architects may have ignored the structural incompatibility and "cultural mismatches" of integrating the peripheral economies of Europe's southeastern countries with the core economies of the north Atlantic (Goddard, Llobera, and Shore 1994). Eurozone governance may favor states like Germany and France that are historically and structurally adapted to global—if uncertain—market-oriented production, but test the viability of peripheral state economies like Greece. In fact, elites' neoliberal promises would prove incompatible with the socioculturally diverse regions, and especially with the most politically and economically peripheral nation-states to which they were applied (Zambarloukou 2015). For example, Greece entered the eurozone as a client state dominated by political parties whose economy fell short of global market standards (Matsaganis 2014).

European integration gained Greeks unprecedented access to capital while their economy's credit rating rose. Wages and prices of domestic products increased, while competitiveness decreased as EU development and trade policies discouraged productivity. However, the state's fiscal mismanagement and misreporting of economic performance, combined with inadequate monitoring by international investors, fueled unsustainable borrowing and excessive public spending. Standard rates of tax evasion, credit growth, and high wages increased mass consumption of imported goods and encouraged a boost in illegal permits in the building industry. A shift by ordinary citizens from meeting necessities to chasing luxuries emerged as a new mainstream pattern of culture.

Greece's adoption of the euro in place of its drachma was a watershed in the country's political economy and its culture. Eurozone governance demands economic deregulation, centralized decision-making, liberalization of trade and industry, and privatization of state enterprise. These policies reflect a political–economic ideology that participation of nation-states in common industries and global markets will benefit all constituencies and stakeholders, including ordinary citizens (Steger and Roy 2010). Accordingly, the Greek state lost control of its monetary policies; the new currency lowered interest rates relative to inflation and encouraged inflows of foreign investment capital. Meanwhile, private sector credit rose as government spending increased, guaranteeing a budget deficit and inordinate levels of debt.

Global Markets

The crisis of the Greek nation-state illustrates the failure of fiscal discipline and breakdown of the eurozone project, but it also recalls the 2007 mortgage crisis in the United States, the 2008 Wall Street crash, and the global recession of 2009 (Stout 2019; Rakopoulos 2017; Öztürk 2015; Ho 2009). Neoliberal principles include a tariff-free, self-regulating global market, where the principle of "profit over people" reigns supreme (Ganti 2014; Rutherford and Davison 2012; Chomsky 1999).[8] Within the European Union, the success of neoliberal models of governance depends on hegemonic, popular consent—that is, on compliance with EU policies by national elite and ordinary citizens (Shore 2000; Steger and Roy 2010). The enactors of EU fiscal policies intend them as an "instrument" by which to effect societal change, and as a "cultural agent" that will change how individual citizens think, feel, and behave economically (Shore and Wright 1997). Yet the eurozone policy package itself is a cultural product: a set of organized and patterned practices, values, and meanings to which entrepreneurial leaders—a cadre of powerful, profit-oriented executives—ascribe, and which they collectively create, enact, and implement.

Greece's incorporation into the eurozone was a political–economic strategy to reinforce the credibility of the European project. Ascendance of Greece in the eurozone marked a milestone in the country's economic and political development. Greek elites welcomed the state's inclusion in EU's economic and monetary union, even if based on falsified qualifications. For their part, EU elites granted Greece membership in the eurozone not because of its economic performance, but because of its symbolic capital as Europe's cultivated foundational legacy (Hanink 2017). Representatives of international banks, the IMF, and eurozone member states, including Greece, formulated personal and class interests into grand neoliberal agendas to which individual state economies were subjected, including those of a vulnerable southern Europe. To be sure, neoliberal policies of economic growth favor the core economies of northwestern Europe at the expense of its southeastern region. In fact, the adoption of eurozone's neoliberal policies by Greece's two dominant political parties, the Panhellenic Socialist Movement (PASOK) and New Democracy (ND), ensured the eventual fiscal collapse of Greece.

The eurozone's centralized executive power subsumed the Greek state's economic policies on the premise—and promise—that Greece would gain stability and prosperity (Mitsopoulos and Pelagidis 2012). In fact, the provision of loans and subsidies would return profits to core countries, such as Germany, as Greeks increased their consumption of imported goods, while the state economy failed in its ability to export goods to other countries. Failure was the inevitable outcome for Greece, a technologically and economically developing society new to eurozone requirements. Greece's vulnerability to a sovereign debt crisis nearly threatened the functioning of the European Union as a supra state. The Greek government's ethically questionable debt policies and practices, and the unmonitored economic strategies of its private citizens, illustrate the inability of the ECB to regulate economies of technoeconomically peripheral societies (Sakellaropoulos 2010).[9] The then-president of the ECB, Wim Duisenberg (1998–2003), asserted cautiously that Greeks would have to improve their economy to earn and sustain inclusion in the eurozone. Did he not think to ask, "What kind of economy is that?"

Neoliberal practices may be the raison d'être of global financiers, but they generally are far removed from the daily concerns of local populations. Technocrats in Brussels propose modes of transnational governance without the participation of ordinary citizens. Greece's integration into the new Europe has been planned and guided by in-dividuals and teams whose personal attributes—cultural background, class, professional expertise—and values inform why and how they wrote the policies intended to govern masses within, and across, dif-ferentially resourced societies. EU elites profess that eurozone policies will promote economic development by converging the cultural orien-tations, practices, and values of people within member societies. The Greek state's implementation of austerity in compliance with eurozone sanctions may have convinced a segment of its nouveau rich to embrace bailouts (Sakellaropoulos 2010). Yet debates concerning the costs and benefits of Greece's inclusion in the European Union, membership in the eurozone, and its place in the global economy intensified during the crisis (Antoniades 2010).

In this work I hope to demonstrate that Greece's current fiscal meltdown must be viewed through the prism of a neoliberal agenda that favors deregulation of state economies, national markets open to trade and global capital, and governments weakened through privatiza-tion. Greece's status as the epicenter of the European debt crisis reflects a global configuration of fiscal policies, economic tenets, and business practices that serve the interests of policy workers, entrepreneurs, and bureaucrats, including Greek elites (Bitzenis, Karagiannis, and Marangos 2015; Harvey 2005; Chomsky 1999). After Greece entered the eurozone in 2001, Greek state officials, ordinary Greek citizens, and EU elites all participated in a process that led to a country in crisis of debt and dig-nity. Much of Greek society has now become downwardly mobile; its citizens have suffered the loss of a familiar and secure lifestyle,[10] and now engage in efforts to cope with and adapt to financial hardships while they construct the aftermath of their country's fiscal collapse.

Thessaloniki's self-identified middle-class residents, who are the focus of this ethnography, are a case in point. Their lived experience of crisis—a generative process of behavioral and ideational transitions during a period of austerity—reflects immediate, experimental coping mechanisms and people's articulations of anticipated adaptive strategies toward more permanent societal changes. Participants' expressed hopes for deeper, long-term, structural outcomes in a post–crisis world requires longitudinal research. However, evidentiary, rational, and affective responses to a precarious economy during 2011–2012 contributes to theories of sociocultural change and continuity.

Crisis Theory

Popular usage of the term *crisis*[11] conveys trouble, risk, and calamity. Scholars also associate social crises with disruption, instability, and decline. Indeed, "crisis talk" on such volatile phenomena as a global crisis, an international crisis, the financial crisis, a constitutional crisis, the environmental crisis, the energy crisis, and the refugee crisis encompasses an array of natural, economic, or political disasters (Holton 1987). Now a universal referent of convenience, crisis narratives signal alarm, analysis, and judgment of hazardous, particularly unanticipated, systemic shifts and humanitarian concerns (Kosmatopoulos 2014). Ongoing, actual catastrophes the world over—natural and human-made—generate multivocal texts and narratives among experts and laypersons who interpret and explain them as crises and who evaluate their immediate outcomes and long-term consequences (Bear 2015; Loftsdóttir and Jensen 2014; Roitman 2014). Times and places of crisis generate different discourses, meanings, and responses—a kind of "work" in which those in crisis engage that lead to new revelations, truths, moralities, and directions (Loftsdóttir, Smith, and Hipfl 2017: 3–7).

Scholars of human disasters have shown that populations in crisis experience an array of intense, often contradictory sentiments and actions related to unanticipated loss, uncertainty, and displacement (Erikson 1994; Shevchenko 2009). Survivors of disasters experience "a vast spectrum of intense emotions . . . anxiety, fear, terror, loss, grief, gratitude, anger, frustration, relief, and resignation—in all their shadings and intensities" (Oliver-Smith and Hoffman 1999: 163). Sudden, threatening disruptions of daily life force individuals into states of shock, displacement, and insecurity. In times of a debt and a moral crisis,[12] fluctuating emotions, thoughts, and actions are particularly pronounced among individuals who, consumed by a precarious present and an ambiguous future, experiment with alternatives to their customary daily routines, personal relationships, and social relations.

As a fluid "conjuncture" of economic, political, sociocultural, and ideological ruptures or shifts, crisis depicts a historical period of cultural continuities and changes (Hoffman 2016). While change is a constant of crisis, its nature is an aggregate of a people's symptoms, emotions, and actions in various degrees from despondency to renewal. We may infer that every natural or human disaster constitutes and manifests itself as a crisis—a process of collective responses by citizens expelled from an ordered and seemingly predictable way of life into vulnerability, social disorder, and recovery. Having experienced a catastrophe, a population moves from a state of stability to one marked by collective instability and ambiguity, followed (hopefully) by reconstitution of society and community (Hoffman and Oliver-Smith 2002; Quarantelli and Dynes 1977).

All disasters are disruptive, but the crises that they unleash can be revelatory and often generate opportunities for societal reconstructions (Button 2010; Markowitz 2010). Indeed, understanding of a human catastrophe must consider "the multiplicity of imaginaries and practices," and "the feasibility of hope—people's temporal orientations, expectations, and engagements with [a] possible future—as the central notion in an analysis of social transformation" (Frykman 2012: 269). Political and economic disasters in particular propel crises that are temporal phenomena of "folded, pleated, and fluctuating time," within which displaced actors navigate new, unpredictable conditions of daily life (Knight 2012a: 354). "The crisis consists precisely in the fact that the old is dying and the new cannot be born: in the interregnum a great variety of morbid symptoms appear," observed Antonio Gramsci (1971: 276). Kazantzakis (1960) characterizes it as a "luminous interval of life"— a space and place betwixt and between complacency and generativity in which not only "monsters," but life-affirming possibilities, may appear. It is this interval—an "inbetweenes" of societal change, an interregnum of contingencies and potentialities—in which Greeks have found themselves (Giesen 2015: 61–71).

I propose that the 2008 fiscal crash constitutes an event, and that citizens' lived experience in the aftermath of this financial shock constitutes *crisis time*: a period and a process of sociocultural transitions. In this work I examine how my crisis-ridden hosts experienced and articulated such transitions from complacency through bewilderment, onward to resilience and intent to "rebuild better" (Barrios 2016). Resilience remains a contested concept, as its multiple iterations in a troubled world attest (Anderson 2015). I am mindful of its treatment as an "operational strategy" to manage risk (Walker and Cooper 2011), a tool of global neoliberal governance (Joseph 2013; Cretney 2014), or a "training system" for individual adaptations to precarious conditions (Coutu 2002). However, I emphasize resilience as fundamental to individuals and societies. In my analysis, resilience constitutes the capacity of disaster-affected urban individuals and communities to survive unanticipated catastrophes, despite overwhelming challenges, through flexibility, solidarity, and other resourceful and innovative strategies that crisis time generates and fosters (Lahad, Cohen, Fanaras et al. 2016; Fainstein 2015; Vaiou and Kalandides 2017).

My focus is specifically on the nature of crisis as a process, one in which actors devise and implement organized, culturally meaningful ways of working, economizing, and living (Narotzky and Goddard 2017). How might ordinary citizens respond when the *habitus* to which they have grown accustomed ruptures unexpectedly, and the *doxa* in which they have been enculturated, and to which they ascribe as the natural and essential social order, betrays them without warning (Bourdieu 1977)? What, if any, interpersonal and intergroup transactions and adjustments in daily life might influence emergent sociocultural patterns, institutional reforms, and societal change?

An anthropological study of social change, posited Fredrik Barth, should begin not with a focus on large-scale social systems but with small-scale, local units of analysis, including individuals and groups interacting and transacting with one another. He argued that macro-level social changes emerge from the collective, cumulative, and recurrent practices of persons, households, and networks (Barth 1967). Moreover, Barth contended that an understanding of social change must include empirical documentation of the following: "the events of change and the use of concepts to facilitate such a study," "the continuity in a sequence of change," and "institutionalization as an ongoing process" (Barth 1967: 661). While Barth's work focuses on small-scale, technologically simple societies, I find his framework useful in investigating the actual process of sociocultural transformation—the mass, collective choices and responses of individuals and families in local communities over time that embody changes and continuities in a global context.

Inspired by Barth's approach, I examine Thessalonikians' lived experience of the debt crisis as a process of daily experiments in cultural continuity and change. I argue that crisis-rooted transitions and adaptations are neither linear nor chronological; accordingly, I investigate how the residents of one urban community in crisis responded at once—emotionally, intellectually, and behaviorally—to imposed, acute financial shortages that tested their material and moral integrity during an acute phase of Greece's economic downturn. Central to Barth's analysis of large-scale social change is attention to how and why people in local settings allocate their time and resources to meet their needs and to solve problems. Critical to my analysis of the debt crisis is the combination of *diminishing material resources* and *increasing leisure time* due to abrupt and forced mass unemployment. How might an increase in leisure time foster personal and collective strategies of recovery? In my discussions with study participants, I explored with them the sentiments that consumed them about being in crisis either in isolated, meditative states in private, or while engaged in animated public debates.

Thessalonikians' heterogeneity with respect to ancestral roots, socioeconomic status, political ideology, and religious activity is understood. How, I wondered, might the fiscal collapse affect them categorically, even if to a variable degree? Dissolution of order defies conventional hierarchies and unifies discrete identities. Could a sense of *communitas* among citizens in crisis[13]—all being in the same sinking boat—compel those forced into destabilizing structures to ponder their common humanity and to invest in collective possibilities? What emotional, cognitive, and practical reconfigurations might occur when societal collapse and agent-driven reconstructions of daily life and meanings occur simultaneously (Horvath, Thomassen, and Wydra 2009)? Might the crisis as a global phenomenon, a national disaster, and a local plight shape Thessalonikians into "threshold people"[14]—formally differentiated individuals awakened to a shared consciousness and a collective predicament of contingency and transformation (Gennep 1960)? If so, what forms of "communalities" might emerge among the indebted through collective consciousness, resilience, and agency (Graeber 2014)?

Guiding my ethnography of Thessalonikians' lived experience of the debt crisis is *liminality*—a social scientific concept that illuminates grounded, in-between human realities that link disruptions in the social order, individual agency, cultural transmission, and social transformation that imply change and continuity (Horvath, Thomassen, and Wydra 2015). As an analytical paradigm of the contemporary world, liminality defies fixed boundaries of a society's before and an after; yet it also reveals the lived human experience of a dynamic everyday in the aftermath of a historically shaped process that ruptured social institutions, and precedes the construction of new, lasting social structures.

In this study I sought to ascertain the particular sentiments, values, decisions, and adjustments to daily life that Thessalonikians expressed when fiscal uncertainty and political security seemed to vanish. What precrash personal habits and social practices may have come to a screeching halt? What customs, values, and rituals did these self-conscious urbanites value enough to preserve in the face of rapid change? Equally critical to this ethnographic investigation is the documentation of reported capacities and ideals that my interlocutors retrieved or invented to reconstruct sustainable and meaningful ways of a material and a moral life during a period of societal transformation (Dalakoglou and Agelopoulos 2017). I theorize crisis as a type of liminal experience—more a sociocultural transition than a sudden event—one marked by a "collapse of order," enduring economic or political instability, ideological reorientations, and sociocultural reconstructions that invade and affect, even revolutionize, a whole society (Thomassen 2015: 48–50). Theoretical analysis of Thessalonikians' experience of *crisis as liminality* may expand our understanding of agentive movements and sociocultural transitions that reshape society in the aftermath of a historical rupture and beyond.

Ethnography of Crisis

This study investigates how people feel, think, and act as participants in two levels of economy: (1) a formal, global economy within which the Greek government is embedded and regulates as a member state of the European Union and the eurozone; and (2) local patterns of economizing—decisions, practices, and beliefs regarding allocation of time and available resources (Narotzky 2012). Ethnography produces systematic data that enhances our understanding of how people experiencing a global transformation make sense of, and respond to, changes in their daily lives for the sake of social and national continuity. My analysis is based on grounded theory: close, inductive, open coding of themes that emerged from individual and focus group interviews (Bernard 2018: 465). I employ ethnographic strategies to gain an overview of Thessaloniki in crisis, and of individual and collective actions and reactions to unanticipated precarious economic conditions and an uncertain future. My fieldwork focuses on narrative inquiry, including thematic, visual, and dialogic analysis (Riessman 1993). The research design included unobtrusive and participant observation of social events ranging from dinner parties and festivals to city hall meetings, political and social protests, and national celebrations, as well as analysis of participants in seven of the city's social networks (Bernard 2018).

I audio-recorded 120 two-hour-long semistructured interviews with men and women between eighteen and seventy-eight years of age. I conducted another five hundred unstructured interviews of approximately one hour in duration, and twenty-five focus group interviews, each with eight to ten adult participants. In addition, I organized two discussion sessions with more than twenty-five participants. One research participant invited me to facilitate a discussion of the crisis at a weekly dinner meeting of the city's Rotary Club. Attendees recorded their individual responses to a list of questions I distributed and subsequently discussed their answers as a small group at their own tables, followed by a discussion with all the participants in the room. Another participant hosted a discussion at his home with members of his extended family and neighbors who shared with me, and with one another, their personal experience with, and outlook on, the crisis. I conducted most of the structured interviews in three locations: participants' homes, the café on the Roof Garden of the Electra Palace hotel (see figure 1.2), and the café of the Byzantine Museum. The staff of each café was fully aware of my work, and they graciously accommodated me and my guest each day, whenever we appeared. I brought them customers, and they provided a quiet corner where I could record lengthy conversations. I also observed the interactions of other patrons at various cafés who carried on their own critical conversations about the crisis for all to hear.

My fieldwork in Thessaloniki involved observation of daily activities by and among its residents, and participation in many of their secular and religious rituals. During that year I became intimately familiar with

FIGURE **1.2 Aristotle Square: view from Orizontes, roof garden, Electra Palace Hotel.**
Source: Photo by Kathryn Kozaitis.

their cultural practices—new and changing behaviors that were crisis-induced, as well as patterns that expressed a continuity or modified continuity of custom, tradition, and beliefs. This account of crisis will reference a range of voices—those of research participants as well as those that have influenced them, including state officials, global experts and elites, and media representatives. My primary task, however, was to note how ordinary people spoke about their experiences, and how they attributed cultural meaning and value to their microeconomic and sociocultural practices.

My hosts understood implicitly that the work was meaningful, purposeful, and collaborative. Many also labeled the interview process as "therapy." They expressed gratitude for the opportunity to unload a burden by talking with me about the threats that austerity was imposing on their household. As Mihalis put it, "We developed such a nice conversation, that is, I said things that I have not said before . . . I had not opened myself before . . . but I wanted to, and this was a very good experience for me." At the end of our interview, one woman remarked that our conversation had relieved her of a distress she carried daily in her heart but was too timid to admit. Others thanked me for the chance to speak openly about anxiety-inducing thoughts and emotions related to an uncertain future. Some expressed relief after the interviews, while others admitted to a level of healing from self-disclosure about the effects of downward mobility on their mental health. My hosts found comfort in talking with me about their experience of crisis. I found comfort in talking with them about my work, and in their willingness to help me quench my intellectual curiosity about a people in crisis by welcoming me to their city and to their homes.

Due in large part to my positionality and identity as a native of Greece (Narayan 1993), I shared with Thessalonikians a "cultural intimacy" that enhanced my rapport with them and that solidified their trust in me. Our conversations often centered on disclosures of personal and systemic violations of state rules and public policies, often concealed from outsiders. My status as a native of Greece encouraged them to share with me aspects of Greek society and cultural identity that they questioned, and even considered a source of embarrassment (Herzfeld 2005). Thessalonikians who met me for the first time recognized me as "one of our own" (*dhiki mas*)—one who understands and empathizes with historical and structural conditions of daily life in Greece.

This ethnography demonstrates that unanticipated loss of money and dignity, despair, and resilience are transforming a nation from one with chronic, albeit ambivalent, dependency on external structures of powers to one that aspires to sustainable and self-determined global integration. I situate this work within the anthropology of and in Europe. The Greek debt crisis is clearly embedded in "processes of Europeanization," the establishment of a "supranational polity," and the (dis)organization of regionally diverse sociocultural groups that its architects sought unsuccessfully to integrate and to govern (Pagden 2002; Shore 2000). The particularly precarious position of Greece is inherently linked to the politically constructed "uneven geographical development" of the eurozone regions (Hadjimichalis 2011).

Yet even in a rapidly changing and interconnected world, my hosts still share an actual and imagined national platform of stories, identities, memories, and symbols. They also claim a beloved physical, topographical, and ethnoecological landscape they call *Elladha*. To the extent and degree that Greece belongs to the European continent—historically, regionally, geopolitically, or culturally (Herzfeld 1982; 1991; 1999; Sutton 1998)—this study contributes to European anthropology and, of course, to the anthropology of, and in, urban Greece. Greece's second city—its beauty, sadness, and vibrancy embodied as much in the lives of its citizens who cherish it as in my own impressions as an ethnographer during a time of crisis—is the focus of the next chapter.

Notes

1. To go hungry is a metaphor for suffering and deprivation. See Herzfeld (1985: 22).
2. See Ehrenreich (1989) for a comparative analysis of financial insecurities of the American middle class.
3. Thessaloniki spans 2,300 years. It was founded in 315 B.C. by Cassander of Macedon. The City is named for Queen Thessaloniki, the daughter of King Philip of Macedon and half-sister of Alexander the Great, who was born on the day that Macedonia won the Battle of Crocus Field (353/352 B.C.E.). The name derives from Thessalos and Niki, which translate as "Thessalian Victory."
4. Dimitria is named after St. Dimitrios, the patron saint of Thessaloniki, the Feast Day of which is October 26. Locals participate in social and cultural activities that promote the performing, literary, and visual arts, while friends, family, and visitors enjoy celebrating with food and spirits throughout the city's cafés and tavernas.
5. Thessaloniki, known as Salonica during the Ottoman Empire, was home to Sephardic Jews who settled in the city following their expulsion from Spain in 1492. The Jewish community thrived economically and culturally during the Ottoman regime, and Jews became citizens of Greece following the country's independence. During WWII, the Germans exterminated nearly the entire Jewish population of Thessaloniki. After the liberation of Thessaloniki from the Nazis in October 1944, those Jews who had joined the resistance forces and those who survived the death camps returned—without family or resources—to reconstruct a vibrant community. The descendants of the resurrected Jewish population are today prominent residents of the city some still like to call "the mother of Israel."
6. See Koliopoulos and Veremis (2010; 2002); Woodhouse (1977); Triandafyllidou, Gropas, and Kouki (2013); Campbell (1964).
7. This period marks the onset of the *Metapolitefsi* (change in regime) and the reestablishment of democracy in Greece following the end of the Greek military junta (1967–1974), and the onset of Greece's dependence on European powers that led to the Greek state's debt crisis.

8. See Boas and Gans-Morse (2009) for a critical discussion of the meanings and applications of neoliberalism.

9. See Bear (2015) for a discussion on the social and ethical implications of sovereign debt policies as depicted in the lived experience and relationships across a set of state officials and civilians on India's Hooghly riverscape.

10. Suffering, struggle, and a generalized tragic view of life among Greeks has been documented by Dubisch (1995); Hart (1992); Herzfeld (1985); Friedl (1962); and Du Boulay (1974).

11. The term "crisis," from the Greek *krisis* or *krino*, denotes decision and judgment among alternative courses during life-altering events to determine favorable outcomes in the face of danger or risk (see Koselleck 2006).

12. See Peebles (2010) on the anthropology of credit and debt.

13. See Turner (1995) for his depiction of a "liminal state," a period during which initiates experience a transformation from one status to another. Here I theorize societal liminality as a transitional period and process of sociocultural transformations. See also Newman's (1999) discussion of downward mobility among America's middle class as a form of permanent liminality.

CHAPTER 2

The City and Its People

The 2008 eurozone debt crisis and subsequent collapse of the Greek economy tested the adaptability of Thessaloniki's middle-class residents. After decades of prosperity, they experienced a rapid decline of their material assets and of their morale. Just three months before the crash, Thessalonikians spoke with me of local history as a series of natural and political disasters, and the cultural transitions through which they and their ancestors conquered adversities. Their self-ascription as inhabitants of a perennial cosmopolitan city speaks to their sense of collective tenacity and grit as an embattled, yet victorious people. In the summer of 2009 my hosts boasted gleefully about their quality of life, save what a majority deemed the "decline in the city's milieu" that they attributed to the influx of *new* economic immigrants and other "foreigners" who had settled in the city's neighborhoods. The city's continued prominence as a center of high culture in the face of abrupt social changes informed the narratives of crises that locals shared with me when I returned in 2011 to work with them in deciphering the roots, ramifications, and prospective outcomes of the debt crisis. Indeed, during an acute phase of austerity in 2012, I found the city experiencing another transformative period. Determined to weather yet another tempest, its residents adjusted their daily transactions in compliance with new and what all deemed "punitive" financial policies. Instrumental in coping with a precarious present were their recollections of an idealized past.

On the Eve of the Crisis

> Thessaloniki is paradise. It has changed . . . newcomers have
> changed it, but we natives live joyfully, and we thrive.
>
> —Athanasia, 45, 2009

On a hot evening in June 2009, while immersed in a pilot study of the
city's milieu, I took my first stroll in Thessaloniki's upper town. This
neighborhood is marked by cobblestone alleys, traditional houses with
colorful gardens, a beautiful Byzantine citadel, and the church of Saint
Dimitrios, the city's patron saint (see figure 2.1). Unaware that Greece's
economy was on the verge of collapse, I focused my attention on neighborhoods populated chiefly by immigrants and on questions about their
socioeconomic integration in mainstream Greece. I stopped and sat on
a bench in the courtyard of St. Dimitrios, a local gathering place and
a tourist destination, to search for natives who might orient me to the
area's milieu. Among a few tourists who lingered there were about twen-
ty residents—young women with babies in strollers, children on bikes,
and elderly folk who arrived alone or with a friend to socialize in the
neighborhood square.

FIGURE 2.1 St. Demetrios Church, patron saint of Thessaloniki.
Source: Shutterstock/Andrei Nekrassov.

Two little girls on their bikes approached me, curious about my whereabouts. Speaking in fluent Greek, they asked me, "What's your name? Do you speak American?" Grateful for their interest, I answered them in Greek that I spoke American English. One of the girls turned to her sister and said in Albanian, "Let's see if she will give us money to buy ice cream." "Oh, you speak Albanian," I said in *Arvanitika*, a linguistic variant of Albanian. "Yes, but I also speak *Romanes*," she said bashfully. "Oh? You are very beautiful," I replied in *Romanes*, in the dialect that I had learned to speak during my fieldwork with Roma in Athens two decades earlier. Startled by my apparent multilingual facility, a boy who joined our group exclaimed, "But in school we speak only Greek!" In Greek, I asked him what he thought of school. "We like school very much," he replied. "We like being in school more than we like being at home," the children chimed in unison. I did not have a chance to probe further about the children's enthusiasm for school. However, I learned from the adults who observed my interaction with the children that living conditions for their parents, including irregular, unpredictable work, low wages, and substandard housing, diminished the children's quality of home life. School, they reported, allows them to socialize with one another, and to play with Greek kids, an experience that facilitates their integration and comfort in Greek society.

Perhaps satisfied with their ploy, the children thanked me for treating each of them to ice cream and ran off laughing, while the adults nodded and smiled at me approvingly. An elderly Greek woman dressed in solid black approached me, sat next to me, and took my hand in hers. "Thessaloniki today is like Australia was once upon a time," she volunteered. In the 1950s she had immigrated to Australia with her husband and young children to find work. There she encountered "many kinds of races, languages, and habits . . . just like Thessaloniki is now," she explained. Her children married and remained in Australia, while she and her husband returned to Greece following his retirement. His death a few years earlier left her lonely in a Thessaloniki she found "unrecognizable."

I learned that this repatriate's impressions of the city as "racially diverse" to the point of "alienation" were quite like the concerns of other residents with whom I became acquainted—young and old, and across the socioeconomic spectrum. Another woman whose family migrated to Thessaloniki in the 1950s from a village on the outskirts of the city complained: "We cannot all fit here; these foreigners live as whole families in a single room or on the ground floor of buildings—even in houses close to the center you see them piled up one on top of the other." Many others echoed such expressions of dismay about overpopulation, congestion, and traffic, which the presence of new minorities exacerbates.

During my forty-five evenings of participant observation on the promenade in the summer of 2009, I had observed hundreds of people passing me—married couples, grandparents with strollers and babies, members of a three-generation family, young lovers, groups of senior men and women, multilingual teenagers, and the occasional athlete who attempted to jog among the walkers. In contrast to the easily recognizable Roma, Africans, and Asians who appeared regularly on the promenade as street peddlers, merchants, or musicians, the passersby were distinguished chiefly by language and dialect. I recorded Greek, Albanian, Romanes, Russian, French, German, and other languages that I was unable to identify. The linguistic diversity intrigued me, as did the cultural diversity that signaled the city's demographic shifts.

Variation in the sights, sounds, and smells of the social settings were striking, while the interactions among those who shared the space were minimal. During my moments of unobtrusive observation of social practices in public places, spoken Greek invariably awakened my affinity for the language and jolted my sense of belonging. When the content of conversations resonated with me, I typically smiled and greeted people with a polite nod, and I was grateful for any affirming glances of acknowledgment. However, I was always conscious that I was one of many self-identified Greeks in a globalized city. The distant view of Mount Olympus on a clear day, the White Tower, or the statue of Alexander the Great were certainly markers of a cultural landscape and a heritage that felt instantaneously familiar. Undeniable and overwhelming were the sensual markers of a new cultural hybridity in an old, multinational city that locals and sojourners alike produced and consumed.

Notable on the promenade was the absence of the middle- and upper-middle-class adults with whom I was acquainted that summer. They gathered instead in certain cafés, tavernas, or clubs in the city center during the week, and typically spent weekends at their second home on the coast. There they patronized favorite venues with their family and friends, and with tourists whom they deemed more desirable guests than the *others* they might encounter in the city's public spaces. Friends confessed that decades earlier they had enjoyed evening strolls at the old seafront, but "the *old* seafront is no longer pleasant . . . it is too congested with all kinds of foreigners now," explained an elderly, upper-class woman. "Once upon a time, the old seafront was a place where the urbane residents appeared for evening strolls," she recalled nostalgically. She described a scene of elegant couples, well-groomed children, and polite sociality that in her view no longer existed. "In contrast, today you see all kinds of people there who look as if they were shopping in the street market . . . not at all gratifying to go out there anymore," she remarked disdainfully. Others distinguished the *old* promenade, which they associated with upwardly mobile Thessalonikians and tourists, and the *new* promenade, under construction during my fieldwork, as the gathering place of lower-income residents, tourists, immigrants, and their descendants.[1]

Whether pro- or anti-immigrant, my hosts agreed that the demographic shift had changed Thessaloniki's cultural landscape, and challenged their historically rooted sense of a *liberal cosmopolitanism* (Hatziprokopiou 2012). The presence of some multiethnic individuals and groups has led self-declared "Greek Thessalonikians" to discriminate in terms of which public spaces are desirable and which to avoid. Locals referenced sociocultural diversity as what some called "indigenous cosmopolitanism." They employed this term as a reference to the city's historical peaceful coexistence among prosperous, urban communities of different national and religious affiliations. Determined to maintain a class-based homogeneity and identity, they expressed appreciation for transnational and international visitors and residents from Europe and the United States. However, they remained ambivalent about the presence of "bottom-up" cosmopolitans—lower-income, working-class migrants and other dispossessed individuals from the Global South (Hannerz 2004).

Indeed, participants contrasted idealized notions of Thessaloniki's historical *cosmopolitanism* as identity with the city's current *multiculturalism*—their reference to the presence of economic immigrants and migrants who live and work among them (Agelopoulos 2000; 2008). Older Thessalonikians' views on cosmopolitanism are rooted in elitist, metropolitan, and hierarchical notions of Western culture characteristic of inhabitants in other Mediterranean port cities (Driessen 2005). Some locals' aspirations and ideals of cosmopolitanism as "transregional solidarity" is particular and exclusive; "the spirit of the cosmopolitan community" does not necessarily embrace today's uprooted, diasporic, and vulnerable populations of refugees and migrants (Chakrabarty, Bhabha, Pollock et al.

2002: 6; Mandel 2008; Anderson 2012). Forcibly uprooted transnationals from multiple localities suggest a "vernacular cosmopolitanism," which a few of my informants preferred to ignore (Werbner 2006).

Thessalonikians claimed a cosmopolitan identity (an orientation to life free of local or provincial practices and ideals), on the one hand, and an allegiance to national culture on the other. Yet most people with whom I spoke in 2009 self-identified as Thessalonikians (*Thessalonikis*) more often than as Greeks. However, locals also incorporated references to European influences in the making of Thessaloniki. They highlighted indicators of their European sensibilities, such as the presence of English, French, and German K-12 schools; multilingual facilities for the city's youth; and the number of local academics, artists, and other professionals who acquired their college and graduate education abroad. As one informant argued, "Thessaloniki has always been cosmopolitan, and, of course, it still is; but then [pre-WWII] life was more graceful, because we lived among accomplished immigrants. They were affluent, well-educated, cultivated urbanites . . . real cosmopolitans."

Locals contrasted a pre-WWII era of a "multinational order" with their "multicultural present." During an impromptu conversation with an elderly couple on the promenade, the man said to me, "Thessaloniki was from its birth a cosmopolitan city, unlike Athens which once was a backward village." Indeed, Thessalonikians expressed an *affinity* with fellow seaport inhabitants by virtue of their locality as a "window on the wider world," and the cross-cultural exchanges and influences that fueled the city's urbanity and cosmopolitanism (Driessen 2005: 130). This couple, and others who shared their sentiments, distinguished cosmopolitans principally according to class-based, elite qualities of culture rather than more "discrepant" national, ethnic, or diasporic identities associated with migrant laborers and other displaced travelers (Clifford 1992: 108). The matriarch of a large old family recalled, "In those years, our culture, our civilization was diverse, but refined. Thessaloniki's Belle Époque—beauty, style, refinement, visible and aesthetic markers of leisure and class, are gone."

Adherence to "hierarchical visions of culture" inspires in some Thessalonikians a sense of being *different* and *better than* the vulnerable newcomers whom they consider as *different* and *less fortunate* by any measure of what they view as upwardly mobile cosmopolitanism (Mandel 2008: 48). Affirming the eternal value of Thessaloniki as cosmopolitan, Yiota, a fifty-six-year-old woman, boasted about the city's 1997 designation as the Cultural Capital of Europe. Apologizing for the effects of immigration on the cityscape, she gestured outward and mused,

> But we still have the seaside, the monuments, the [Aristotle] university, museums and exhibitions, like the Biennale, the international film and music festivals, the new concert hall . . . Thessaloniki has culture, civilization; these features will keep Thessaloniki cosmopolitan forever.

For middle-class Thessalonikians cosmopolitanism connotes privileged, highly mobile, and professional citizens of a globalized world with which they identify or to which they aspire, especially since the country's inclusion in the European Union (Heiman, Liechty, and Freeman 2012). They recognize that globalization drives waves of immigrants and refugees who now seek citizenship or asylum in a new, host society. They also are critical of globalization, and the culturally based violence, genocides, and wars that plague societies the world over. However, they believe that the recent economic immigrants and refugees who now share their public spaces challenge, rather than enhance, the nostalgic, historically rooted cosmopolitan character they wish to sustain.

Emotional, often wistful claims of a changed Thessaloniki characterized conversations I held in 2009 with everyone who was willing to speak with me. Typically, locals spoke nostalgically of a former Thessaloniki as a peaceful, multinational, multireligious city in which Christians, Muslims, and Jews coexisted harmoniously. As Mazower notes, "Most striking and unexpected was the high degree of residential mixing . . . how intermingled the religious communities of the late Ottoman city were" (2006: 285). Markos, a retired scholar, argued that "even after Thessaloniki was liberated from the Turks, we were one community [*mia kinotita*]." Tasia, a forty-five-year-old woman whom I met on the bus one morning, had this to say about her city: "Thessaloniki has changed very much . . . once upon a time it was beautiful, elegant, cosmopolitan; in the last couple of decades it has fallen . . . well, it has diminished in value as a city due to an influx of new minorities." Her words reflected a popular sentiment of an often memorialized "old Thessaloniki," an imagined epoch of prosperity, romance, and congenial interethnic relations. Their idealized, nostalgic accounts highlighted past cooperation and fellowship—a multiethnic but convivial milieu, unlike the Thessaloniki of the early twenty-first century, and unlike the city that would soon be changed yet again by the debt crisis.

Perceptibly still financially secure in the summer of 2009, a middle-aged couple spoke enthusiastically about a high quality of life, access to "every good" (*ekhoume ola ta aghatha*), and the prevalence of good times (*pername kala*), which they attributed to their professional success as architects. Other financially established acquaintances invited me to join them for a respite at their vacation villas on the coast of Chalkidiki, or to dine with them at a neighborhood corner café. Birthday and name day celebrations with new friends at charming tavernas by the sea were festive and costly events. More impressive were wealthier informants' references to leisure travels abroad, ownership of second and third homes, and rental properties in the city center—all indicators of an affluent community, or at least one whose members "have captured the meaning of life," as some less fortunate observed resentfully.

On the eve of the country's fiscal collapse, people brushed off my questions about economic conditions. Money was not a source of concern for anyone with whom I spoke in the summer of 2009. Prophetically, "Greece is a poor country with rich people," they insisted, distinguishing between the nation-state's comparatively low GNP per capita and its citizens' high quality of life.[2] Others stated that "there's plenty of money, and money buys a good life; we work, and we spend our money to live well!" In fact, my experience of being in Greece periodically up to 2009 was that money was always available and a means to living well. Friends demonstrated financial well-being through their ability to hire domestic servants, travel abroad, purchase expensive automobiles, and entertain regularly and lavishly. After all, even as the financial collapse was looming, their Prime Minister, George Papandreou, announced, "Money exists!" Until it did not; until living well became a challenge even for those who weeks earlier claimed good health, lucrative careers, and reasonable pensions. By 2010, even those who were ensconced in loving and supportive relationships with family and friends had become vulnerable and insecure. In 2011 I returned to study Thessaloniki and its people who, two years after the crash of the state economy, displayed the dire consequences of enforced austerity.

Times of Trouble

> We sense the howl of a raging storm about to engulf us. We tremble in anticipation of what will come next.
>
> —Fotis, 51, 2011

As my plane began its descent into Macedonia airport in August 2011, a lighted Thessaloniki and the sight of its shining coast mesmerized me. The passenger next to me remarked that my tears must signal a sad arrival—surely to a family in financial duress. Mine were tears of exhilaration, I replied, while I validated the man's empathic interpretation of my emotional state. Nearly two years of alarming media updates on Greece's financial calamity and friends' accounts of personal economic ruin had only increased my eagerness to study a phenomenon that haunted me personally. The neoliberal assault on Greeks was too close for ethnographic comfort, and my new acquaintance's ambivalent welcome confirmed it. His declaration that the country was experiencing economic warfare alarmed me, yet it impressed me as an exaggeration. Was the global debt crisis destroying a nation that two years earlier boasted of prosperity and well-being? Recollections of proud, gregarious hosts who in previous visits charmed me with lavish receptions contradicted this man's assessment of "a constrained people." His reference to crying, hungry children "in some places" contrasted with the boisterous laughter that I remembered among parents who chastised their children for overindulging in fast food at a beach taverna in Chalkidiki two summers earlier. That the generalized sense of social, physical, and emotional wellness that I observed among Thessalonikians two years earlier had dissipated, and that disaster reigned instead, seemed implausible. Within weeks of living in the city, I realized that this man's assessment did reflect a nation-state in transition, and a collective consciousness of a people in peril.

Later that day, I set out to secure a place to live and to delimit what would become the field site of this ethnography. But not before I made my pilgrimage to the seashore for breakfast. I delighted in the sound of the waves and the taste of my first *koulouri* (a bagel-shaped crusty bread, covered with sesame seeds). Among Thessaloniki's street foods, the *koulouri* is a staple. The kind vendor asked me if I was a Thessalonikian or a tourist. It was from this man that I first learned about concrete, local "tragic circumstances" that some of his friends and neighbors confronted because of the fiscal meltdown—notably the eviction of one family, and a suicide of a distant associate. "Things are horrific today; we don't know what tomorrow will bring," he said softly. I left him with a cart filled with *koulouria* wondering how long he would be able to earn his daily bread by feeding passersby on the run to their own jobs, while they still had jobs, or while they were doing errands each morning.

As I continued my stroll, I observed the city waking up to its daily rituals. Shopkeepers washed their sidewalks, café owners wiped down tables and chairs in anticipation of their first customers. Street cleaners attempted hopelessly to empty the too-small, overflowing bins of trash next to the gulf. A more pleasant sight was that of elderly men taking an early morning stroll by the sea before they settled with friends at a café or sat on a bench gazing at the water to talk about grandchildren or to debate the causes of the crisis. One morning I struck up a conversation with three senior men on Aristotle Square. They spoke proudly of their families yet they were deeply troubled about their children's future, a future that in 2011 appeared to them uncertain and unforeseeable. They lamented not only their children's precarious circumstances, but they agonized about the fact that they were unable to bail them out of their debt. Perceived helplessness among parents to rescue or to support their children unconditionally, I soon discovered, was a new experience that proved more tortuous than the loss of their own security or prospects for their own future.

On that first morning, I also saw cheerful students in colorful outfits playing happily on the schoolyard before classes began. This, too, was a joyful sight, and contradicted the despondency that plagued their parents and their teachers. I also spotted Roma beggars gathered outside the courtyard of St. Gregory Palamas Orthodox Church waiting for alms from the faithful. Other beggars, particularly young children and elderly women dressed in black, emerged with hands outstretched to passersby asking for money or food. In time I learned that the number and frequency of beggars on the center's streets had risen exponentially since 2009. While informants were convinced that some of these beggars were "foreigners that opportunistic businessmen have planted there," the sight of Greek elders and youth seeking alms for their families disturbed me as much as it agitated their fellow neighbors.

Hair and nail salons opened their doors for business, and I was surprised to see that customers trickled into these places of beauty throughout the day. "Women in Thessaloniki," my research assistant Ioulia Kazana[3] informed me later, "maintain their well-groomed appearance, even if now they indulge in aesthetic services more rarely than before [the crisis]." In fact, whether running errands first thing in the morning, meeting friends for coffee in the afternoon, or out on a stroll in the evenings, men and women appeared well put-together—clean, tidy, and neat, projecting an effort to appear attractive and fashionable.

As friends confirmed later, austerity measures forced Greeks to pay unanticipated taxes, and unemployment prohibited them from shopping for new material possessions. However, these individuals held on to their stock of clothes, shoes, and accessories, which they displayed in public, as some admitted, even "with fallen faces" and an "agonizing mind."

By midmorning, brisk walkers populated the city. Hundreds rushed to the Kapani and Modiano public markets—dozens of stands and shops where one can purchase anything from cheese and olives, fruits and vegetables, and fish and meat to clothes and cleaning supplies (see figure 2.2). Window shoppers admired garments and accessories that graced the vitrines of designer boutiques in the center's thoroughfares, while automobiles and motorcycles encroached on streets and sidewalks. The lush colors of flower shops and the piercing aroma from the bakeries at every turn was enough to get me out early each morning to meet research participants and to document the visual markers of a city in flux.

FIGURE 2.2 **Kapani and Modiano markets.**
Source: Photo by Kathryn Kozaitis.

Field walks through Thessaloniki in 2011 drew me again to the architectural markers of the city's cultural past, including those signifying Roman, Byzantine, Ottoman, and Sephardic Jewish presence. Few tourists appeared to be visiting archaeological and modern sites of cultural display, while natives crisscrossed the narrow streets and inviting squares seemingly oblivious to the battles, celebrations, and cultural meanings that such monuments represented. I also identified other public spaces of city life, including neighborhoods, parks, squares, and cafés where I might establish contacts with locals who would be sympathetic to my study, and who might agree to set up interviews.

Navigating the city was easy. I began at Aristotle Square and used the central thoroughfares, including Tsimiski, Egnatias, Nikis, Sophias, Mitropoleos (on which I lived), Venizelou, and St. Dimitrios Avenues, to guide me through neighborhoods. Westward of the city center I passed the port[4] and old warehouses, now home to art exhibits, other cultural activities, and trendy eateries. I paused at the Holocaust Monument on Freedom Square that commemorates the victims of the holocaust. Ladadika, the former Jewish quarter whose name refers to the presence of olive oil shops, is a lively destination with entertainment venues, cafés, and restaurants, and was a delightful place to have lunch after many interviews that I held at the café of the Electra Palace hotel on Aristotle Square.

Past the court district, I reached the country's largest and busiest International Railway Station, built in 1961. Established in the 1920s was an industrial area in the northwest of the city—factories and residences of the working poor that have been converted into cultural centers and green spaces. I climbed the narrow streets, passing unremarkable multistory residential and commercial buildings. Striding onward, I reached upper town, a UNESCO World Heritage Site and the highest point of Thessaloniki, with a view of the entire city and the Thermaic Gulf in the distance. Tempting me momentarily to make upper town my home were its narrow stone-paved streets, quaint tavernas with spectacular views of the city and the sea, charming neighborhood squares, and renovated old houses with flower-filled balconies that from a distance appeared to be suspended in midair.

Landmarks of the city's east side include the universities, the International Exhibition Center, the football stadiums, the Hellenic Broadcasting Corporation, the archaeological and Byzantine Museums, and the new City Hall, built in 2006. The southeastern part of the city is home to a majority of the city's middle-class residents. Eventually I reached the coastal area called *Exoches* (country homes or holiday destinations), where until the 1920s the most affluent Thessalonikians lived and vacationed. Their villas, including Villa Bianca, Villa Modiano, and the Hatzilazarou Mansion, reveal another, some say "more glorious" layer of the city's history. The Concert Hall of the Performing Arts, at which I enjoyed concerts, a play, and an opera, is situated on the southeastern coast and was built in 2000. From a distance it appears to be floating on the glistening sea.

By end of my first weeks in the field, a self-determined map of my field sites emerged: residents of the city center and surrounding neighborhoods. Some research participants lived in Kalamaria, a municipality about four miles southeast of Thessaloniki's center, and others resided in Panorama, a nearby affluent suburb. Having established the sites of this ethnography, I proceeded to observe and participate in public life. Initial stages of fieldwork focused on unobtrusive observations of people's treatment and uses of the built environment, particularly archaeological sites turned backdrops for commercial transactions; recording of public discourses of crisis; impromptu chats with strangers about current events and personal struggles; and documentation of public behaviors and symbols of a city in crisis. Within my first month as an ethnographer in residence I was integrated as a participant-observer in local events and family celebrations and immersed in two or three structured interviews each day, which by evening left me exhausted, but exhilarated. Participants' disclosures of a private struggle raised my awareness of a humanitarian crisis in the works that public displays of anti-austerity and evidence of new intimacies and support networks revealed (Rakopoulos 2014a; Margomenou and Papavasiliou 2013).

Nightfall in Thessaloniki

> There is chaos, darkness, and confusion everywhere; we cannot see ahead.
>
> —TAKIS, 48, 2011

By 2011 Thessalonikians were fully enmeshed in confronting the effects on their daily life of eurozone financial pressures and austerity policies. The Greek economy was on a downward slope; the government was failing to meet its deficit targets, and financial vulnerability threatened households across Greece. Sophia, a thirty-two-year-old small shop owner, captured the sentiments of many residents with whom I worked in the coming weeks and months.

> If you had come to Thessaloniki a few years ago you would have seen a different city. Since 2008–09 the city has changed, the people's look on the street or on the bus has changed . . . they are frowning, they are distressed; things are not what they were . . . we are all worried.

Of course, I had visited Thessaloniki several times before the crisis and was a witness to the changed affect and physical manifestations of crisis among my hosts. On the street, clenched jaws were more common than smiles. Walkers with arched eyebrows, eyes lowered, and head forward and down outnumbered those who acknowledged others with a pleasant glance or cheerful greeting. The city now accommodated innumerable individuals who had lost their jobs, whose salaries or pensions had been cut, and whose savings had turned into unanticipated property taxes. The city that so many deemed consumable was no longer affordable.

People accustomed to investing their disposable income in cultivating and consuming a festive urbanity now grieved the loss of income to meet essential needs, and worried about their survival. They struggled emotionally with the shock that the sudden financial decline had imposed. I found friends of good means who suddenly were unable to pay their utilities on time. Other higher-income individuals resented being forced to forego costly food, including meat and seafood, that they had previously consumed with ease. Financing their children's education and paying taxes on properties that yielded increasingly lower incomes preoccupied those who counted on property income to finance the educational advancement of their children.

Locals were also concerned with the impact of the crisis on their national reputation—their place as a society vis-à-vis other countries, most particularly Western Europe and the United States. No label offended them more than the stereotype of all Greeks as lazy that found its way in international discourses about the Greek crisis. Such insults demoralized and angered Greeks across the spectrum, and compelled small business owners who worked at least nine to ten hours a day to defend their work ethic. People sought to manage the crisis through small adjustments to daily choices and practices. They also considered explanations, causes, and accountability for the dismal state of affairs, and pondered alternative paths to overcoming the fiscal disaster.

I recognized and appreciated the change in locals' priorities and concerns of daily living. Experiencing unanticipated and immediate loss of income, the same people who had celebrated "living large" two years earlier now projected a conservative disposition toward consumption, and resentment at their inability to maintain their standard of a "proper lifestyle." Preoccupations with meeting basic needs and protecting the future of their children replaced their dismay about immigrants and minorities. "All the immigrants are leaving now," they replied to my questions concerning the topic. In fact, some acknowledged the ironic parallel between immigrants from the Balkans who sought a better life in Greece decades earlier, and their own children's current search for economic refuge abroad in the face of Greece's fiscal collapse.

As the downturn pierced their pockets and wallets, people admitted to me—still a relative newcomer to their community—their new inclinations to distinguish needs from luxuries, and to reduce the consumption of what they now deemed "extras," such as clothing and eating out. My informants modified their personas and behavior to ensure the continuity of those cultural ideals and practices they held dear, most prominently family, moderation, solidarity, and civic duty. As resources were diminishing, I witnessed a renewed commitment among parents and children to care for one another, especially the more vulnerable members of the extended family, even as financial burdens strained relationships. Social time among friends gained in value, as much for emotional support as for fun.

The crisis stirred passionate discussions about the pros and cons of European integration, particularly the implications of common monetary policies on Greek national identity and the juxtaposition of globalization and national identity. Protests against austerity measures were regular fixtures of the city's streets, and small aesthetic modifications of the urban landscape marked a shift in civic consciousness. Mutual, generalized reciprocity in sharing resources among family members and friends increased. Artists and educators volunteered their time and talents both for the benefit of their audiences and students and for their own self-expression and meaning. Professionals lowered or waved fees for services rendered to regular and new clients. Young people continued to work for decreasing wages; others waited months for salaries; some even kept on working without pay. Explained one graduate student turned waiter, "Being out among friends and colleagues, even if in desuetude, trumps staying in a gloomy home alone; at least when you are out, you live!" Some discussed with me prospects for moving abroad to escape what one young and aspiring diplomat called "the cataclysm" that threatened his generation. Common in narratives of crisis were personal strategies and solutions to a precarious economy that left most wondering, "How will the crisis affect the country's youth?"

Urbanites Out and About

> We still embody the city . . . we walk it, we meet our friends for coffee in it, and we heal through it and with it. When we see the closed shops our mood falls, but the city's [ancient] treasures and cultural features lift our spirits.
>
> —ANGELINA, 31, 2011

Upon meeting me, random citizens readily volunteered to educate me about their city's formidable historical, urban, and cosmopolitan heritage. They promoted particularly Thessaloniki's archaeological sites, if only to accentuate their belief that Thessaloniki's civilization and that of Greece in general could not possibly be at risk. The state may go bankrupt, they figured, but the nation could not, and would not suffer annihilation. I learned quickly that while the past figured in their discussions of life in times of crisis, everyone was much more preoccupied with visual markers of economic decline in the present, notably the closed shops and increasing number of men and women rummaging through garbage bins. People acknowledged that the stability of the city's social order was crumbling, while others wondered whether the crisis would extinguish their city's exalted legacy any more than had previous economic and political disasters.

While implementation of austerity measures impinged on households and small businesses in 2011–2012, Thessaloniki remained a vibrant and gracious milieu. Every day I observed in the city center a continuous, interwoven stream of workers and shoppers (see figure 2.3): men and women in small groups socialized together in public spaces, rushed to their shops or offices, dropped their children at school, stopped at the street market for fresh produce, or sneaked into a pharmacy for something to ease their physical or emotional discomfort. Even before the 2015 capital controls, people piled like sardines at the door of a bank waiting for the green light so that they might enter it, and stood in long lines waiting for a clerk's attention to cash a check. Customers of all

Figure **2.3 Navarinou Square, residential and commercial district and archaeological site of Galarius Palace.**
Source: Photo by Kathryn Kozaitis.

ages leaned bored against the walls of the post office with too few chairs to accommodate everyone waiting to be served. Middle-aged women asked passersby for domestic work in the early hours of the day, while young adults filled the streets in the afternoon and evening on their way to a favorite hangout (*steki*).

Prominent scenes of public culture were cafés and bars that young and old alike patronized throughout the day, while locals and visitors strolled on the expansive promenade. Rarely did I encounter a person sitting alone at a café or any public place. "Passing the time alone is meaningless," friends reminded me, while they stressed that companionship (*parea*) "is in the Greek DNA." In various public places people engaged in animated, critical debates about the eurozone, the Greek government, and ways to cut expenses without compromising quality of life (Habermas 1989). While the subject of conversation was invariably the crisis and its consequences, the speakers interjected jokes and self-deprecating stories into their narratives. They teased one another with such endearing humor that even insults evoked laughter, relief, and amusement that may have compensated for the fear and anxiety that loomed within them.[5]

Throughout the year the tempo of city life was generally congenial, even festive at times. It is no wonder that visitors from the United States claimed oblivion to any evidence that the country was in crisis. However, evidence that the financial meltdown was taking its toll on individuals and families was unmistakable. The visual stimuli of movement, color, and textures did not always hide the undercurrent of a people in distress that became vivid in face-to-face interactions and personal relationships. Without exception, discussion of the crisis led every conversation I had with locals—regardless of context, speaker, or solicitation. "We no longer talk about family, work, education, recreation, or anything joyful. We sleep with the crisis, and wake up with the crisis," exclaimed a frustrated health professional and mother of two adult daughters. A distressed father of two teenagers told me, "My dream for my children's future has become the nightmare of our present. I am an engineer, yet I watch my family go from paradise to hell." Locals admitted that one of the debilitating effects of the fiscal collapse was its power over every aspect of their life, every relationship and every daydream.

Ubiquitous, disconcerting visual markers of the city in crisis were abandoned properties, graffiti-covered facades of storefronts, new pawnshops, street-dwellers and beggars, and transients who scavenged garbage bins for food and drink. Research participants identified the closed shops on the city's three main thoroughfares—Nikis, Tsimiski, and Mitropoleos, which comprise the heart of Thessaloniki—as the chief indicator of assault on the urban middle class. A woman who resides near Aristotle Square, which some locals refer to as "the city's living room" (*to saloni tis polis*), noted sadly that before the crisis, the center shone. "Now look at it, suddenly, and without warning, it darkened," she said somberly.

Adding to the visual assault offered by the closed retail shops were the many "For Rent" (*Enikiazete*) and "For Sale" (*Polite*) signs (see figure 2.4). The signs in the windows of boutiques and department stores indicating clearance prices (*Ola sto ksepoulima*) attracted customers who hoped for a deal, yet they regularly walked out empty-handed. One evening I stopped to admire the designs in the windows of Max Mara, the high-end Italian boutique. An elderly woman whom I did not know approached and stood next to me. She remained silent while she stared at the vitrine with its display of fine garments. Then she held my arm

FIGURE **2.4 Closed shops and abandoned buildings with "For Rent" and "For Sale" signs.**
Source: Photo by Kathryn Kozaitis.

and uttered in disbelief. "So, have they [the retailers and consumers] lost their mind" (*Kala, afti ksekoutiathikan*)? She figured that given the state of the economy, anyone who sold or purchased a jacket for 850 euros ($1,100 at the time) must be insane.

Owners and sales clerks in specialty boutiques and some designer shops, including Armani, Max Mara, and Dolce and Gabbana, remained idle throughout the day, waiting for customers who never appeared. Some small-shop owners sat solemnly alone behind a desk smoking; others set up tables and chairs on the sidewalk where they chatted with friends or passersby over a smoke or coffee. One sales clerk at a designer boutique, dressed in a fine dark suit and tie, stood daily with hands clutched on his back and legs slightly parted, in the same position, staring out the window. For months I observed this figure, always alone, never smiling. I wondered if he was a guard and was surprised to learn he was a salesperson when I saw him helping a customer with a sweater and matching scarf. That customer eventually left the shop empty-handed.

Prominent on the seaside promenade, tourist sites, street corners, and squares of the city center stood illegal street vendors who competed with local merchants and specialty shop owners by selling often counterfeit accessories, handbags, sunglasses, toys, and trinkets. I heard many of them speak Greek with their Greek customers and English with tourists. As many Albanians and other immigrants began to leave Greece at the height of austerity, Thessalonikians' xenophobia intensified in the scapegoating of undocumented immigrants from the East and from Africa. Informants complained that these foreigners tested their patience as they watched them earn a living illegally on the street while Greeks were closing their shops to save on operating costs or abandoning their rented spaces altogether because they could no longer afford the space.

Throughout the year, the landscape changed gradually to reveal symptoms of a citizenry in peril. Long lines of sedentary taxicabs circled whole blocks, waiting hours for a customer. Most drivers stared impatiently at the crowd of walkers who opted for a bus; others surrendered their attention to a newspaper and some dozed off, until the next horn alerted him to move up in line another half meter or two. Public demonstrations in the city center were normative events. In June and October 2011, garbage strikes protesting new austerity measures demanded by the European Union and IMF filled Thessaloniki's streets with piles of trash, a pungent indicator of systemic failings. An actual or imagined increase in petty crime and xenophobia in a city once proud of its grace and safety threatened the security of a people whose streets and cafés are extensions of their salons and dining rooms.

Media Madness

> I am hooked. I watch multiple news channels at once every day all day; then I feel worse than I did the day before. And yet, the next day here I am again—glued to the television.
>
> —ASIMOULA, 62, 2012

Alarming updates about eurozone-enforced bailouts and austerities dominated the mass media, whose power and presumed authority shaped audiences' interpretation of the crisis, informed public debates about its impact on the country's future, and influenced individuals' perceptions and responses to new developments. Many of my acquaintances considered television viewing as an addiction." Others, critical of the economic and political interests that control media networks (Zaharopoulos and Paraschos 1993), condemned journalists for exacerbating their uncertainty and fears with contradictory messages about the state of affairs in Greece and in Europe, even as they engaged actively in decoding the messages of crisis that they consumed daily: "We don't know what awaits us tomorrow," explained a local baker, "and the parrots on television confuse us more. Whom can we believe?" Critical of the partisan political and sociocultural production structures of media outlets, informants argued among themselves about the meaning and validity of the information that broadcasters disseminated throughout the day. Some discussed the demoralizing experience of having to confront kiosks plastered with newspapers and magazines whose alarming headlines fed them scripted sound bites that proliferated as collective imaginaries of reality.

As finance ministers negotiated a second bailout for Greece in February 2012, many Greeks vowed to ignore all media lest they become ill, despondent, or insane. "I just can't watch anymore . . . I fear that I will have a stroke if I continue to listen to all the traumatizing updates from journalists and correspondents," stated a neighbor who was forced to close her music shop due to a serious drop in sales. Like so many others, she struggled to decipher the facts from the messages that "state-bought" reporters and broadcasters delivered. Elites used the media to shape public assessment of the crisis. My study participants admitted to such manipulation. Even those who reported being glued to their television sets told me that media updates confused and terrified them, rather than inform and reassure them.

The media's cacophonous depictions of Greece as the epicenter of the EU financial crisis, economic conditions as "tragic," and sensationalistic depictions of a society paralyzed by disorder acerbated citizens' insecurity and fear that a cultural cataclysm was in progress. The media stressed the crippling effects of the eurozone crisis on the citizens of Greece and other Mediterranean member states. Newspapers and radio broadcasts highlighted threats to Greece's national sovereignty. Television anchors warned of more austerity measures and the country's possible fiscal demise. Journalists wrote evocative essays about rising unemployment, and published stories about and images of poverty-stricken families and children who had fainted in their classrooms because they had not been fed for days.

News about violent protests and workers' strikes offered the world an image of Greece in revolt. Highly disturbing, even to those who felt comparatively unthreatened, were reports of increasing suicide rates among men in their fifties who had lost their jobs or were on the run from loan sharks. Melodramatic accounts on television of the fiscal crisis as a national tragedy influenced and shaped the views of media consumers who were eager to know more about the global recession. The personal and collective anxieties that Thessalonikians expressed reflected as much the sentiments inspired by the media as everyday sights of urban blight.

The promise of the Treaty of Maastricht to further European citizenship through a common currency, defense system, and foreign policy fell short from abolishing nationhood and nationalism across Europe's nation-states. Emblematic of the global recession and sovereign debt crises was a rise in European populism and nationalism. Greece's financial and political disintegration gave impetus to the People's Association Golden Dawn (*Khrisi Avghi*), an ultranationalist right wing political party founded in 1980 (Kirtsoglou 2013). In May 2012 it received 6.97 percent of the vote in parliamentary elections, and in June 2012 won a municipal council seat, a marked increase in popularity from the 5.29 percent of votes it received in the 2010 elections (Ellinas 2013). By January 2015, the party gained 6.9 percent of the vote and ranked third among political parties.

Like fascist organizations the world over, members of the Golden Dawn employ a rhetoric of protection and nationalism to garner support from a populace confused and in distress (Stanley 2018). Societal disruptions and transitions generate such peripheral, dangerous, and transformative figures—*imitation tricksters*, who emerge in times of chaos and social disorder. Tricksters rise among vulnerable populations, cultivate myths about a society's past and future, scorn social conventions, challenge established boundaries, and cultivate a new ideological and moral order (Hynes 1997; Babcock-Abrahams 1975). Media depictions of Golden Dawn's fascist ideology and acts of violence on the one hand, and protectionism on the other, enraged my informants. The increasing presence of Golden Dawn representatives in public debates about Greek vulnerability alarmed viewers seeking a way out of social disorder. Even some center-left informants pondered aloud, ambivalently and apologetically, whether Golden Dawn might be "the only way" to protect the Greek nation.

Among the many epithets attributed to Thessaloniki is "mother of the poor" (*ftohomana*), a status the city gained in the 1920s when it embraced Asia Minor's dispossessed and newly impoverished refugees. Absorption of immigrants by the thousands from countries of the former Soviet Union reinforced Thessaloniki as a desirable destination for displaced peoples eager to work and live in peace. During the eurozone debt crisis Thessaloniki struggled to take care of its *new poor*—exiles from a state of relative abundance to one bereft of security and integrity (Panourgia 2017). Bombarded by severe austerity measures, these Greeks felt multiple levels of betrayal and states of confusion, rage, and fear. Research participants acknowledged that "the crisis is global first," and that their lived experience of it locally was "threatening and life-altering." As a thirty-nine-year-old educator put it, "We are in a state of transition. We are no longer who we were, and we don't know what will become of us, or where we will end up." Participants also noted that while the prospective aftermath of the debt crisis was "frightening and uncertain," a history of disruptions and rebirths had taught them that crises force transformations. Human beings possess the intellectual abilities and cultural means—behavioral and ideational plasticity—that allow them to respond and adapt to conditions that punctuate their equilibrium. As we will see in the chapters that follow, during a time of instability, disorientation, and uncertainty Thessalonikians sought to find their bearings as citizens in flux and to kindle hope to overcome a crisis that so many viewed as both a threat and a salvation.

Notes

1. The waterfront and the city's most exalted aspect of its landscape is about 4 km in length. The old side of the seafront starts at the warehouses that now host cultural events (e.g., art exhibits and the International Film Festival), continues past Aristotle Square, the center of social, political, cultural, and humanitarian activities, onward to the White Tower, the most prominent landmark of the city and now a museum of its history, embellished further by the famous statue of Alexander the Great. The new waterfront, now completed and marked by social spaces, including parks and playgrounds, continues until the Concert Hall of Thessaloniki.

2. Greece's GNP per capita is at about $28,000, compared with Italy's at $40,000 and Turkey's at $27,500 (2017). The country's infant mortality rate is 4.3 compared to 4.7 for Turkey, 2.9 for Italy, and 5.9 for the United States. The average life expectancy for men and women combined in Greece is 81.2 years compared with 81.0 in Germany, 82.9 in France, and 78.7 in the United States (2018).

3. Ioulia (Julia) Kazana, a native of Kallikrateia, a municipality in Chalkidiki, Greece, oriented me to Thessaloniki, introduced me to many women and men who became my interlocutors, and transcribed verbatim all the recorded interviews in Greek. Dr. Kazana completed her PhD in 2018 at the University of Surrey. Her work examines the lived experience of crisis among women in their twenties and thirties in Thessaloniki and Athens. View her dissertation on line at http://epubs.surrey.ac.uk/849594/.

4. See Katsiardi-Hering (2011) on Thessaloniki's port as a geopolitical, historical, and economic landmark of the city during its occupation by the Ottomans, and its instrumental role as a gateway of interregional commerce in the livelihood of varied religious communities within a multiethnic empire.

5. See Bakalaki (2016) on the centrality of laughter in surviving adversity.

CHAPTER 3

Assault Without Warning

During an acute phase of austerity in the winter of 2012, talk among my hosts of heart palpitations, headaches, insomnia, melancholia, nervousness, and depression dominated private conversations and public discourse. Whether internally generated or externally imposed, unanticipated societal upheaval engenders an array of fluctuating psychological and physiological states among even the most self-possessed of citizens. Loss of wages, reductions to pensions, and increases in property and other taxes threatened family security and individual stability. Study participants reported feeling trapped in an unsettled state of existence that left them psychologically insecure and physically vulnerable. During the limen of the debt crisis, my hosts articulated seemingly incongruous and contradictory feelings. Emotional states such as fear, rage, guilt, regret, helplessness, relief, empathy, and hope reflected their struggle with financial embarrassment, uncertainty, a precarious future, and declining health (Simou and Koutsogeorgou 2014). Equally burdensome was the loss of personal dignity and the sense of national pride as a resilient people, which only a modicum of hope for recovery alleviated. Informants' affective accounts of life in flux reveal their efforts to cope with the disruption of past customary ways of life and to manage a chaotic present. In this chapter I examine the prevailing emotional experiences of men and women in 2011–2012 as state-imposed austerity measures ravaged households throughout Greece. Those measures continue to burden Greek society in 2019.

Fiscal Embarrassment

> The sudden decline in assets shocked us to the point of pa-
> ralysis . . . it is as if some force struck us down from an un-
> known place for unknown reasons.
>
> —EFFIE, 67, 2011

A bankrupt Greece was unimaginable to upwardly mobile professionals, even as their own household incomes were vanishing. Unanticipated fiscal embarrassment was the principal concern among locals as state-mandated austerity measures invaded their bank accounts. Decreases in or loss of salaries, wages, and pensions and lack of other earning opportunities paralyzed a community of middle-class urbanites whose identity and worldview reflected the privilege of once having lived a comfortable life. Striking was the high degree to which husbands and wives, fathers and mothers shared the agony of diminishing resources and related costs to their household. The household (*nikokirio*) is an economic, political, and conjugal unit in Greek society, and its success is a source of pride and identity (Loizos and Papataxiarchis 1991). As urban, credentialed professionals and (former) income earners, men and women share, and exhibit, social freedoms and form complementary partnerships (Faubion 1993). Thus, they were equally preoccupied with financial losses that threatened the stability of a respectable household and their family's well-being (Dubisch 1991; 1986).[1]

Adults claimed to have encouraged their children to pursue higher education as an end in itself, and as a path to economic and social upward mobility. By 2011, these parents feared their children's long-term economic dislocation while they faced an unprecedented array of fiscal constraints that threatened their own security. Some young parents hoped to emigrate for jobs, though they regretted having to forego raising their children in Greece, close to family and friends. Middle-aged parents agonized about the disappearing opportunities for their educated children's professional advancement, in which they had invested heavily. For their part, young adults grieved the loss of meaningful and lucrative careers, a trajectory they had taken for granted. Consistent with traditional, albeit modified and regionally varied rules and practices of inheritance and postmarital residence in metropolitan Thessaloniki, young adults anticipated parents' transfer of property and other material assets to them as a form of dowry (*prika*), an asset that austerity measures and increased property taxes transformed into liabilities (Allen 1979; Du Boulay 1983).[2] Unmistakable was the discouragement, disillusionment, and resignation of elders who had counted on growing old independently, safely, and gracefully.

Thessalonikians attributed their shock to their unawareness that an economic collapse had been brewing. Elena, a thirty-six-year-old medical technician, reported that she and her peers were "still consumed by shock, rage, and fear," mainly because they did not feel prepared to tackle a financial crisis. "We are experiencing a sudden disturbance to our security, wellness, and moral character. There was no warning from anywhere that a catastrophe awaited us," she shared. Elena's words summarize the collective experience and sentiments of middle-class professionals, including civil servants, attorneys, physicians, architects, and engineers. Previously assured that the state economy's integration in the eurozone was secure, owners of small businesses, such as art galleries, tavernas, grocery stores, hair salons, and flower shops, were equally despondent. They claimed to have "overextended" themselves financially, oblivious to any threat of a recession. There was consensus that individuals suffered as much from a global recession that threatened any prospect for a quick recovery and a mismanaged, fraudulent state economy as from their own personal, unanticipated financial decline linked to unwise fiscal decisions and random financial mistakes.

Their prosperous, precrash living conditions only exacerbated their postcrash financial anxieties. My hosts reported that life since WWII had improved across all social strata, and families thrived. Homeownership was a universal standard, and a coastal vacation home was a given for members of the middle classes. Several participants owned rental properties, the income of which afforded them luxuries that wages or a salary alone could not secure. Young people realized their aspirations for higher education, "a precursor to a life of working with your mind, not your hands," as they liked to say while imitating their parents. Retirees claimed to have enjoyed well-pensioned, leisurely lifestyles, heightened by the upward mobility of their own children. Prosperity was within everyone's reach, or so it appeared. By comparison, in 2011–2012, more common was the collective realization that for three decades Greece had been subject to a delusive scheme, and that the bubble in which citizens lived had burst without warning (see figure 3.1).

FIGURE **3.1 Pensioners queue outside of a national bank waiting to cash up to 120 euros on July 1, 2015.**
Source: Shutterstock/Ververidis Vasilis.

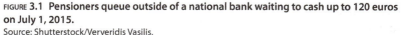

Participants' experience of the economic shock corresponded to their age grade and location in their life course. Professional parents in their thirties and forties faced high levels of distress due to what some called "impediments to proper childrearing," the priority of which was "the best education that money could buy," including extracurricular activities, music, and foreign language training. Young parents were on track to attain a comfortable and "dignified way of life" when the government pulled the rug from beneath their feet. Having secured gainful employment, they felt confident to take out a mortgage and to use credit cards for luxury items, including vacations and holiday celebrations. Convinced that a Greece embedded in the European Union would thrive for a long time to come, protecting themselves against an economic recession had not been a concern. Those who claimed fiscal conservatism as a personal strategy were as bewildered at the economic meltdown as were those who had borrowed to invest in real estate. Austerity measures paralyzed even those families who reportedly had not overextended themselves and had avoided debt.

The financial meltdown forced couples to choose between paying the mortgage and denying their children basic needs and other valued resources, most notably private lessons in academic subjects and in the arts. Credentialed professionals and other educated workers, explained Dimitra, a worried grandmother of three, "are prepared to settle for a job as a server or even a busboy in another country, but at least the family will have something to eat!" Referring to her daughter, an attorney, and her daughter's peers, she continued:

> Here, professionals' normal way of life has been disrupted and their path to success has been closed! Abroad, they imagine new beginnings and new opportunities that may provide them with some comfort. But leaving is not a choice. It is a necessity. As well-bred kids, accustomed to all that is good in the world, they dread descending to a life of barely meeting basic needs, and of being preoccupied with whether they will have food tomorrow.

Newly married couples and those with young children attributed their anxiety to being trapped between a bleak future in their homeland and an unknown future abroad. Moreover, these men and women ascribed passionately to a "life–work balance" as standard practice. Suddenly, they struggled with a dilemma: Should they stay in Greece, to care for their aging parents, who in turn would provide child care, or should they emigrate in pursuit of a more secure livelihood that would ensure the safety and prosperity of their children? Such questions evoked chronic nervousness and sleepless nights among parents of young children who felt incapable of meeting the demands of adulthood.

Loukas and Adriana, a couple whose three sons ranged in age from two to fourteen, confronted loss of income and an unanticipated increase in property taxes. Adriana lost her job as a researcher in a biotech company, while Loukas's salary as a civil servant was reduced from €1,700 to €1,000 euros a month. Furthermore, they had a mortgage and credit card debt. Loukas referred to the latter as "small consumption loans" of approximately €5,000 "to cover holes," such as purchasing clothes and shoes for his growing children. One day, a representative of his bank called to offer him the chance to refinance his consumption loan. Out of desperation he agreed, only to face an extension of his debt by five years with interest that totaled €9,500.

His predicament tormented this forty-two-year-old man, who felt that he had complied with his society's rules of adulthood: he had acquired a college diploma, pursued a career, purchased a home near the city center, and built a family. Most Greeks with whom I spoke emphasized the instrumental value of income in acquiring "a proper lifestyle" (*mia zoi kathos prepi*) and maintaining their dignity (*aksioprepia*), marked, they argued, by material and symbolic indicators of upward mobility such as a favorable reputation, homeownership, a college education, and professionally bound children.

Young adults whose parents still lived in small towns on the peripheries of Thessaloniki felt privileged to be pursuing undergraduate and graduate degrees at the city's universities, typically Aristotle University of Thessaloniki and the University of Macedonia. They shared with me their dismay at being forced to interrupt their educations because their parents could no longer afford the rent of an apartment in the city, or the reportedly carefree lifestyle to which some college students were accustomed. A professor at the local agricultural school cried as he related his friend's confession that he could no longer afford to educate his son who had been admitted to the school of engineering at Aristotle University. He confided, "Instead of training to become a mechanical engineer, his son now works for 15 and 18 euros a day for his own pocket money [*khartziliki*]." The son of another friend, he said, lost his job as an engineer and took a part-time job as a server. "Now he is reduced to carrying ice cubes in nightclubs!"

Parents spoke anxiously about the precarious futures of their adolescent children whom they had enculturated to pursue higher education as a path to a professional, lucrative career. "Never did it occur to me that we would find ourselves—as a family, as a nation—in such vulnerable and tragic circumstances," said Vicki, a psychotherapist and single mother of a seventeen-year-old son. I spoke with Vicki at her modest two-bedroom apartment, which she shared with her teenage son after her divorce. Away from her parents and siblings who lived on an island, she struggled to support herself and her son on reduced wages of 500 euros a month, 70 percent of which went to rent. She had been looking forward to seeing her son in college in 2013. That her plan was no longer feasible financially was psychologically "maddening." The help she had been receiving from her ex-husband and her parents, now financially strapped themselves, became increasingly sporadic. I asked her about her clients and changes to her workload. Leaning forward and raising her voice, she replied in tears, "People now are hungry themselves; they don't have food to feed their own children . . . Who will pay me to listen to their problems?" At a time when Vicki's clients most needed her skills, they could no longer afford to seek her help.

Vicki described her son as "a victim of business greed," and regretted having "fed him Americana" in the form of unmonitored consumption of American television programs, an emphasis on lucrative career trajectories, and discussions about images and symbols of material wealth. The thought of her son living in the Thessaloniki of a "black future" horrified her. She also lamented that she had encouraged her son to embrace eurozone soccer, which she viewed as another symptom of "Europe's chaotic lawlessness." All matters related to Europe made Vicki anxious. She bemoaned her own mental health, and her son's decreasing options. She also wondered if Greece, as a nation, would ever become "disentangled" from the European powers and their Greek allies who had colonized her nation and betrayed her generation.

Two years into the debt crisis, men and women generalized their state of mind as "still in shock," and their social selves as "disoriented" and "displaced." No longer assured of material security and social safety, which they all deemed to be the norm, they calculated alternatives to ensure survival. When Athena's father was still alive, he supported three households—the family home where he lived with his wife and their youngest of three daughters, and two apartments that each of his other daughters rented in the city center. Athena, at twenty-six years of age, considered her family's multiple residences a marker of "well-being" and "normal" social status. However, at the time of our interview in March 2012, her family had agreed that "in such perilous times, throwing money on rent for two of those three homes was irrational." Athena's parents considered college education for their daughters a priority. The family had a plan: when her parents aged, and if they needed help, Athena and her sisters would be financially equipped to care for them.

The plan that all three daughters would be financially secure, through careers and marriage, was not to be realized. "The crisis has changed all that, and now we only seek to survive," admitted Athena. Her recently widowed mother was searching unsuccessfully for work to make ends meet. Meanwhile, the family understood that should the mother find gainful employment, she would lose 30 percent of her husband's pension. Athena explained that her father's pension was no longer sufficient to meet monthly expenses and pay for the unanticipated property taxes. Her mother and sisters continued to look for "something, anything to do" so that together they might increase their chances of surviving the crisis. Athena lamented having to forego her middle-class standard of a "decent and respectable lifestyle" and to settle for mere survival. Faced with dismal prospects at home, she decided to move to Canada and live with an aunt. There she would secure work as a personal trainer. Meanwhile, the dreams of higher education and professional careers for these young women, and their mother's graceful aging, would be deferred indefinitely.

Financial embarrassment—something that once was a private matter in Greek society—permeated public discourses of crisis. On a sunny Saturday morning I walked into the neighborhood bakery for my weekend supply of crusty black (whole wheat) bread and yogurt. I found the owners, a couple in their fifties, anxious that their livelihood and their children's future were in peril. Fearing a decrease in demand for store-bought baked goods, Mrs. Erini asked rhetorically, "How long do you think it will be before women start kneading their own loaves?" On another occasion, this mother of adult, formally educated but unemployed children recalled a time when she and her husband had tried unsuccessfully to convince their eldest son to complete his college education and to grow the family business. Instead, he chose a career as an accountant; he was now unemployed and despondent, admitted this worried mother.

Other shopkeepers lamented that their (six-day) workweek, which previously had secured their livelihood, was yielding barely enough to survive. Shopkeepers were disheartened that the rewards of their years of hard work—baking bread and pastries, repairing shoes, painting houses, driving cabs, or grooming others' appearance—were turning into penalties. No goal was more laudable for these citizens than for their children to become educated and to secure professional "clean jobs" (*kathares dhoulies*). Like many others in the same predicament, these parents regretted deeply their failure to anticipate the economic decline that would divert their own, and the nation's children, from the intended path to an upwardly mobile and dignified way of life.

Equally distraught were retirees and senior citizens who insisted that they had "worked hard and lived a full life," but now worried about "an ugly end [to their life course]." Kostas, a sixty-two-year-old agricultural economist, claimed in 2011 that had anyone warned Greeks "ten years ago that we would descend to such precarious financial circumstances, we would not have believed it. The shock is drastic, the change threatens us, and the fiscal uncertainty scares us all." Others feared becoming "third world peoples" or a country in "the Balkans."[3] Maria, sixty-five years of age, had traveled abroad regularly and lived for a time in the United States. With her lower lip protruding in disgust, she recalled "Bulgaria during my visit in 1990 . . . closed shops, dusty and dirty windows covered with newspapers and flyers . . . full of filth. That's what Thessaloniki reminds me of now." She recalled nostalgically the precrisis historic center's vibrant movement of joyful residents shopping and socializing, and the lights and music that created a perpetual festive ambience.

To be sure, even at the height of austerity, I observed a city center saturated with social activity. Political rallies, improvisational theater (in which I participated), holiday parades, Feast Day celebrations, and campaigns for humanitarian causes were common. All were magnets for hundreds of participants and spectators who filled the squares and the streets with talk, transactions, and laughter. Yet Maria still could perceive a "dramatic decline" in the conspicuous consumption by a privileged middle class of the city's pricy material, cultural, and sensory goods. She and her peers considered prosperity, dignity, and progress as givens of European integration, and conditions that they, as elders, had earned and ought to possess. Seniors reported having embraced Greece's membership in the eurozone, without questioning the sustainability of the economic and cultural developments it promised. During the crisis men and women in their sixties and seventies saw themselves as preparing for, or being in, an uncertain and precarious third phase of their life course *(triti ilikia)*, contrary to their ideal of graceful aging.

Citizens who had planned for a financially carefree old age now complained of chronic vulnerability. At sixty-two, Spyros admitted to feeling insecure for the first time in his life. The state had cut his pension significantly, and he feared that he might lose his retirement altogether, leaving him unable to meet his monthly living expenses. Like other retirees, he expressed indignation at the unexpected financial bind in which he found himself at his age, "after years of working hard and saving." He explained:

> Before the crisis I used to pay €5,000–6,000 in income taxes. Suddenly, a month ago, they [state officials] asked for an additional €600. The state's position is based on the premise that "the government doesn't have money, so we will take it from the citizens." Then, without warning, they also added another €900 in property taxes. In other words, while all these years I was doing fine, suddenly I ask, "What is happening?" And no one knows!

The fact that they neither anticipated nor fully understood the financial meltdown enraged these middle- and upper-middle class urbanites, who before the crash had led a life of relative predictability and control. Manolis, a retired accountant in his mid-seventies, has two single, un-employed adult children who a year earlier moved back home to live with their parents. Manolis returned to work, seeking new clients to support his expanded residential family. "This shift in the economy be-wilders me," he admitted. "We lived well. Suddenly we don't know what is happening to us. Our money disappears from our hands. We never expected to end up like this." Like other seniors, Manolis was mystified that even educated adults, like his children, had been oblivious to euro-zone policies that would subject Greece to its current agony.

Plagued by Uncertainty

> What concerns me is that there is no framework, no pro-gramming, no direction, and no light on how to proceed . . . we are nowhere, we are in transition . . . there is uncertainty all around.
>
> —Yiannis, 75, 2012

Exacerbating Thessalonikians' financial concerns was uncertainty about daily actions, personal decisions, and their future as private citizens and members of a nation on eurozone's red list. Study participants were per-plexed "by a heavy darkness," of not knowing "what we will wake up to," or being unable "to predict what awaits us tomorrow." Uncertainty plagued even those who claimed to have led a "rational, well-ordered, honest, and informed life." There was a popular perception of "suddenly living in chaos," or "marching on without a light to guide us." Loss of control and the ability to plan stirred fear, helplessness, and hopelessness in many. Speaking for his peers during a coffee break with three proud grandfathers, Yiannis protested, "Messages from outside [eurozone pol-icies and mandates] and the state's negotiations [with eurozone officials] threaten us constantly without guiding us . . . we are unsure of how bail-outs of the government debt will benefit our country or us personally." To be sure, these men, and most of my study participants, admitted to having benefited financially and socially from Greece's membership in the eurozone. However, these middle- and upper-middle-class men and women resented being "victimized" by a system that had tricked them into serving simultaneously as its beneficiaries and its pawns.

Uncertainty led to confusion and disorientation, a condition that Margo, in her mid-thirties, described as "extremely spastic." Having lost their jobs within a year of each other, she and her husband relied on temporary unemployment benefits to meet their expenses. Barely established as members of the rising middle class, they were suddenly unable to pay utilities. Increasing debt and "still incomprehensible taxes" paralyzed Margo, who turned into what she termed "a frightened and bitter" person. Anticipating that unemployment benefits would end soon, the couple lacked other sources of income. "We are losing our minds, we are irritable, and we function in fear and madness," said the husband. "Uncertainty and doubt about financial recovery" distressed them and alienated them from each other, she cried.

Fantasies of returning to their ancestral villages to live off the land became for some increasingly popular. Unemployed professionals wondered if survival might mean abandoning city life and instead cultivating their grandparents' fields, which their parents and grandparents had abandoned years ago for more promising urban livelihoods. Second- and third-generation urbanites, who previously had looked down on villagers as rustic hicks, now pondered the possibility of living off the land. The village that also served as a temporary leisurely retreat from the hustle and bustle of the city they now valorized as offering a viable economic strategy.

Revealing an economically driven shift in ideology, younger hosts further rationalized that pursuit of village life would be an ecologically responsible adaptation. Farming, even as a hypothetical economic strategy to being unemployed or homeless, grew in value within a generation that months earlier had labeled it as "immigrants' work."[4] With easy access to the American Farm School of Thessaloniki, some contemplated enrolling in classes to learn about planting and cultivating fruits, vegetables, and legumes for a healthier diet, and to earn a living by selling their products to other urbanites. One fifty-five-year-old college-educated son of rural migrants who had lost his jobs as a part-time musician and retailer now considered life as a farmer. His knowledge about his family's olive groves and vineyards was vague, and he had "no idea" how to cultivate crops. His parents responded to his plans sarcastically, pointing out that he was considering a lifestyle without appreciating the time and skills that farming requires, and the physical stamina that he and his entitled (*kalomathimeni*) peers lacked.

Across age and gender groups, participants compared their lives "before the crisis," pre-November 2009, with the predicament they faced two years later. Uncertainty about how best to prepare for the future distresses all Greeks, said Froso, a twenty-eight-year-old philologist.

"We all talk about how well off we were, and how the worse may be ahead of us . . . this is what scares all of us, not knowing what we may encounter . . . how much further we may fall! We have not reached the bottom of the barrel yet." Like their European counterparts, younger adults felt that eurozone policies were fueling a dismal financial future (Antonucci, Hamilton, and Roberts 2014). For younger adults, economic displacement had quickly shifted their status from "the generation of promise" into "the lost generation."

Christos, an engineer in his fifties and father of two adult sons to support, had been forced to shut down his private office. He and his colleagues were outraged at "the darkness ahead." He wondered:

> Where will this madness lead us? Someone is taking the money right out of my pocket. Soon they'll be grabbing at my balls! Will they continue to take it until I don't have any more to give? Then what? Will they take everything that I own, that my father and I worked so that my children can live well? This is why we can't relax. We are constantly bewildered because we don't know what awaits us ahead!

I met Dina, a divorced teacher in her fifties and mother of a teenage daughter, at a neighborhood grocery store. She felt that she was "sliding in downward spiral without anything to hold onto to avoid hitting the bottom." Like other professionals, Dina had lived a comfortable life. She had gained upward mobility through higher education, a career, and her family's connections. Now, she confessed, "Nothing is familiar, predictable, or comparable with the past of just two years ago . . . we don't have a name for what we are experiencing now . . . we are simply numb—in utter shock [*aposvolomeni*]."

Elders worried about the country's youth while they felt vulnerable and threatened by an uncertain economy. Yiannis and his friends envisioned a precarious future and talked about the irony that even in their seventies they could not predict it. "I thought the crisis was still on paper," he admitted. "However, when loss of income and new taxes knocked on my own door, I felt as if the epidemic had reached me, too!" Uncertainty caused Sandra, an eighty-year-old woman who never married and worked for the Hellenic Telecommunications Organization for thirty years, "persistent migraines and nightmares." During a coffee break one afternoon, she explained to me that she had made monthly payments to a retirement plan for those thirty years. In 2011, her "decent pension" of

€900 a month dropped to €650 a month. She prayed that "they don't cut any more," fearing that as a loner without any other sources of support, another cut would put her in danger of hunger. She began to cry, oblivious to onlookers at the café where we usually met for a mid-morning cappuccino. Sandra called me three weeks later in shock to tell me her pension and holiday "gift" would be reduced further. "The gift" refers to the bonus that employees receive before Christmas and Easter, which citizens consider integral to their annual income. Accordingly, many of my informants referred to the elimination of the bonus not only as another cut in their annual income, but as another indicator of uncertainty.

Zack and Alexia, a couple in their seventies, were accustomed to self-sufficiency and now admitted to living day to day in agony and despair. I interviewed them together at their elegant, well-appointed home in Panorama. Alexia began with this revelation: "We fear what will happen next. I look around me and everything is crumbling—shops are closed, people lose their jobs, and professionals shut down their private offices." She was particularly traumatized by media reports that people lacked food and were sending their children to school hungry without breakfast. "There does not seem to be an end to this calamity," she cried. Of course, clarified her husband,

> We don't know anyone who is hungry, but we hear that people don't have food to eat, that children are starving! I am typically a positive and optimistic person and I want to believe that we will get through all of this, but the tragic circumstances, as the media portrays them, and the uncertainty about the future, traumatize even me!

The couple also disclosed a painful living situation. Their recently divorced daughter and their granddaughter, both of whom lived with them in the lower level of their home, now relied fully on their financial and moral support. The angst of which they spoke reveals their disillusionment and grief that their daughter and granddaughter are not only unlikely to live in the style to which they had become accustomed, but that their future appears unpredictable and perilous.

Overwhelmed by uncertainty today, my hosts feared a precarious tomorrow. Parents faced pressure to adopt frugality as a new value in childrearing, while young adults grieved their lost hopes for prosperity in their homeland. Elders worried particularly about their increasing physical and mental vulnerability in the face of diminishing resources and an unforeseeable future. However, and unlike their younger counterparts, elders often recalled difficult periods in their past and the recoveries that followed to ease their angst.

A Precarious Future

> We fear that everything that we accomplished will be lost
> forever . . . that we will become part of the Third World.
>
> —Maria, 55, 2011

Collective grief and insecurity in an uncertain present also revealed a generalized fear of a precarious future. While beset by chronic anxiety, my study participants were also preoccupied with forecasting an aftermath of the recession. Descriptions of daily life in 2011–2012 highlighted chaos and disorientation, yet hosts' foresights also revealed sentiments that ranged from fearing the country's annihilation to hoping that from the trauma would emerge a stronger society. "There's great fear all around," informants claimed, and it is associated with not knowing if "we will come out of this national calamity." Recalling the occupation by Ottomans and Nazi Germany, some argued that the "economic war" of the time would obliterate Greece as a sovereign nation-state (Argenti and Knight 2015). "That's how whole empires disappear and are lost forever," insisted an ophthalmologist. When I inquired about the prospect of reforms, he, like most others, expressed cautious optimism and hope for a brighter future, only to shift our conversation to a darker present.

Perceptions of impending doom preoccupied everyone. Niki, the mother of two sons in college abroad, echoed others' opposition to globalization and Western interventions in Greece's institutions (Kirtsoglou and Theodossopoulos 2010). She argued that external powers had already decided on a war against Greece, and that citizens were learning about it gradually. "We are without an opportunity to prepare for it. And we don't know the enemy. I don't have an enemy in front of me!" She shrieked: "Too many people are losing their homes. Others are giving up their cars. We can no longer afford car insurance . . . This is a catastrophe, and who will survive this war to see a future, only God knows."

Forced to close his engineering firm, Christos was also convinced that "We are fighting a war, and that the enemy is invisible! How can we fight back?" Vera, a twenty-eight-year-old economist, frequently discussed with her friends "the potential outbreak of WWIII." She spoke with me nervously about the "inevitable anarchy" that may come from "this one crack," a crack that she felt was tormenting people, while not yet reaching the level of "total destruction." Talk of feeling the terror of a fiscal war in their sleep and contemplating suicide punctuated conversations, as were occasional references to the need for no longer affordable psychiatrists and other sources of formal support. A professor of education shared her assessment of her peers' perspectives on the future:

> We are all confused and vulnerable. We are disoriented about the future because we don't trust our political leaders who brought us here. We are scared because we don't know what dawn will bring. We don't see improvements on the horizon. We don't see light, that's why we are scared and hopeless. We all fear that the way things look now, our country will become bankrupt. We fear chaos in the future . . . we fear that we will become the Albania of the 1950s.

Even those who claimed to be temporarily immune to financial ruin depicted the crisis as a form of ethnocide—terror that shattered the spirit of a people without rescue in sight. Yioula, a widow in her fifties, felt alienated and defeated by what she viewed as "a cultural calamity." I asked her to elaborate.

> My mind just can't accept what is happening. We don't know where to look for support, what to call *patridha* [homeland] anymore, or from whom to ask for justice. To whom can we complain? I can't trust anyone anymore, so sometimes I just scream, and scream, and scream, but no one listens.

She admitted to being chronically exasperated at what she saw as injustice—"the punishment of ordinary people for the crimes that elites committed." Most disturbing to her was her tendency to "explode because you don't have a person in front of you to shoot [symbolically]," she cried, recalling the popular impulse "to banish all the parliamentarians." Those in her social circle, she claimed, experienced the crisis as a form of terror that disrupted the rhythm of daily life.

For others, a future of rapid downward mobility might generate civil unrest and violence. A woman in her late sixties feared "an internal revolution," in which "Greeks will destroy Greeks." Like her, many people hypothesized that economic decline might lead to poverty across socioeconomic strata, and that strategies for survival might include violence among and against friends and family. Tom, an instructor at a technical school in his thirties, recalled Aristotle's words: "Poverty is the parent of revolution and crime," he declared. Echoing rural perceptions of "the limited good," he worried that continuing austerity would now force urbanites to compete with their neighbors for increasingly scarce resources (Foster 1965).

Austerity measures, many speculated, might lead to a future in which "people who will go hungry, who will not have 10 cents in their wallet to buy bread . . . will do anything to eat." Mina, a sixty-nine-year-old and proud consumer of the fine arts, dreaded the inevitable outbreak of violence and warned,

> You might run into such a person on the street, and he will hurt you. He might think, "Even if I die, who cares?" Instead of having coffee with friends, or taking medications to feel better, desperate people might find relief in attacking others, like terrorists do!

Describing people who are indignant and enraged, she mentioned economically displaced young men who use profanities in public and threaten to kill people. "Such rage drives people to extremes and if pushed to the limit, they will not be able to control themselves. They cannot think clearly and rationally," she argued. Others also speculated that when people suffer enough, internal violence is likely to erupt. One father, whose daughter was an undergraduate at Harvard University, pondered a scene when one "would soon hesitate to sit at a bench on the seashore to eat a sandwich out of fear that another, hungrier fellow Greek might assault him for his lunch." All my interviewees feared that conditions were likely to worsen, and some believed that it might take decades, even generations, for Greece to find its balance again.

The cessation of salaries, insisted Vera, constituted "the collapse of the whole system," a threat that kept her and her husband, both of whom were still employed, grateful but anxious. Among her friends and peers, she shared, distress and anxiety escalated with each passing day that a societal calamity was inevitable. A popular refrain was, "We don't know how and where we will wake up tomorrow . . . if we survive at all to see a future." Some insisted that Greece was a pawn rather than a beneficiary of European integration—which perhaps had turned out to be a poisoned chalice for all but the elites of Greek society.

Through some responsible media reports and organized lectures by researchers and social analysts, people gradually gained more clarity about the eurozone debt crisis and their government's role in the economic meltdown. However, this increased understanding did little to reassure my hosts that conditions for their families, and their country, would improve. In fact, many older adults reported feeling a declining strength, initiative, or willpower to act. As Dimitris, a sixty-nine-year-old physician, put it, "We have lost our way, and there is little hope of finding it . . . there's no perspective now on how to overcome this catastrophe. We've lost our confidence in ourselves and our ability to control our lives and to plan our future."

Anticipation of a precarious future often left even confident and more informed individuals feeling defenseless. A sixty-two-year-old electrical engineer referred to himself as incapable of securing gainful employment now that retirement was no longer an option. "At this moment I feel that I can still work, that I can make more money, but who will hire me? And besides, there are no jobs now, and will not be any in the near future!" He and his friends talked about how frustrated they were because they did not know what to do and how to direct their own destiny. Said one gentleman in a focus group: "We are smart people, we have skills, yet we are looking at the problem and we don't know how to solve it."

People who were accustomed to planning ahead felt an unfathomable inability to know how to respond to the crisis, whom to trust for information, and where to look for hope. References to a crisis aftermath that is veiled in "darkness" interfered with locals' ability to conceptualize and plan for a future. They lacked reliable information on which to base decisions. As Maria, a sixty-two-year-old administrator, put it, "We don't know how to protect ourselves because we don't know the cause of the disaster, or what is coming at us other than sheer destruction." Concern about an unknown future dominated everyone's daily life as people's projections of a national decline seemed as plausible as the prospects of recovery and national renewal.

On Being Unwell

> People are suffering, they feel melancholy constantly. There is misery all around. It is as if there is mourning everywhere, that something bad will occur. As if terror awaits us.
>
> —SERAPHIM, 53, 2012

People's impression that worse things were in store affected their health. Discussions about austerity measures revealed anecdotes about "being unwell," a state of chronic emotional and mental suffering (Economou, Madianos, Peppou et al. 2013). Most sought solace in one another's company, while few withdrew from social obligations lest their vulnerability show. To my question regarding symptoms of a community in crisis, informants invariably mentioned people's facial expressions that conveyed distress, a depressed tone of voice, and slouched posture when sitting, standing, or walking. They instructed me to pay attention to passersby who appeared to them "worried," "lost," "anxious," "nervous," and "in a daze." "Look around you," a friend prompted me while frowning; "lowered faces everywhere, many, many lowered faces and crouched shoulders . . . a sullen crowd . . . you would never see people in this condition before [the crash]."

Headed toward the seashore for an evening stroll, a woman and her friend shared with me their observation of a man whom she diagnosed as "unhitched and traumatized." He was holding the hand of a little girl, whom they assumed was his daughter, who was skipping joyfully and talking with him. The man impressed them as despondent. He had stopped abruptly in his tracks and gazed in the distance as if he had lost his way, oblivious to his daughter's presence. Scenes like this troubled informants who insisted that people's faces and bodies projected a generalized, collective sense of disorientation and dejection that had been uncommon before the crisis.

Contrary to my interactions with study participants and random strangers, whom I found worried but consistently congenial, friends insisted that certain neighbors, colleagues, or relatives who were happy and generous before the crash had become moody, depressed, and uncharacteristically rude. Gregoris, a high school teacher in his fifties, shared with me the following scenario:

> One summer evening, a neighbor and I hung out and enjoyed food, beer, and conversation, etc. The next day, on my way to work, I ran into the same man. I said, "Hello, Andrea, how are you doing?" He turns around and gives me this angry look, and says, "What's it to you? What are you, a doctor?"

The camaraderie that Gregoris had enjoyed with neighbors and colleagues before the crash was declining. Some individuals were careful to conceal the emotional and physical ills that financial troubles had stirred. However, others found relief in complaining publicly about eurozone policies, self-serving parliamentarians, and the tragedy in which they were protagonists. Others found self-disclosure of their own ill health or that of family members therapeutic. My own observations confirmed informants' assessment that people were talking incessantly and publicly about being ill. A graduate student of history confirmed this:

> Everybody in public cafés and the bus talks about being sick. How they are depressed and anxious . . . they reference fear of a nervous breakdown. They say we look like people looked in Bulgaria years ago, when they were miserable because they were denied the good things in life.

"The problem is as much financial as it is psychological!" acknowledged Petros, an attorney in his forties. He reported that his clients now spoke with him more about their emotional disorders than about their legal cases.

Hearing about fellow citizens who contemplated, attempted, or committed suicide "distresses even the most rational of persons," admitted a nervous wife who worried about her husband's mental state and talk of suicide following bankruptcy. The suicide by handgun of Dimitris Christoulas, a seventy-seven-year-old retired pharmacist, in Syntagma Square alarmed a nation. People empathized with his accusatory remarks about politicians and his final words: "I have debts, I can't stand this anymore." In fact, while suicide rates in Greece have historically been among the lowest in the world, incidents increased rapidly in the aftermath of the 2008 recession and the 2009 eurozone debt crisis (Fountoulakis 2014; Antonakakis and Collins 2014).[5]

During a group interview, Angela, a personal coach and owner of a fitness facility, reported that she and her friends and clients attribute wide psychological instability and suicidal ideation to the crash—"not so much of the market, but the crash of our lifestyle . . . of what we deem normal." In fact, comments about abnormality and chronic irritability were common references to how daily life had changed. During a bus ride, a widow who relied on her husband's dwindling pension admitted this to me: "Something has broken inside me. I can't walk straight and normally anymore . . . I am sick . . . I feel as if I have a rock in my stomach." Indeed, my questions to informants about their lived experience of debt invariably led to narratives of depression (*katathlipsi*), a condition exacerbated by the inability of many to afford anti-depressants or psychotherapy to alleviate the pain.

Individuals reported that they, along with friends and family members, suffered psychologically but that seeking help from a mental health professional was neither customary nor affordable.

A sixty-two-year-old man put it this way: "There is no psychological support for depression . . . the problem in Greece is that we have not learned to ask for professional help. A person must become crazy before any formal intervention takes place, and only when family and friends fail to help." An elderly widow whose wealth had sheltered her personally from the crisis nevertheless complained that the national predicament had caused her so much nervous apprehension that she feared she might die of apoplexy.

Some compared the eurozone debt crisis to the Great Depression of the 1930s that devastated state economies and families across the globe.[6] "I don't know if this catastrophe is like the crisis of the '30s, but the desolation and insecurity that we are experiencing today is sheer torture," said sixty-eight-year-old Eleni. She admitted that the "cloud of debt" was making her physically and mentally ill. She complained to me of chronic headaches, panic attacks, and heart palpitations. Others reported various aches and pains, agitated nerves, and sleep apnea. Jenny, who graduated with a master's degree in anthropology and who worked part-time at her family's restaurant, described her mother's condition:

> I hear her get up in the middle of the night. She walks out to the balcony, she smokes one cigarette after the other, and she cries. She cries because she is scared, she cries because she is angry, she cries because she fears tomorrow.

Fueling this woman's angst was the insurmountable debt that her husband had accrued in high-interest bank loans to build multiple rental properties, without her consent. Faced with empty units and financially strapped tenants, Jenny's mother was "mad with wrath" and resented her husband for putting her family at risk of bankruptcy.

Members of lower-income households were predictably more vulnerable than their more fortunate counterparts. Vaso, a forty-two-year-old social worker, shared with me insights gained through her practice with working-class families. Her clients had expected the crisis to last two to three years. When it persisted, her clients anticipated further declines in their mental health and family stability. Vaso shared with me her professional assessment of the crisis:

> There were always poor people, of course, but now the rates of poverty are increasing significantly. These are people who lived just fine, but now they have become poor; they are the new poor.

This poverty is different, unrecognizable. We're talking about extreme poverty. People don't have heat to keep warm in the coldest winter we have seen in years . . . they may not have enough food to feed themselves. That's what scares us . . . that for them, this worse situation has already arrived.

Chronic anxiety, Vaso told me, included her own concerns and those of her middle-class peers. "We, too, are anxious because the money is disappearing." She and her colleagues commiserated about diminishing salaries, while an increasingly indigent client population demanded their services more than ever. During our interview a couple of Vaso's colleagues, also therapists, joined our conversation. They told me that their own downwardly mobile clients complained more and more of emotional and psychological disturbances, attributing their declining mental health to fear of an even steeper fall. Many expressed fear that "Greece will become like the Albania of the 1950s," she said, echoing a popular perception of their country's destiny. In general, people equated poverty and poor health with conditions in the Balkans, to which they had been exposed directly or learned about from immigrants.

The Indignity of It All

> A person may sacrifice everything but must maintain her dignity. One does not need a lot of money. Middle-class people can live well. A middle-class person must be able to meet her basic needs . . . have a home, have a car, be able to appear in public and to navigate society. That's dignity!
>
> —Yioula, 62, 2012

One morning, on my way to the Byzantine Museum to conduct an interview with a bank clerk, I noticed a well-dressed man lean carefully into a dumpster while he held his tie away from the overflowing trash. Within seconds he pulled out a paper cup, still with the lid on it and a straw intact. He opened the cup, lifted it to his lips, and drank to the lees whatever leftover beverage was still in it. He then threw the resealed cup back in the bin and proceeded to scavenge, presumably for other eatables. On another occasion, I observed a woman with two small children approach a dumpster on Tsimiski, one of the main thoroughfares in the city center. She instructed her children to sit quietly in the shade, next to an upscale boutique, whose large windows were plastered with discount signs. The woman pulled various objects out of the dumpster, including a crib blanket, children's clothes, and overcoats in various sizes. She placed these items on the sidewalk and continued searching for more. I watched her fill large bags, which she threw over her small shoulders, grab her children by the hand, and walk away. Passersby stared at her solemnly and shook their heads in ambivalent approval. Such scenes troubled my hosts, who claimed an increase in the number of beggars throughout the city, because they signaled not only poverty, and hunger, but also shame. The frequency of these incidents signaled assault on the nation's dignity—an affront to a proud people for whom self-respect and social standing equate with individual accomplishment and family stability.

Hindering their struggle to sustain a semblance of dignity was the cacophony of stereotypes and insults directed at the Greek population by the international media. Indignity manifested itself as embarrassment, shame, and guilt among both those who considered the recession to be a neoliberal attack and those who viewed it as an outcome of personal indiscretions. Even two years into the crisis, my informants concealed from their friends and neighbors detailed accounts of their financial woes, lest it cost them their social image. "Imagine my humiliation," admitted a sixty-four-year-old physician in tears, "when my mentor in medical school called me from Germany to offer me financial support!" Economic security is a core value and a signifier of moral character among these middle-class urbanites. Publicly one neither brags about the specifics of gaining wealth, nor discloses the particulars of losing it.

Individuals whose bank accounts were depleted and whose refrigerators were emptier than usual liked to maintain a well-groomed appearance. While locals reported that purchases of new clothes and accessories had ceased in the wake of the crisis, public displays of expensive and fashionable apparel already in their closets continued. The well-groomed men and women who filled the streets and cafés of Thessaloniki challenged tourists to confirm that the crisis about which they had heard and read was real. Of course, tourists were unable to decipher the nuances of new forms of sociality. The well-dressed young adults whom they saw engaged in spirited conversations in the cafés now sipped their *frappé* for hours. Hundreds of couples avoided the expense of a table at a bar by opting instead to stroll on the promenade.

Others watched the romantic sunset from the city's Pier 1 port while they shared a bottle of beer or wine purchased at the nearby kiosk or a sandwich from a bakery. Such creative adjustments to loss of income facilitated sociality and saved face for a people who prize being out in the city ensconced in their *parea* of dear friends and select relatives. Showing up, being present, and partaking in public social gatherings, always groomed and fashionable, displayed one's dignity even if at their disposal was the last euro of their weekly allowance.

Downward mobility was moral anathema to many, including Yiannis and his comrades, who had entered their senior years in comfort and respectability. At the onset of crisis these retirees denied that the economy was as fragile as the media indicated. Like others in his social circle, Yiannis explained to me that even as financial hardship permeated all levels of society, he "suddenly" became conscious of his own at-risk status. In a trembling voice he continued: "I had a certain profile to maintain. Now I feel overcome with shame . . . imagine reaching your seventies and then losing your dignity!" Yiannis felt that a decline in his financial security threatened his social status—the honor and prestige he felt he had earned through his financial success. He recalled to me Greeks' preoccupation with one's public image relative to cultural constructs of honor and shame. "Greeks are a proud people," he told me. His comrades agreed in unison. Saving face was a cultural practice that my hosts insisted must be maintained.

Referring to some wealthy friends and colleagues, a middle-aged architect observed that although the catastrophe had not yet knocked on their door, anticipation of the aftermath of the bust still preoccupied them. "Shame will come when your neighbors notice that you don't have money, that you no longer operate like you used to," he explained. Yet references to relatives, friends, and neighbors who were especially hard hit by austerity reflected compassion and empathy. "People are ashamed to admit they can no longer afford to eat meat and fish, heat their house, or pay for children's tutorials," a neighbor told me. Even people who needed immediate help meeting basic needs still wanted, and were expected, to maintain their dignity.

For those who still felt able to lend a hand to less fortunate friends and family members, the calamity was too close for comfort. Crossing the center daily, a woman noticed that more and different people appeared "still clean, walking around with their little suitcase who live on benches." She spoke of a neighbor who could not pay her rent of 500 euros and other utilities after her monthly pension was reduced by

750 euros per month. Someone can go from living well to being poor when their household income diminishes or disappears. Such circumstances force some elders to turn into beggars, I observed.

For days, I spotted an elderly woman dressed in solid black, her head wrapped in a scarf that covered part of her face, and her trembling hand outstretched for alms. Each morning she appeared seated on the same corner and near a bus stop on one of Thessaloniki's busiest thoroughfares, an avenue lined with shops, office and residential buildings, and tourist sites (see figure 3.2). When one day my eyes met hers, she signaled me to approach her. When I leaned near her, she produced a glossy wedding photo and pointed to her son and his bride who, she said sorrowfully, had been killed in an automobile accident. In the local Greek dialect, she identified herself as "a crippled widow," who was now responsible for two young grandchildren. So dire were her circumstances that she had resorted to begging for money to feed her family and to purchase her medications. From her pocket she took out a few empty prescription bottles, and two prescriptions dated weeks earlier that she

FIGURE **3.2 A grandmother waiting for alms.**
Source: Photo by Kathryn Kozaitis.

could not afford to fill. I listened to her story sympathetically, left her some money, and walked away.

A shop owner a few meters away from this unfortunate woman stopped me. "You just threw your money away," shouted the man. The old lady, he went on, "does that for a living. Her story is nonsense . . . I observe her daily . . . this is her profession." This spectator's depiction of the elderly beggar as a rogue may have been accurate. However, her visible predicament alone revealed an unconventional profile of a Greek grandmother. In time, I observed more elderly women, always dressed in solid black, whose children could no longer support them and who now relied on charity. "Such indignity is new in the streets of Thessaloniki, and it is growing every day. The indignity is a national problem," confirmed a doctoral student of history who guided me through a tour of the city one hot afternoon.

The conspicuous presence of urban beggars alarmed locals, who suspected that among the foreigners might be residents of metropolitan Thessaloniki. "Now there are Greeks among the street beggars, and the number is increasing daily," said twenty-four-year-old Dora, a recent graduate of a local university. She was startled when she witnessed a well-dressed elderly man rummaging in a dumpster in her upscale neighborhood in Panorama, presumably looking for food. Especially alarming to observers was seeing faces of people they thought they recognized who had lost their homes and lived on the street. "We could be next," they feared.

Another new sight that signaled concerns with saving face among locals were the bags and "solidarity baskets" filled with groceries that others left unattended on the side of the road or against a wall near the public market. Through this new form of gifting citizens aided the needy, but did so discreetly to preserve their dignity (Rozakou 2016b). A local hair stylist recounted the following scenario:

> One time I went to the fresh market and I noticed that there were bags that had things in them—full of bread, apples, and clothes. Further down I saw a bag with oranges. Then I noticed that a woman went and took the bags quietly and walked away. No one spoke to her. But everybody knew that she and her family must be struggling.

Those who knew families in dire need helped them as a matter of *anthropia* (humaneness). "We leave the bag there and walk away, knowing that we are helping a family that suffers," said one of my neighbors. For each witnessed case of fiscal hardship that my informants provided, they emphasized the psychological, emotional, and spiritual toll that it took on those unable to preserve their dignity or to hide their shame.

Hope Heals

> We need to have hope. We need to create hope. If we assume that we have reached the bottom of the barrel, we can only move up!
>
> —HARRIS, 59, 2012

When people focused on immediate events and news of the day, a sense of hopelessness usually conquered their spirits. Yet when I asked them to imagine possible favorable outcomes of the crisis my hosts mentioned hope for change, both as a feeling of anticipatory emancipation from adversity and as an act of resilience that inspired resourcefulness and a will to survive (Bloch 1986). Recalling Theocritus's (270 b.c.) words, "Where there is life there is hope," a thirty-four-year-old lab researcher pondered. "As long as we are alive, we hope" (*Oso zoume elpizoume*). Some prefaced their narratives of hope by apologizing for rationalizations, wishes, and fantasies of a brighter future, while others linked the inevitability of recovery to the basic drive for political transcendence of human nature. Others emphasized the power of hope as a basic human attribute, and a vehicle for helping individuals and populations in despair to change their thinking and their habits (Zournazi 2002).

In her late sixties, and the widow of a once successful attorney, Eleni was outraged, but thoughtful and hopeful. She felt that difficult days, even tragedies, are part of life and that one learns to adapt. She philosophized: "The rule in any crisis is that you can choose to give up something but still enjoy something else. One must learn to live with less . . . that the crisis may be a temporary condition that requires adjustment." Accustomed to a gracious lifestyle as a resident of the city's historic center, Eleni was outraged that predictability and control, privileges she had taken for granted her entire life, were being "snatched" from her and from other "decent, dignified people." Still, she insisted, "We are resourceful people; with hope and determination, we will overcome and rebuild. Let our youth be healthy, and all with be well with our country."

Others shared Eleni's optimism that recovery is possible. A cab driver who struggled to support his family was sure that even though people were despondent now, their love of country and their identity as Hellenes would give them the strength to overcome. Resilience, he felt, was on the side of young Greeks who looked to solidarity as a weapon of revitalization. A retired attorney hoped for "a miracle," and likened the economic crisis to a life-threatening disease. He posited that through proper treatment and interventions, the patient survives, even after a lengthy period of recovery. If we remember our history, he argued, we can hope for a better future. And a twenty-eight-year-old historian and would-be anthropologist found solace in the following ancient Greek words: "*Τί κοινότατον; Ἐλπίς. Καὶ γὰρ οἷς ἄλλο μηδέν, αὕτη παρέστη (Ti kinotaton? Elpis. Ke ghar is allo midhen, afti paresti)* What is a given? Hope. When all else has vanished, hope remains, he said with certitude.

Some advocated compliance with recommendations by global economic experts and adoption of neoliberal principles as a way out of the crisis. Observed one accountant, "eurozone technocrats saw that we are crooked, and they are telling us to straighten out. It is up to us now to readjust our ways and, I believe, we will overcome these difficulties. Once we prove ourselves as honest and good eurozone partners, then we will reinstate our economy." Describing the "Greek character" as impulsive and improvisational, an instructor of philology argued that Greeks are agile and accustomed to surviving crises. He reasoned, "As a people, we have not learned to live according to protocols and programmatic instructions . . . The state is completely disorganized, so we have learned to adapt and adjust and solve problems daily, often based on the problem of the moment." Despite these self-orientalizing statements, most of my hosts believed that recovery and an eventual sustainable economy depended as much on EU policies and state practices as on personal accountability.

One young woman self-identified as an optimist. She questioned conformity to global markets and recognized instead Greeks' agentive potentialities as a resilient people.

> Even if we have to return to the drachma, or be subjected to yet higher rates of unemployment, even famine, we will survive through a rebirth and, hopefully, we will move forward as an organized people. It is a matter of getting through this transition, and through our wits, and by fishing and hunting, and gardening, we will reinvent ourselves. Perhaps we never should have abandoned these ways of life and given in to neoliberalism. Let there be hope and we will persevere as a people.

Her sentiments echo others' confidence that structures and institutions may die, but that Greeks will prevail as a society. Such discourses of hope often highlighted the promise of agentive, grassroots mobilization in revitalizing Greece.

Even the most skeptical and cynical of study participants expressed hope that Europe would not sacrifice Greece, if only to save itself. Greece has been vulnerable to worse conditions since its inception as a modern state; it has managed to survive because of the legacy of its classical civilization, which the entire West has adopted, they argued confidently. A retired businessman in his mid-60s who received his formal education in northern Europe spoke of the West's cultural debt to Greece:

> European culture and spirit were launched by the ancient Greeks. Western Europeans understood our civilization and adopted it . . . enlightened leaders were inspired to create a united Europe that includes Greece. Even though Greeks have behaved badly, and are punished for it, Europe wants to save itself, so Europe will save Greece. Let us hope that that's how things will turn out.

Others insisted that disruptions or shocks to any new geopolitical system are par for the course, and that Greeks ought to remain patient and hopeful that the crisis will yield social and cultural reforms. "We elders know that we are in flux, that everything changes," asserted the businessman. He recalled the ancient aphorism "Πάντα ρεῖ" (Pada ri), everything flows, to convey his belief that hope, patience, creativity, and intentionality will see Greeks through this new, but temporary disintegration of their society.

The turmoil that permeated Greece in 2011–2012 mirrored the emotional responses of Europeans across Portugal, Italy, Spain, and of Americans a few years earlier. All were victims of a financial bust and its attendant sociocultural transitions (Bremer and Vidal 2018). Financial exploitation by elites, rampant unemployment, and unanticipated downward mobility stimulated conflicting emotions in citizens ranging from despondency to relief, from despair to hope, and from indignity to resilience. Popular and critical assessments of European integration as a failed economic project did little to console individuals whose personal fortunes were disappearing, or whose families risked hunger and homelessness. The consensus among all participants was that mass, crisis-generated psychological disorders were evident all around, and that the economic recession had turned into a social, humanitarian crisis. Alarming rates of suicide threatened the emotional state of my hosts, as did conspiracy theories of national obliteration through economic warfare or another German occupation of their homeland. My observations confirmed a generalized cultural malaise rooted as much in a destabilizing, uncertain present as in fears of a precarious economic future. The complex, varied, and fluctuating emotional states depicted in these narratives are implicit symptoms of *crisis as liminality*, and reveal participants efforts to confront and manage what they experience as a dissolution of normal social order and uncertain postcrisis outcomes. While distressed by gnawing economic anxieties and societal instability, informants sought simultaneously to ascertain the causes of the disaster and to gain some control over its effects on their state of mind. Their perceptions and declarations of blame and accountability are the focus of the next chapter.

Notes

1. See Campbell (1964), du Boulay (1974), and Friedl 1962 on gender roles in rural localities of Greece.
2. Dowry is an important institution that throughout rural Greece is associated with the transfer of property, including agricultural fields, livestock, and household materials from the bride's family to the new couple as a form of inheritance. The practice changed to coincide with the rural to urban migration of the 1960s and early 1970. Among middle-class urbanites the practice continues, but involves the transition of property from parents to their children, typically in the form of apartment homes or business, and money, that individuals or couples may acquire before or after marriage. See du Boulay (1983); Dimen and Friedl (1976) on variation in postmarital residence and correlate inheritance patterns.
3. See Neofotistos (2008) for a discussion on Western depictions of "the Balkans" as Europe's "Other within."
4. See Koutsou, Patsalidou, and Rajot (2014) for an account on young farmers' pursuit of rural development models as a response to global markets.
5. According to Basta, Vgontzas, Kastanaki et al. (2018), while Crete has the highest mortality rate in Greece, there was no significant increase between 1999 and 2013, which includes the period of acute austerity. The study also concluded that there was an increase of suicides among middle-aged men (forty to sixty-four years of age) and the elderly, and an increase of suicides among residents of Eastern Crete, who lack formal support services, and a decrease in western Crete.
6. For a discussion on the Great Depression and its impact on the daily life of those who lived through it see Elder (1974).

CHAPTER 4

Days of Reckoning

In this chapter the focus shifts from feelings to thoughts, as participants consider the roots, nature, and causes of the crisis. In the wake of state-enforced fiscal austerity in 2011–2012, I found Thessalonikians consumed not only by emotional turbulence, but also by cognitive deliberations of cause and effect as they tried to make sense of their plight. This form and process of intellectual work is typical of liminal actors who seek order out of chaos. Public discourse on accountability for the crisis was prevalent, but highly variable.[1] It reflected the influence of alarming media accounts as well as citizens' own critical introspection. Forced, tumultuous disruption of daily realities exacerbates symptoms of social liminality—a people's collective experience of living in limbo, a state that is neither fully conventional and customary nor absolutely new and enduring. My interlocutors' interpretations and explanations of a personal and a cultural economic upheaval they did not anticipate reveal their concern with understanding and responding to the crisis thoughtfully and resourcefully. The following categories of actors, and the transactions that link them, figure in their ruminations: state officials, eurozone elites, Greek citizens, and global financiers.

State Officials

> The [Greek] state must have known. Why did the govern-
> ing officials permit us to extend ourselves so freely, put us in
> extreme levels of debt, and then crush the whole economic
> system?
>
> —Vaso, 42, 2011

In 2011, people were suspicious that officials had known all along that a fiscal bust was imminent, and that austerities would continue and would become more severe. Without exception, participants accused their officials of bearing principal responsibility for the collapse because "they knew the truth from the beginning, and they lied to us." A sixty-two-year-old clerk lamented that "the political parties that govern the nation now are the ones that led us to the financial crisis . . . and yet they continue to govern." Some theorized that the Greek state's compliance with eurozone policies protected the already privileged parliamentarians at the cost of ordinary citizens.

The state's conventional disregard of widespread tax evasion compelled even those who had avoided paying property taxes to complain about "living in a country with a negligent, disorderly, and reckless government." They criticized the authorities for their failure to monitor citizens' lack of compliance with public policies, including legal transactions and tax evasion. Greece's unregulated tax system reportedly protects wealthy individuals and families, who may display their assets in the form of large and multiple homes, expensive cars, international leisure travel, yachts, and private jets, yet declare €10,000–15,000 as their annual income. Informants repeated to me the popular claim that more than 80 percent of self-employed citizens declare an annual income of €10,000, while civil servants are obligated to pay the required percentage of income taxes.

Others claimed that the state gave pensions illegally, including "thousands of euros to dead people." Reportedly, children, grandchildren, and neighbors collected the social security funds of deceased persons without having to provide proof of identity. Yioula, a middle-aged schoolteacher, explained the scam:

> When a grandmother dies, someone must declare her death to
> I.K.A. What if the old lady lived alone? What if she had direct
> deposit? Who knows who had access to her checking account?

> It could be her kids, it could be her neighbors. No one monitors the distribution of social security funds. This could have happened to thousands of people . . . investigators determined that thirty to forty thousand people were receiving social security checks in the names of "deceased" parents. Now when we go to the bank as retirees we must show our identification card and sign that we are alive [*en zoi*].

Another scandal that my consultants attributed to the state is the distribution of disability benefits to healthy people. Some bribed government officials to confirm by signature that a recipient was disabled. A famous case took place in the island of Zakynthos, where a person who received disabilities for being blind was caught driving. Another much-abused government program provided compensation to (real and purported) wounded warriors.

The parliamentarians, claimed my friends, control access to public offices and appointments in civil service settings. Many spoke disparagingly about political connections (*ta kone*) and social cliques (*klikes*), the dominant mechanisms by which politicians afford civilians access to all strategic resources, including professional posts in public institutions. A middle-aged teacher recalled a job interview with a government agency following his graduation from college. The interviewer said to him, "We need to figure out to which party you belong, so that we can determine how to proceed," to which he responded, "I don't think this will work out."

There was broad consensus among participants that state officials are incompetent, myopic, reckless, or at best, uninformed about the political process: "One declares that he is running for office, negotiates and bribes people for votes to become a member of parliament, and then proceeds to live the good life—he secures a good salary, resourceful social connections, access to advantages and entitlements, and entertainment of his choice." A sixty-seven-year-old retired artist with a keen intellect doubted that "anyone in parliament has actually researched or understands the depth and responsibility of proper governance." She continued:

> The politicians are as ignorant and complacent as the rest of us. They too, have been sleeping. All the economic bliss that we have enjoyed without any concern is due to lack of information. The French, the Germans, and other foreign powers manipulated our officials to conform unwittingly to policies that they may not have understood, or cared to understand.

Equally critical were others' depiction of politicians as weak creatures or "little people" (*anthropakia*)—persons without the education, talent, or ambition to pursue an honest profession. Such characters, my hosts argued, choose politics instead: a career based on greasing the palm for favors (*lathoma*), a form of bribery, and other informal exchanges of resources for votes. Grigoris, a fifty-year-old instructor of agriculture, did not mince words:

> At this moment 99 percent of the politicians who govern us pursued politics to make money, and not to produce, because they don't know how to produce, or they don't consider themselves competitive, and they are afraid to get to the pavement to sell [compete in the open market]. So, they go into politics where bribery dominates!

I stopped counting the number of times I heard people angrily imagine the mass assassination of all public officials as an expedient response to the country's decline. In the words of a rather dignified elderly gentleman, "The politicians have killed Greece! Shouldn't they be executed? They are criminals! What they are putting us through is a huge crime!" Citizens' critiques of politicians as "ignorant," "out of touch," "corrupt," "self-serving" and "lazy," typically included the popular closing statement, "Of course, we elected them!"

Lack of trust in their representatives did not originate with the crisis. Friends lamented their dependency on politicians on whom they have always relied "to get things done," even if illegally. State officials in Greece have historically maintained an instrumental and illicit relationship with civilians, an exchange of often unwarranted employment in the public sector or illegal favors and services for votes. A young woman shared with me the predicament of her cousin, a public servant accustomed to earning a monthly salary of 3,000 euros. "She realizes now that she had neither earned those wages, nor stolen them; the state gave the money to her," she argued. Based on her salary, the woman took out a bank loan, with which she purchased a house and a car, and helped her daughter to set up a home of her own. When the state cut her income by 30 percent, the woman felt as if she had been left "floating in the air." She also risked foreclosure of her house. My host expressed sadness for her cousin, while she accused the state representatives of "taking from her all she had," after setting her up for a fall. Like so many others, not only was this young woman unable to pay the mortgage, she also struggled to pay the newly implemented property taxes. In 2011 the state imposed this property tax levy by adding it to the electricity bill, forcing home-owners to pay it or have their power shut off. My interlocutor felt that the state "fooled us multidimensionally."

Participants blamed state officials for the debt crisis, which they viewed as the inevitable result of politicians' greed and incompetency. A thirty-six-year-old psychotherapist was pessimistic about the state's past injustices and current role in forcing citizens into deeper, "presumably irreversible destruction through debt." She asked, "What can we expect from a state that for so many years we viewed as a generous father who fooled his family and betrayed his children for his own good?" As a school principal put it, "They tricked us! They did what they did consciously and defiantly."

Citizens' complaints seemed to go unheard by parliamentarians who, as my hosts insisted, live in a world of their own (*zoun ston kosmo tous*). The fact that these perpetrators of the crisis escaped punishment enraged even the most stoic of study participants. A popular reference of contempt for all politicians was Apostolos (Akis) Tsochatzopoulos, a founding member of PASOK who served as a minister in several PASOK cabinets (1981–2004). He was convicted on October 7, 2013 on multiple economic scandals, including accepting bribes from offshore companies for the procurement of a Russian rocket defense system and German submarines.[2] Accused widely of "eating [stealing] public money," he had become an infamous symbol of Greece's crooked and debased political and economic elite. "And he is not alone, he is just the one who got caught and will be punished," claimed a disgruntled bank clerk.

Former PASOK loyalists articulated their deep disillusionment at George Papandreou (2009–2011), in whom they once had placed confidence to represent Greece to the Europeans. Similarly, Antonis Samaras, the center-right leader of New Democracy (2009–2015) and prime minister (2012–2015), had energized his supporters only to leave them deeply disappointed and hopeless. Talk of the left-wing SYRIZA party coming into power in 2015 thrilled those who adopted its anti-austerity rhetoric, while infuriating others. Indeed, reliance on any head of state to protect the Greek citizenry from foreign exploitation seemed futile. Sentiments of blame against politicians often conveyed a sense of personal betrayal and assault. Asked many a despondent voter: How can citizens function and thrive when the political environment is a chaotic mess (*bahalo*)?

European Policymakers and Eurozone Technocrats

What business did we have in the Eurozone? Did we not get
along just fine, before?

—SORITIS, 35, 2012

Greece's perennial economic and political dependence on foreign powers, and misallocation of strategic resources by state officials, compromised the country's economic development and its productive workforce. Threatening to disgruntled citizens, who found austerity measures
to be punitive and arbitrary, was the popular rhetoric of an ultimatum
rooted in Europe: "Austerity or drachma. You choose." This threat came
from what some considered to be invisible webs of influence—EU policies, and eurozone politics. Participants blamed eurozone elites for manipulating Greek officials (*lamoghia*) in transactions driven by a commission that politicians receive, such as those made from purchasing
weapons from foreign parties on behalf of the Greek government. German bureaucrats, argued some, have exploited Greek leaders of PASOK,
the New Democracy, and the Communist Party, knowing that they all
"swim in filth and corruption." Northern Europeans, they insisted, are
the superior crooks. They took advantage of Greek counterparts and
others in Europe's south who did not stand up to implicit patronage by
Europeans of the north.

Thirty years after Greek officials negotiated the conditions of
Greece's inclusion in the European Union, eurozone elites dictated and
Greek authorities imposed austerity measures that would oppress ordinary Greeks. References to Angela Merkel and Wolfgang Schäuble as
contributing actors to the Greek crisis were common. How, my hosts
wondered, do eurozone elites dare to demand such sacrifices by ordinary citizens to bail out a bankrupt state economy? One self-employed
accountant in his late sixties confessed, "Wherever I turn my head I see
misery." His adult children, who are credentialed with graduate degrees,
are unemployed and dependent on him and his wife. The men and
women who work for him live in fear that their days of gainful employment are numbered. Meanwhile, the demand for his own business, on
which the livelihood of his entire family depends, decreases by the day.

This gentleman vented about his predicament as he sat in the quiet,
dark office of his small family business:

Troika orders reforms for Greece by claiming that our nation is
corrupt and disorganized and requires rebuilding. Our officials

insist that "we have to fix the economy," but how? Punishing ordinary citizens who depend on wages to feed their families? Today I fired half of our employees. We had seven, and now we have four. I also reduced their wages from 1,000 euros to 850 euros. And I decreased their hours; now they work seven instead of eight hours a day.

The incongruence of a "deep socialist nation" within a "neoliberal supra state" bewildered him. He mocked prime minister George Papandreou for his incompetency, and former minister of finance George Papakon-stantinou (2009–2011) for the response to EU elites' invitation to join the eurozone: "Since you [Europeans] have the recipe, we'll follow you and we'll adapt." Of course, he argued,

> We did not adapt from the start, and we struggle to adapt now. Troika has our officials by the neck, telling them, "You are an unaccountable nation! We have to give you money to bail you out of the mess, but only if you agree to cuts in salaries, pensions . . . you need to become more competitive so that one day you may lift your head again."

Like many others, this gentleman was convinced that the Troika subjugates Greek officials, and that those officials in turn subjugate the Greek citizens without remorse. This form of structural violence is familiar to all who understand that since the birth of the modern Greek state, European guardianship has always crushed the Greek citizenry.

As a retired former employee of an international bank argued, with George Papandreou at the helm following the 2007–2008 fiscal collapse, "[Northern] European leaders found fertile ground [*pros-phoro edhaphos*] to exploit. In him the foreign powers found a conduit to turn Greece into 'the black sheep of Europe.'" I asked her to elaborate.

> He brought corruption to our society with his lie that "There is money" [*lephta iparhoun*] . . . Greece did not have to reach vassalage if Georgie [*Ghiorghakis*] [Papandreou] had been economically savvier, more honest, and more responsible. Instead, he betrayed his constituencies with short-term gifts so that his friends and relatives could profit.

Citing her expertise as a banking professional, she declared this: "Money and the banks rule the world now. There are no longer visionary, social, moral leaders. Europe does not have social leaders. Mrs. Merkel is not a leader, but a captive of the banks and one of the beneficiaries of economic profits . . . there is no Franklin Roosevelt any more." Brussels (the de facto capital of the European Union and code for eurozone elites), she argued confidently, had enticed Greek government officials by including them in their mission to dominate the continent's economic peripheries, including Italy, Spain, and Portugal.

Along with public frustrations about yet another "foreign occupation" were shared grievances against eurozone technocrats who seemed to be immune to punishment for illegal acts and immoral indiscretions. Middle-aged participants of a focus group expressed outrage at all eurozone elites and eurozone-minded Greek leaders who they felt escaped punishment for their immoral deeds. A man who was forced to shut down his kiosk and only source of livelihood complained: "The fact that those responsible for bringing the country to this disaster are not punished, perhaps even benefit from their political maneuvers makes me feel like a dupe [*malaka*]."

Most participants agreed that European policymakers deliberately sought to repress or paralyze the Greek public with talk of a Grexit.[3] Some argued that Eurocrats lead people into a state of vegetation or hypnosis, even as ongoing social protests and demonstrations against austerities were held throughout the country. While all study participants feared the destruction of the Greek nation-state, most were certain that Grexit was not a true threat because, as one schoolteacher put it, "They will not let us exit from the euro, because it suits them to keep us in it. The rest of us will have to live with 300–400 euros a month, and they will claim, 'That's more than you deserve!'" Eurozone policymakers, she feared, were determined to turn Greece into "a poor society, so that they may control us as they want, so that we are dependent on them—so that we become the Third World. Germany will turn us into its farmland." In a similar vein, a social worker was certain that the very rich, those who "ate [stole] the people's money," will not feel the fiscal drop in their life style because they possess hidden assets abroad.

Global Bankers and Corporate Financiers

> A bank clerk would call and offer you money. You felt as if you had won the lotto.
>
> —ANTIGONE, 49, 2011

Discourses of blame and accountability also extended to representatives of multinational corporations, global financial institutions, and European banks. Most participants admitted to unfamiliarity with global economics, yet they theorized that the Greek state economy was subject to neoliberal requirements and global markets controlled by opportunistic tycoons and predatory lenders. People acknowledged their own naiveté about international monetary exchanges, and a generalized negligence in understanding and conforming to global fiscal policies and practices. Others spoke of the "global bubble" that engulfed them and their "discovery of the stock market," in which novice investors lost savings and homes. Broad consensus among my interlocutors pointed to the multinational banking firms, such as Goldman Sachs, and rating agencies, such as Moody's Corporation, as the ultimate perpetrators of the Greek crisis. The vulnerability of Greek officials to ruthless big business moguls was a popular account of why "Greece folded." As the elder accountant acknowledged, while the recession is a global disaster, "the stone fell on us." Like his contemporaries, this man viewed Greece as the epitome of a failed neoliberal experiment.

Monetary predators exploited a public vulnerable to consumer credit with promises and images of a more affluent way of life (Placas 2018). Most debtors claimed that bank representatives had convinced them to accept holiday loans (*eortodhania*) and vacation loans (*dhiakopodania*). Bankers reportedly told prospective borrowers that the first payment for any of these loans would be due three years from the date of borrowing. With reassurance that "we have time" to repay the loan, some first-time automobile owners celebrated a marker of upward mobility, with typically a jeep, BMW, or a Porsche Cayenne. Citizens reportedly accepted car loans and mortgages without considering the implications of contractual terms regarding the amount and timing of repayments of principal and interest. Pointing to a neighbor who had borrowed money to purchase three jeeps, one for each adult in the family, a woman compared her own, more sensible decision to share a car with her two adult children. Yet she quickly justified her neighbor's actions as "naïve," blaming instead the predatory bankers that subjected her neighbors, and thousands of others, to a lifestyle based on debt.

Predatory bankers victimized citizens who did not understand the procedures of formal, legal loans and those who lacked experience with living on credit. Borrowers who did not qualify for loans financially, or who were unlikely ever to be able to repay such loans, had assumed various degrees of debt on the premise that "God willing, we'll pay it back one day." Speaking rhetorically to a bank, Marina remarked:

> You are principally responsible. Why do you allow him [the citizen] to purchase what he cannot afford? Why do you give him money and tell him that he has three years to make the first payment, and you don't ask him, "Mr., do you have the money to buy this car or this house on these loan conditions? And if so, show me the money!"

"Isn't this how lending works in America?" she asked me. "First you demonstrate your assets, and then you borrow. Nothing like that occurred here." In fact, the subprime mortgage crisis in the United States also resulted from bankers offering easy and ambiguous terms that convinced Americans to accept risky mortgages in anticipation of refinancing with even easier terms. However, rising interest rates and a decrease in housing prices subjected thousands of would-be first homeowners to default and foreclosure. Marina recounted how "hyper happy" everyone was as "free money" floated through households. She concluded, "We now realize that global financiers turned Greece into a sucker [*koroidho*]. Of course, we allowed the bankers to harm us. In return, they have stolen our money and our dignity."

Would-be lenders promoted credit cards as forms of "free purchases." Credit cards became accessible to the Greek masses at the start of the twenty-first century, claimed two lunch companions. My hosts admitted that most borrowers, including members of their family, were uninformed about eligibility requirements, repayment conditions, and late fees. Some argued that they had been "tricked" by bank representatives who convinced them to accept a credit card without explaining the conditions. Reportedly, bank clerks called people at home to inform them of their privileged access to credit. A former banker, retired for several years, reported that even she had felt invaded by calls from colleagues who insisted that she take out a credit card. Such cards were promoted to help meet expenses associated with life rituals, such as a baptism or a wedding, special feast days like Easter, or to fund a luxury vacation for the whole family.

Reportedly, bank officers did not assess fully their clients' borrowing status, neglected to inform clients adequately about repayment plans, and failed to monitor how money was spent. Some admitted to having accepted such offers willingly, albeit naively. Others recollected getting into an argument with the persistent caller. A woman described how she had received a call from a bank representative who told her that she was "eligible for money," an offer that she rejected repeatedly to no avail. "But I don't want a loan!" she resisted. Yet the caller attempted to convince her that the loan was a benefit, an asset that she could repay at her leisure at some distant future. "You'd think that I had won a prize!" she exclaimed. In the end, and not quite certain of her decision, she rejected the offer of a credit card.

The cards increased mass material consumption of creature comforts and status symbols that shifted people's core value orientations and shaped identities (Placas 2018). We changed "from living well, in a more holistic, integrated way, to seeking money indiscriminately as a means of accumulating material possessions," suggested Adriana. "Suddenly, we were all chasing money without necessarily questioning its sources." Another woman, Anna, denounced the practice by adults of giving their children money at whim, arguing that "we have taught them [children] to chase money from the age of fifteen . . . to find ways to gain as much money as possible, because bankers convinced us that everything worth having requires money. That's how we became greedy." She then chastised her fellow Greeks for "forgetting what the ancients used to say": "The man who is not engaged in the public, common well-being, is a useless idiot!"[4]

Others argued that the social cost of such materialism was loss of ethics and morality—neglect of *anthropia*. "Access to easy money, and the accumulation of purchased luxury goods and services, corrupted our moral compass," concluded a pharmacist who was struggling to maintain her business. She argued that bankers and representatives of multinational corporations exploited the country's entire social hierarchy. Heads of state and their allies "ate [stole] first and most," so the middle and the lower classes followed suit, she explained. Old and young alike faulted their representatives and business elites for failing to regulate banks and other lending agencies. A seventy-four-year-old art historian argued that global corporate elites tricked the masses while they protected their own assets by transferring them to Switzerland.

Having enticed Greek politicians into "signing dirty contracts," she continued, financiers then controlled them [*na se ehoun sto kheri*], as in to be in someone's pocket. Speaking for her contemporaries, a retired philologist shared this:

> We cannot wrap our heads around this. We don't know whom to hold accountable, whom to call on, from whom to request our rights. Against whom may we protest? How does one confront [Goldman] Sachs or Moody's? So you yell, and you yell! You yell at Papademos[5] and he responds, "That's how things are; take it or leave it!"

Others referenced allegations of fraudulent accounting practices by Lehman Brothers, and wondered if protesting the investment bank's financial malpractice in front of the US embassy would be productive. Some concluded that the primary cause of austerity measures is "business, not politics," insinuating that money trumps policy. Indeed, neoliberal restructuring, and its attendant policies of deregulation, privatization of state assets, and reductions in welfare provisions fueled the financial and moral ruin of a nation already vulnerable and enmeshed in a dependent socioeconomic system (Kallianiotis 2013).

Greek Citizens

> What can we say? That we didn't know what we were doing? We knew, and looked the other way because [the system] benefited us. The politicians ate well, but we accepted the crumbs that fell from their tables.
>
> —ADRIANA, 67, 2011

Greek debt to foreign powers is as old as the Greek republic itself. Subjugation by foreign rulers, and default of debt obligations to dominant foreign states, have been defining attributes of modern Greece since its birth. "If you want to make sense of what we are going through now, look at our past," noted a fifty-five-year-old engineer. Elaborations invariably included brief references to the region's Roman, Byzantine, and Ottoman past. The country's historical tolerance of informal rules, personal interests, and patronage involving state and religious elites are evident in the systemic everyday corruption that still plagues the Greek state (Gounaris 2008; Haller and Shore 2005; Pardo 2004).[6]

There was also broad recognition among my interlocutors that internal, individual, and collective complicity by civilians helped fuel the country's current fiscal collapse: "We, too, are at fault" (*phteme ki emis*) was a universal refrain across age groups in private and public discussions about the why and the how of the crisis. Middle-aged and older study participants were particularly adamant about having failed to be more accountable for the national well-being. Others emphasized their accountability and obligation by virtue of their privileged position as urban, educated, and critical consumers of world events and local opportunities. Such claims contradict notions of *efthinofovia*, fear of responsibility, or avoidance of blame for disasters great and small, as characteristic of all Greeks (Herzfeld 2016b).

Various participants saw contemporary corruption to be a "residue" of life in the Ottoman Empire. To illustrate internal corruption, they cited such practices as accepting bribes from state officials, including (*rouspheti*) for votes, kickback (*miza*) to solve personal problems, and the provision of unrecorded cash in a small envelope for professional services (*phakelaki*). Such systemic, illegal, and unethical social transactions persist in Greece today, explained a retired employee of the Hellenic Telecommunications Organization S. A. (Organismos Tilepikoinonon Ellathos). "We haven't unlearned the ways of living under the Ottomans . . . Now we live under the Eurozone chiefs." Wrinkling her face in disgust, one woman declared: "The police are bribed, the tax collectors are bribed, the municipal officers are bribed, the customs administration is bribed, the land administration is bribed; we are all bought and sold! There is no morality. Blame the Greek mindset [*nootropia*]." Bribery, as conventional value and practice in Greek society that precedes the debt crisis, reportedly increased rather than decreased during the period of unprecedented affluence. A fifty-eight-year-old physician summarized the "Greek mentality" as a lack of accountability between the state and its citizens:

> Greeks for four hundred years lived under an Ottoman regime, so they always viewed the [Turkish] state as the enemy. The state took from them part of their production, collected taxes, so the Greeks were forced to cheat the state. Even after we created our own state, the mindset remained the same . . . so the state is still an opponent, and the citizens are subjects of the state who continue to trick the state in order to live. That's how the system works.

References to "the Greek mindset" and "Greek mentality" (*nootropia*) as prone to patronage or corruption, and as a partial cause of the crisis, do not signify collective pathological inner states among Greeks, or an absolute internalization of the stereotypes that outsiders ascribed to them. Patronage in business and politics is not unique to Greece, and corruption is certainly not a biogenetic condition of Greeks. It constitutes a mainstream cultural practice of socioeconomic transactions that exists to various degrees within, and across, all societies, including the core member states of the eurozone. Greek *nootropia*, a motif in locals' discourses of accountability, denotes Greeks' acknowledgment of learned, customary, and patterned habits, dispositions, and attitudes that guide and reflect daily strategies to meet practical needs and to solve problems, all within the constraints that state and international structures of power impose. Recognition of *nootropia* as a malleable property with which all humans are endowed, is precisely the basis for Greeks' insistence that in times of crisis "a change of mentality," that is, agentive ideational and behavioral alternatives to established, albeit now maladaptive cultural patterns, is both possible and required for sustainable recovery.

Public perceptions of the Greek state depict it as exploitative from its inception and negligent of the rule of law. Informants insisted that the rivalry between state and citizen, and citizens' mistrust of state officials is justified. The state strives to exploit the citizens, and citizens in turn are forced to trick the state. Corrupt transactions with officials reflect citizens' learned convictions that playing the game of securing one's interests by any means is productive and rewarded. Citizens comply with corrupt leaders, my hosts said, because they rely on patterns of patron-client arrangements, the idea "that someone somewhere will help them, that politicians will protect them, and that elected officials will accommodate them and their own family." As Herzfeld argues, Westerners accuse Greeks of corruption, even as "the system of patron-client relations within Greece reproduces the client status of Greece itself in relation to the Great Powers" (2016b: 11).

Some hosts also pointed to the strategic role of religious elites during the Ottoman occupation in mediating the subjugation of the Greek population by Turkish officials. A social scientist and professor at a local university theorized that "leaders of the Church held a higher status in the Ottoman Empire compared to that of ordinary Christians." Clergy served as administrators and cultural brokers between the Turkish state and the Christian masses. The middleman role that priests occupied fostered access to state privileges, while it permitted them to organize the masses religiously. Is the Greek state to the Eurozone Empire what the Orthodox Church was to the Ottoman Empire? Do clientelist practices among ordinary people reflect the clientelist transactions characteristic of global financial institutions?

Penelope, seventy, believed so. Her perspective integrates historical, political, religious, and cultural references to Greek society:

> Greek society reflects Byzantine values of Orthodoxy. We are still a theocracy . . . the patriarch and the emperor are bound together. Our culture is medieval, Byzantine, and theocratic. Well, this theocratic system ought to rot and be replaced!

Penelope was not alone in arguing that it behooves the politicians to promote the Church because, "With one whistle to priests the politicians earn three million votes!" Indeed, that the Greek Orthodox Church is wealthy, and that state representatives avoid recording or taxing its assets, is a common assumption among Greeks.

Without exception, people argued that daily practices of solving problems and meeting needs contributed to the country's socioeconomic calamity. Patonage, in all its manifestations, reflects "societal realities," and is "necessary to survival" in Greece. The country's economic disaster, study participants declared, was the result of normative Greek values that reflect and drive instrumental relations of exchange. The boom and bust of our three decade-long economic bubble "stank of corruption," claimed some of the more self-critical study participants, who viewed ordinary Greeks as accomplices to political and economic injustices. In fact, patronage dominates all levels of government and sectors of society within which civilians operate, most notably the tax administration and public procurement. Vaggelis, a fifty-year-old educator, assessed Greek mainstream culture as follows:

> The crisis is a curse on our race, because we chase easy money, we succumb easily to bribery to meet our needs, we seek and find ways not to work hard, as long as we don't have to work, we are fine . . . this is characteristic of my generation—the *Homo hellenicus*; we are children of consumption.

The peers of whom Vaggelis spoke belong to the well-known "generation of the polytechnic" (*politekhnio*),[7] a term for students who rebelled against the military junta government (1967–1974) and went on to thrive and define mainstream Greek society and culture. Vaggelis claims that this generation reached the top of the socioeconomic hierarchy, but that it did not know how to manage or sustain it. Now, he hypothesized, the same generation suffers from "a state of free fall . . . This generation, blurred with power, destroyed Greece." A fifty-eight-year-old attorney, who claimed marginal participation in the protests against the military junta, also criticized his more active peers of that movement:

> The Polytechnic generation was supposed to bring about re-
> forms and to democratize Greece. It failed miserably because
> the dominant orientation of change was not knowledge, cul-
> ture, and education, but rapid enrichment [in material ways].

The fifty-six-year-old president of a cultural center concurred. Access to easy money, she claimed, "shifted our values from moderate comforts to beliefs that material goods bring happiness. We lost our way [*ksestratisame*]." This woman blamed Greek citizens who accepted the politicians' affinity for corruption and greed. However, she concluded, "Every act comes with a price, and hubris invites punishment." While citizens may criticize and condemn politicians, she continued, "We must remain strict and critical of ourselves, when we, too, possess such proclivities of corruption and greed without being conscious of it." Indeed, to historical and structural explanations of the fiscal downturn, informants added a *cultural schema*—shared and taken-for-granted mores, feelings, and experiences to interpret the national crisis (Nishida 2005).

"The crisis is a matter of culture," insisted Adriana, an upper-class matron, referring to core beliefs, values, and actions among mainstream Greeks. Many others shared her perspective and acknowledged that explanations of the debt crisis must consider "the Greek mindset": a set of cultural values and norms transmitted through generations that they consider practical, yet now critique as misguided. They highlighted "traditional," ruthless self- and family-centeredness in all business transactions, and a precrash mania for consumption. My hosts noted that members of the middle classes embraced material consumption because it allowed them to demonstrate choice and taste (Bourdieu 1984). "There was a time, before Europe, that we celebrated more simply and hosted more modestly at home with good friends and family," said Georgia nostalgically. She contrasted styles of entertainment before

Greece's incorporation in the eurozone with lavish and conspicuous hosting of dinner parties at restaurants that followed integration. Participants' articulated such conceptual and cognitive *models* that as members of Greek society they have created, internalized, and on which they rely to understand and to cope with precarity (Strauss and Quinn 2001 [1997]).

Money floated in, my friends said, so "we ordered dishes indiscriminately without looking at the menu . . . we would tell the waiter, 'bring this, bring that, bring the other,' as if we were eating free . . . we paid no attention to the prices." Some hosts mocked themselves and admitted that looking at a menu might indicate to companions that one is unaccustomed to eating out frequently, or that the cost of any main course might determine the order. Such an act would not only embarrass one but would "ruin everyone's joyful mood [*kefi*] of the moment." Indeed, when people described overconsumption of food and drink, whether while shopping at the super market or dining at a restaurant or a taverna, gluttony was not the driving force. Conviviality and conspicuous consumption was the goal.

Some shared popular generalizations of "foolish overconsumption," such as taking out bank loans to purchase a "huge jeep land rover" to drive on Thessaloniki's narrow roads to show off. Some admitted to their own habits of filling their carts with groceries only to throw away much of the food that was not consumed each week. Some older respondents, however, reported that all along they had objected on financial and moral grounds to the idea of living with debt, having been accustomed to paying cash for furniture, a car, and vacations. Consumer credit was an innovation that perplexed elders who viewed it not as a signifier of having money (credit), but of losing it (debt).

A woman in a focus group claimed "to speak for thousands of Greeks" when she asserted that citizens share the responsibility with their politicians for the country's economic demise. "We let all of them govern with our vote, and our indifference . . . by not getting out on the street and protesting our leaders . . . we gave up our voice. I say [the crisis] is our fault, too!" Impunity toward politicians, people argued, breeds corruption and cunning as norms of Greek society. The sense that citizens accepted bribes from state officials troubled everyone with whom I spoke, including those who had benefited from early retirement with high pensions, salaries without positions, and good wages for an undisciplined and capricious work ethic.

In formal interviews and casual conversations with me, participants asked, "What have we done for Greece? What have we done for our homeland?" An attorney in his mid-sixties liked to repeat the following question: "Millions of [employable] men and women in our country lived comfortably. What did they produce?" Given the lack of viable economic opportunities and the failure of social institutions to protect citizens, Greeks generally have cared less about individual productivity, social responsibility, and national well-being, and invested more in securing the prosperity of their family. Many argued that "Greece's problem is that we are by necessity a culture of *me* and *mine*, rather than one of *us* and *ours*." The political structure rewards citizens who, by complying with state policies and practices, solve their individual problems and meet family needs. As one participant put it, "The truth is that we are a self-serving people [*partakithes*]. Personal accommodation [*volema*] dominates in our society." The notion of self-interest over civic duty as a cultural orientation was a recurrent theme as informants sought to explain critically the dismal state of their household, their city, and their country.

Participants' assessments of blame and accountability revealed considerable political awareness and self-critique. While several claimed to have avoided credit card debt and recreational loans, most confessed to having engaged in clientelist practices as a matter of practicality (*ek ton praghmaton*), even as they deemed such operations "inappropriate," "backward," and "third-worldish." Some conformed to illegal habits, such as adding extensions to vacation homes without a lawful permit. Interpretations of the fiscal disaster as reflection of cultural erosion were common. People reflected on a "moral decline" as a correlate of Greeks' desire to "play with global money." Availability of government benefits, bank loans, and credit shifted citizens' priorities from "living well" to "living it up."

When informants discussed economic matters in the abstract, they noted the unpredictability of markets, the cycle of economic expansions and retractions, and the global integration of national markets. However, efforts to articulate the mechanisms of the Greek economy ultimately reached the conclusion that "the Greek economy was a lie," and that it was a "bubble" that was bound to bust without prospects for recovery. "Greece does not have the necessary foundations [for industrial production], it lacks programmatic direction, and our acceptance of easy money did not help," noted a seventy-four-year-old man. His wife added, "They [the newly rich] want to buy Rolex watches, Jeeps, and other expensive cars with money they borrowed." This couple blamed the economic downturn on ingrained beliefs, stereotypes, scenarios, and models of all Greeks: the leaders, they contended, for lacking skill, knowledge, and ethics, and the Greek citizens too willingly complied with a fraudulent system.

A group of middle-aged friends at a dinner party acknowledged self-blame for their financial troubles, even after admitting to me that they knew better. They pointed to debts that they incurred by purchasing luxuries to keep up with wealthier friends.

> Why should Marinela have new boots this year? Why should she have a new coat? I want these too! Why should Harry buy his wife a new car? I'll get one too! Tzeni and Takis went to Dubai on holiday. We must do it next year! But we can't, so we turned to credit cards. This is what ruined us! We are auto-masochistic! We did not think critically about who can and cannot afford luxuries, so we got ourselves into debt, which we now must pay, whether we like it or not.

Fiscal constraint has shifted values among consumers from excess to moderation. As Anna put it,

> What were we thinking? Because we wore these clothes last year, we can't wear them again this year? Or even when the car functions just fine, we want to throw it away and buy a new one? Is that what it means to be European?

My hosts embraced debt to increase their standard of living on the premise that they were gainfully employed, and that their finances, at least until 2009, were stable. Some surmised that Greeks were naïve or ignorant to have gotten into debt and to have participated in inordinate displays of consumption uncharacteristic of their precrisis personae. All with whom I spoke expressed personal regret and admitted to collective misguidance in complying with the state's improprieties and transacting with bankers and state officials by way of accepting partial blame for the fiscal catastrophe.

Some were especially critical of a self-proclaimed ethos of expediency, a process of seeking favors, meeting their needs, and realizing their goals through political negotiation and with minimal or no conflict. This cultural practice may also be infused with a tinge of manipulation or exploitation of circumstances or persons to achieve a selfish outcome.

Strategic accommodation in business, legal, or personal transactions is not a cultural ideal, but a response to structural conditions rooted in failed economic policies and bureaucratic inefficiencies. Youla shared the following experience:

> My daughter received social security benefits following her father's death while she was in college. When she graduated, she contacted "I.K.A." (Ίδρυμα Κοινωνικών Ασφαλίσεων [the Social Insurance Institution) to inform the clerks of her change in status. She was told that she must send confirmation of graduation from the university "to Europe." They did not know what paper we needed to file, or to whom to address it exactly, or to what office in Europe I should send the paperwork. It took me three months to gather the required documents. Meanwhile, my daughter continued to receive the money illegitimately as direct deposits to her account without alerts from any [legal] office. She went to the bank to ask if she should return the money to the Legal Treasury. The banker responded: "Lady, how can I send the money? What is the code?"

Thwarted, yet not surprised, by the apparent indifference of the bank clerk, Yioula replied, "How shall I know the code? That's your job, you should know! You are the bank representative! The Legal Office told me to tell you that I should send the money to Europe!"

This lady expressed her frustration with the familiar, disorganized, and inefficient bureaucracy that humiliated and alienated her (Herzfeld 1992). It also cost her inordinate amount of time and energy on the telephone unable to communicate and to figure out how to return 1,200 euros. Generalized absence of merit-based hiring and promotion processes, neglect of professional ethics, and the prevalence of political interests in the appointment of often incompetent and, I would argue, utterly bored employees and executives are normative practices in the public service sector. Such bureaucratic inefficiencies encourage ordinary citizens to ignore rules or to avoid contact with high and low echelons of government unless it becomes necessary. Degrees of resignation and indifference permeates civic and business transactions, at the expense of a productive and sustainable economy. To live honestly, locals declared, would single one out as an idiot. Besides, it is impossible to live honestly when "the system" requires corruption. Informants theorized, naively, that such scams would never occur in Europe or in the United States.

Participants also emphasized the practice, across all sectors of society, of paying for small favors. A fifty-year-old radiology technician provided the following scenario:

> One goes to the theater with his wife. The clerk at the ticket counter tells him that there are no more seats left in the most desirable location of the theater. The man slips 20 euros to the clerk, and suddenly, two seats become available.

"*Lathoma* occurs in many societies, but here in Greece it has become a part of our self," noted Grigoris. Indeed, exchanging money for access is a widely accepted practice among individuals across the social hierarchy of Greece. Thinking more broadly, a seventy-three-year-old businessman surmised, "We [Greeks] were the bohemians of the Mediterranean, the bad kids in the European Union. Tourists wondered, 'Don't these people ever work? They party all night long!'" What outsiders may not understand, he reasoned, is that Greece is "a nation-state of nepotism and patronage, in which all citizens are socialized and educated." He proposed that in the face of socioeconomic precarity, Greeks must adopt habits to reflect legal and moral principles and transmit such cultural practices through childrearing practices and formal education. The Greek mindset is complicated and difficult to change, he said, concluding that this complexity lies in the cultural hybridity of Greek mainstream society. "We must change our mentality. Otherwise we are at risk of a cultural cataclysm," concluded a retired notary public.

> We created a society that consumes what it does not produce, and does not deserve to have. We created a society of corruption by voting for—by caressing—gentlemen with ulterior motives, and supported politicians on whom we could count to serve us when we needed them.

The collective finger of blame points to the system, yet my hosts acknowledge a considerable degree of constrained agency in micro-practices that ultimately might alter the country's trajectory. They also recognize that structural conditions and systemic policies limited the extent to which they could exercise autonomy or volition. Universal was the sentiment that the crisis must mobilize younger generations to pursue productive and sustainable cultural practices so that the country might recover from the recession and the nation may smile again.

In 2011–2012, at the height of the eurozone debt crisis and oppressed by grueling austerity measures, my hosts sought to make sense of their vanishing security and the sociocultural limbo that consumed them. Our conversations inspired them to ponder the external and internal causes of the unanticipated recession that had disrupted their otherwise congenial way of life. A botched European integration process, some asserted, was the primary reason for the crisis. Informants' discourse on blame highlighted a European Union managed by greedy financiers, a corrupt Greek state, and an exploitative Greek business elite. Most Greeks, my hosts claimed, were ignorant about eurozone policies and practices, investment banking, and the structuring of loans. Their government officials exploited their ignorance. Greeks experienced a cultural calamity that many claimed traumatized them, marked their consciousness of a "collective identity," and altered their future as nation. Those who blamed predatory bank representatives for leading them into debt also attributed their predicament to their own ignorance of lending institutions and processes. Even more passionate and heartening were locals' narratives of their own personal and cultural practices that reinforced systemic corruption across sectors of Greek society. Cultural oppression during Roman, Byzantine, and Ottoman periods, and now the Troika, and fueled by a dependent state system since the inception of modern Greece, explains a Greece in danger today. Sustainable recovery from this disaster, asserted my liminal hosts, increasingly eager to stabilize their nation and to reintegrate a stronger Greece in the global order, depended principally on a radical, citizen-driven change that is in the hands of young Greeks.

Notes

1. For a critical discussion on anti-austerity discourses of accountability and blame as unifying and empowering see Theodossopoulos (2014).
2. Tsochatzopoulos is serving a twenty-year prison sentence, which he periodically appeals.
3. Grexit stands for "Greek exit," and refers to Greece's potential withdrawal from the Eurozone and reversion to the drachma, its currency until 2001.
4. The words "We alone regard a man who takes no interest in public affairs not as harmless but as a useless character" are attributed to Thucydides's Funeral Speech of Pericles, Book 2, section 40.

5. Loucas Papademos is an economist who served as the prime minister of Greece from November 2011 to May 2012. He led a provisional government following George Papandreou's resignation on November 11, 2011.

6. See Campbell (1964) and Loizos (1977).

7. The Polytechnic is an institution of higher education in Athens that consists of departments of engineering. On November 14, 1973, students of the School of Engineering participated in the famous Polytechnic uprising against the Greek military junta of 1967–1974.

CHAPTER 5

....

Solidarity to the Rescue

Crises reveal people's coping mechanisms and adaptive strategies when faced with sudden and threatening conditions. As earlier chapters demonstrate, my hosts' narratives of *unanticipated, forced social change* were at once replete with emotional responses to, and diagnostic explanations for, the perils of recession. However, they were also interspersed with evidence of hope, agency, and renewal. Even as informants philosophized that social change is constant, the unanticipated economic decline left them unsettled, yet resourceful and determined to secure equilibrium. Their insistence on gaining some control of the direction and outcomes of the crisis through new ideals, strategic decisions, and actions was undeniable. In this chapter, I focus on participants' behavioral responses and philosophical outlooks to effect *intentional, volitional cultural change* during a period of financial decline. Paradoxically, rapidly diminishing wealth produced a growing leisure class—men and women with less money but more time to invest in alternative and creative thought processes and pursuits. Analysis of participants' allocation of meager incomes and abundant leisure reveals the power of human agency to cope and to promote more enduring efforts toward what they viewed as societal revitalization and progress.[1]

Conspicuous Frugality

> Money is disappearing. We all are changing the way we
> think and the way we live.
>
> —Krista, 58, 2012

Periods of economic deprivation may generate thrifty and efficient use of resources (Cappellini, Marilli, and Parons 2014). As the eurozone debt crisis permeated Greece, and as state-imposed austerity constrained consumption, frugality [*litotita*)] emerged as a new core value and norm. An ideology of temperance now guided domestic fiscal decisions, and thriftiness fueled private conversations and public discourses about surviving the crisis. Austerity measures forced citizens to manage spending to ensure daily meals, pay standard utilities, and, when feasible, to settle *haratsia*,[2] the Troika's newly imposed taxes. Participants spoke of "rationality" and "necessity" as changing their consumption habits, as forcing them to return to or adopt simpler, more moderate ways of living to regain their security and dignity. Constraints in spending habits dominated their personal and public narratives of coping as living conditions deteriorated. Yet public acts of charity became increasingly common as more and more members of the middle classes acknowledged that while "everyone is suffering," financial disparities were unequally distributed (Doxiadis and Placas 2018).

Reflecting on individual strategies of frugality, a professional editor recalled the ancient Greek phrase "μη κρίνεις εξ ιδίων τα αλλότρια" (*mi krinis eks idhion ta allotria*/do not judge others by your own standards). By this form of relativism, he intended to convey that adjusting to new conditions will vary from one person to the next, and that compassion (*sibonia*) must inform interpersonal relationships in precarious times. Feeling helpless, yet convinced that coping with external assaults requires investment in solidarity *and* self-reliance, the editor had this to say:

> From now on, I need to make sure that I survive and to do so
> I must invest in my own microcosm—my home, my family, my
> dog—and to insist on quality in people and in situations. I do
> not have the capacity to do anything else . . . the public sector
> is corrupt. In the past, each time that I have sought to collaborate with colleagues in the public sector, the message I received
> from them was "quick and dirty gets the job done" [*kane ena
> pasalimma na telionoume*].

Frugality implies not only rational choices, but humility and modesty, continued the editor. "I uphold the Greek expression λάθε βιώσας (*lathe viosas*/live discretely),[3] and avoid provoking attention from others . . . now I try to live my life inwardly, and with minimum cost to my person," he explained. Indeed, developing habits of conspicuous frugality emerged as "prudent decisions," "wise choices," and "responsible conduct"—a mainstream value orientation that recalls a pre-eurozone urban Greek middle-class identity and performance.

A new sense of conscious, and often conscientious, spending manifested across age groups. Economizing required discriminating choices, product valuation, and cost-benefit analyses. Indicators that individuals were changing their habits and values were evident and encouraging, noted a seventy-three-year-old man. He referenced the ancient Greek aphorism γνῶθι σεαυτόν (*ghnothi seafton*/know thy self), to convey his observation that in times of crisis, people must engage in a self-assessment of sorts in order to determine what and how they must change to cope with adversity. "I am changing my habits, and I see my friends changing . . . we all are becoming more aware and more responsible citizens," he told me.

In anticipation of lean months and years ahead, frugality dominated people's management of preferences, decisions, and practices. Cuts targeted consumables deemed to be "extra," such as new clothes, leisure travel, and any "money spent foolishly" (*koroidhistika lefta*), such as on lavish entertainment. My hosts were eager, and often proud, to share with me alterations in their consumption habits. They boasted about their new and creative ability to live with less, while also preserving sacred and religious rituals, enhancing primary relationships, and sustaining their dignity.

Home and Hearth

Conspicuous frugality was first of all a family affair. Decline in financial resources prompted some nuclear and extended families to reunite under one roof. Young adults left their apartments and returned to their childhood bedrooms. Some elders, whose children needed their now-reduced pensions to make ends meet, left nursing facilities and reintegrated into a multigenerational household. Participants viewed the reunification of the extended family as a symptom of financial embarrassment. However, they labeled the interdependence of the Greek family as the only reliable form of support in perilous times. Some saw the affirmation of family unity as a "reminder" that blood relationships save lives. Framed as the positive consequences of the fiscal crash, family ties gained strength and value. Mutual support also gained currency as a form of resistance to what so many viewed as "a distancing of family bonds" during the precrisis decades, and the "individualistic and materialistic way of life" that preceded the chaos of the times.

For some households, economic survival entailed the emigration of some members abroad or back to ancestral villages. Young adults spoke of outmigration to Western economies as a plausible response to the high rates of unemployment. Parents spoke wistfully about their college-educated and professionally credentialed children who sought to leave Greece for any employment opportunities abroad. Determined to flee a dismal local economy and a seemingly bleak future, single individuals and young couples spent their days reaching out to contacts abroad in search of any lead for work. Fearing an emptying Greece of young, talented citizens, some lamented that Greece would become "only a country of old folks and of foreigners" (Dzenovska 2018).

Until 2009, middle-class young adults had believed that higher education guaranteed access to professional positions and lucrative salaries. While in crisis, many college graduates were willing to pursue careers abroad, or "any jobs" that required international travel. A philologist, who had gained new appreciation for any kind of work among members of this educated class, asserted that "every job is a way out; we must stop underestimating the value of any job!" Conscious that such measures are adaptive in times of financial crisis, she recalled the popular idiom "We [must] move forward as cabin boys or as captains" (*porevomaste pote os moutsi, pote os kapenani*). Both kinds of workers are capable of happiness. "One must look in one's soul for joy, and offer joy to one another," she proclaimed. She also reiterated the popular sentiment of the times that "all work is good work" even when it does not pay. Indeed, young adults continued to work even after they were officially laid off, regardless of cuts in their salary, or after months without wages. During this liminal period, the structural hierarchy of the employer–employee relationship gradually diminished as each side recognized and empathized with the plight of the other.

To compensate for severe reductions in his salary, one man was willing to emigrate west even temporarily, and "to do any job so as to ensure that my family, my wife, my children, and my parents will not be denied the basics—food, safety, survival," he clarified. Others advocated a temporary emigration of young adults to Western countries to learn new, different careers, with a conditional return to Greece after becoming "skilled and knowledgeable, to save the country." Said a rather optimistic elder:

> And those who will go abroad will be better off and do great things. The country will feel lighter since it will not have to take care of all these people, and later the young people will come back and bring their cultivated brains back to their homeland.

Undeniable was the ambivalence of parents who urged their well-educated children to emigrate after having invested in their future as prospective leading citizens of Greece.

Discouraged by the loss of work and wages, and unable to meet the increasing costs of austerity or to afford emigration expenses, some families migrated temporarily or intermittently to their ancestral home in towns outside of Thessaloniki. Others abandoned their city apartment altogether and relocated to an ancestral home in a nearby village. One's village-based parents or grandparents welcomed such refugees from the city center. Most considered the sojourn from Thessaloniki to village life to be a viable solution after the loss of a job or if unable to afford an urban lifestyle. A thirty-six-year-old special education teacher reported that her colleagues had secured transfers to smaller towns or now commuted to the city for work or school. Now divorced with two children, an administrator of a cultural center whose earnings had diminished contemplated migrating to her ancestral village to live off the land:

> Three years ago, I bought a vineyard in the village, and I cultivate it. Living next to it would cost me nothing, and I would have my grapes, my wine, my *tsipouro*, and my *petimezi* with which I could make *retselia*, and I could earn something from selling these products.[4]

She recalled, "In the past and [in the] old times, people in my village used to say that the winter will pass as long as we have wood and flour." Forced to direct their focus on basic needs and priorities for survival, the old rural saying affirming the value of heat and bread among poor peasants now resonated even with urban professionals.

A Well-Groomed Persona

Greeks value and are inclined to enact an attractive public appearance. However, as household incomes plummeted, so did the purchase of "the seasonal wardrobe." Expensive clothes and accessories were now superfluous possessions. Such indulgences, argued a seventy-seven-year-old mother of three daughters, must end.

> The crisis has forced us to hierarchize our true needs and values. We do not need to have twenty-five pairs of shoes . . . we must change our way of life by prioritizing our basic needs so that we may adapt to the conditions of the crisis.

Men and women still prioritized a fashion-conscious, well-groomed public appearance. Women managed this by exchanging clothes, bags, or accessories with friends and close relatives. Such forms of frugality signified new definitions of prudence and well-being amid financial ruin (Pipyrou 2014). The creative composition of articles and accessories—be it with old clothes, items from consignment shops, or accessories borrowed from friends—was central to a young woman's public persona and in making a good impression. Some remembered disdainfully their frequent precrash visits to jewelry stores where they spent money on gifts of gold and silver for relatives and friends. Jewelry is a highly valued and popular gift in Greece, noted one woman who reported that the city is as full of jewelry stores as it is of bakeries. That the demand for bread now trumped the desire for jewels reassured even the most nervous bakers, while it worried the rightfully pessimistic jewelry storeowners.

People referenced former affluence to accentuate current distress. Questioning of childrearing habits was common among parents who regretted having raised their children to be entitled (*dhistihos ta kalomathame*). Those who only a few years earlier had purchased second homes and raised their children as "princes and princesses" now contemplated the prospect of foreclosure. "Linear understandings" of prosperity—that money was, and would be, available to complete projects and repay loans—was no longer valid (Sabaté 2016). Patterns of gift-giving were rethought. Purchasing clothes, school supplies, and toys for young children had been a regular preoccupation of grandparents. As one fiscally conservative grandfather explained, "One cannot go to visit a grandchild empty-handed. You bring a present to the child whose name day or birthday we celebrate. But what about his siblings? They will be jealous, so we bring a present for every child in the house. This is wrong, of course," he noted, "but normal for us Greeks. Such habits must end!"

Another grandfather, who admitted to indulging his grandchildren, hoped that the crash would teach all a lesson of moderation. "When you take the child outside for a walk, it does not mean you have to buy him an ice-cream. This is the time for a walk, it is not the time for ice-cream . . .

This has to change!" A grandmother who had been accustomed to subsidizing her daughter's children through material gifts was aghast when her five-year-old grandson scolded her for bringing him a present from one of her excursions to the city center. The child's words—"Grandma, you should not spend your money on toys for me anymore"—shocked this grandmother, but it also alerted her to the possibility that new economic principles of enculturation were taking root. More important now, she concluded, was "the time we spend with our family, and helping our children find their way, not grabbing whatever our eye catches on the market place." The decrease in money curbed expenditures for gift exchanges and luxuries as expressions of love. It also shifted the values of old and young alike for whom in this time of uncertainty, frugality, and moderation, sharing time now signaled a favored form of responsible love.

Commensality

Common before the crash were elaborate parties and feast day celebrations at home with bountiful buffets of food and drink that were sometimes facilitated by hired help, typically an immigrant woman. "Once we opened our homes, we invited people to parties. Those days, too, are over," declared a seventy-nine-year-old former retailer in the fur industry." Elaborate entertainment during the crisis, she said, is "more obligatory than amusing." She described a recent dinner party for sixteen guests that she had been forced to manage two days earlier without hired help:

> First, I croaked. Second, without a woman [hired help], I died. Third, I am still cleaning up dirty dishes, and fourth, too many expenses. Once we never had to think about such things, we invited people for coffee, for meals, for parties. Without money and without a woman to help, elaborate festivities have ended.

Paying for a housekeeper now was an extravagance, she reported, even as she complained that at her age she could no longer maintain a proper home. She also missed her groundskeeper, but she recognized that it was no longer feasible to hire help. "A housekeeper demands 50 euros a day, which is nothing, but what can she accomplish in a day? It has been years since I ironed anything; now I iron," she said resentfully.

Now nearing eighty years of age, and after a fifty-year career as a successful businesswoman, she felt obligated to keep house and to support her three adult daughters, whose income as owners of small shops was disappearing. Yet without missing a beat, she assured me that commensality within her household had intensified. To economize, she and her daughters spent more time together and shared household chores. They also regularly shared meals that she planned prudently and prepared creatively so that the "food is flavorful and healthy, but inexpensive." Decreases in gainful employment of the daughters and the cuts in the mother's pension left this family with fewer amenities, and with more time to invest in one another and other loved ones. While disposable income decreased, creative and affective commensality increased.

Individuals claimed that precrash they generally neglected to dine on leftovers from lunch. The bread had to be fresh, and the evening meal required grilled food, which preferably would be consumed at a neighborhood grill or popular taverna by the sea with friends. Looking back, a couple assessed their former food spending as pretentious and reckless. "We need only half a kilo of feta, not two kilos!" My neighborhood butcher complained to me that his customers bought less red meat and less frequently, with the exception of small portions of ground lamb and "a chicken here and there," leaving his meat products "to putrefy in his freezer." I observed, and participants confirmed, that substituting beans, lentils, and chickpeas for meat was financially feasible, nutritionally healthier, and a wiser way to feed the family.

Participants in a focus group reported that before the crisis they made fun of people who cooked enough for two to three days, freezing portions for later meals. During his travels abroad, one man claimed to have scoffed at locals whom he observed buying "one tomato, only two chicken thighs, and two slices of cheese to consume without waste." Now he was certain that "they knew what they were doing." A public consultant insisted that urbanites must now adopt the simpler food habits of village life.

> We have forgotten our diet, the Mediterranean diet, and have been tempted by fast food. We should eat homemade frumenty (*trakhanas*) and egg noodles (*khilopites*), which are delicious and super good for you. What else do we need? We must become more inventive with how we conduct our life, and not accept easy solutions from outsiders [Westerners/Americans], like fast food industrialists.

Going out, getting together, and sharing food and spirits with friends is a core cultural practice among Greeks, and one that they maintained by modifying it in line with financial constraints and newly constructed values. Casual and impromptu gathering in one another's homes gained momentum as an alternative to going out. "Now we all bring something to share," disclosed an instructor at the local agricultural school. Flowers, sweets, and spirits are mere excesses now, explained a sixty-two-year-old teacher of foreign languages. "Now we exchange real food with friends, like rice, nuts, homemade bread . . . we bring a box of *koulourakia*[5] or a container of stuffed grape leaves to share."

Prioritizing needs and virtues over indulgences and vices dominated narratives of frugality as both a private and a household strategy, and as an emerging pattern of culture. Informants imbued the exchange of food with such sentiments as empathy, sympathy, intimacy, and fun.[6] The shift in local gift-giving etiquette inspired my own practices. When I had an opportunity to visit a colleague who hosted me for an overnight visit in Athens, I ordered a can of honey from a friend at my native village who manages a small bee-keeping operation. My hostess was delighted at my thoughtful gift, and grateful that I did not add one more dust-collecting bibelot to her collection.

The conventional exchange of expensive Christmas presents was no longer feasible, and offering self-made and more modest and useful gifts gained popularity. Kostas skipped a Christmas vacation abroad so that he could save the money to meet other "more necessary expenses" related to the holidays, such as a festive meal with family and small, "symbolic gifts" for the children. The customary exchange of gifts in the form of purchased pastries, alcoholic beverages, and personal accessories burdened some who felt unable to maintain the practice. Others who could no longer afford to reciprocate in kind felt embarrassed and avoided social events, including invitations to spend holidays with friends.

Prudence

By the fall of 2011, international travel for leisure had also become a thing of the past. "There was a time when we could do everything; now we have to choose how to spend what little we have left. The way things are going, we don't even know if we will have anything left at all to celebrate the holidays or to vacation abroad," worried a thirty-year-old woman who was accustomed to a life of privilege. She admitted distress for having to rely fully on her parents, who supported her lifestyle. However, she was adamant about spending "at least one more summer break in two islands." She feared that the summer ritual of playing with friends at islands away from the critical eyes of parents and relatives would be her last.

Knowing that her family owned a second house on the coast of Chalkidiki, I intimated that she would always have a vacation destination

by the sea. She explained that staying at the family home does not constitute a real holiday break (*dhiakopes*) from the daily routine—what a
"proper vacation" ought to be. "Of course," she contemplated, "the family weekend home may have to suffice in such times of crisis." Indeed,
most of my hosts reported that their recent holidays were not extrava-
gant, and that summers in the near future would be limited to short
respites at their natal home in a nearby village or at their vacation property on the coast. Others admitted that financial constrains would force
them to rent their beach home to foreigners; they hoped that they could
still enjoy that home between tourists.

The winter of 2012 was brutal, Thessalonikians insisted. The aver-
age temperature there in January 2012 was 37 Fahrenheit. The unusually
low temperatures compelled my acquaintances to sacrifice another basic
comfort: warmth. Shocking to an elderly mother was the prospect that
her adult daughters spent winter nights in their "icy palace" in Panorama
because they could not afford to pay the heating bill. A 40 percent increase
in the price of heating oil led urban middle-class families to find alternative forms of heating, such as wood-burning stoves popular in villages, or
to go without heat. Unfortunately, many pointed out, the overwhelming
use of wood-burning stoves increased air pollution, and the dangerous
particles found in smog exposed citizens to respiratory problems.

People gathered in kitchens that on the coldest days often functioned
also as living rooms and bedrooms. Other coping mechanisms in a cold
winter included wearing multiple layers of clothing indoors and staying in
bed covered in wool blankets. New energy taxes, including a property levy
on electricity bills, forced many families to resort to room heaters, which
they also used sparingly. Kostas, who likes his home environment "hot,"
reported, "This winter I *prefer* to wear more layers in the house than to pay
for heating my house." Some residents of large homes in Panorama walled
off part of the house, or a whole story, to reduce heating costs. Finding
such measures humiliating or burdensome, some participants opted to
spend most of the day outside, where the sunshine "warms our bones."

Another popular savings strategy was reduced auto usage. Many
people opted for public transportation, formerly deemed a lower-class
marker. Now people flock to the bus stations, pushing one another to
secure a seat before someone else occupies it (see figure 5.1). By leaving their cars at home, they save money on maintenance and parking.
Others park free far away from the city center's garages, where they
would be forced to pay. Cabs, the most conventional and popular form
of transit for upwardly mobile urbanites, in times of crisis became a

FIGURE **5.1 Busy bus station at Egnatias Avenue, reflecting a rise in public transportation.**
Source: Photo by Kathryn Kozaitis.

luxury for all, and a necessity only for the old and frail. Walking, use of public transportation, and the popularity of bicycles increased noticeably as people found driving their expensive cars to be financially prohibitive.

Ownership of an expensive automobile, which once indicated affluence, became a burden in postcrash times. In 2012 people reported a notable decrease in traffic and an increase in the masses of pedestrians compared to previous years.[7] "Selling my car," reported a fifty-eight-year-old physician and father of two young children, "was a step to changing my lifestyle, and adjusting to the new conditions." While people admitted that selling or reducing the use of their cars was a financial decision, they also acknowledged the ecological and civic responsibility of returning to public transportation, and the health benefits of walking more and transporting themselves by bicycle to work. Car-pooling, like the potluck dinner, became a new and popular adaptive strategy. Participants took turns driving others or their children to and from destinations. They infused these gestures with such moral sentiments as social responsibility and environmental consciousness—a new form of "vernacular humanitarianism" that reflects grassroots responses to precarity (Rozakou 2016a).

Transitions from excess to moderation reveal a mass acquiescence to a precarious economy that many perceived as destined to have "a bad ending." However, people in general did not confront their fate with absolute resignation. Uppermost on the collective consciousness was the prospect of a return to a more predictable lifestyle, more characteristic of Greeks before membership in the eurozone: life without debt. A forty-two-year-old recently unemployed bank clerk viewed debt as a public menace to be eradicated. He argued that before the country joined the European Union, ordinary Greeks considered debt a personal disgrace and anathema to one's social standing. A return to "frugality, simple frugality must become the new norm. Death to debt!" he declared.

Rise in Transnational Solidarity

> A new Greece requires investment in solidarity, kindness, civic duty, and mutual respect as normal cultural practices, not just ideals.
>
> —Fotis, 58, 2012

The road to recovery from austerity, many locals argued, requires investment in social solidarity—an emphasis on internal cohesion and such sensibilities as egalitarianism, general reciprocity, philanthropy, reciprocity, and voluntarism (Rakopoulos 2016). Solidarity, as an impulse and a practice of unity against and resistance to external threat, has been intrinsic to a segmentary Greece, as the ethnographic record attests (Herzfeld 2016a, 2016b; Papataxiarchis 2016.) New, and characteristic of an urban, educated class of actors amid a global crisis, is *transnational solidarity*—a principle and practice of unity that transcends national boundaries and relies on a shared struggle against a common, international enemy. The solidarity I witnessed among Greek young adults in particular, who self-identify as "global citizens," encompasses a community united by an experience of the Great Recession that they share with their counterparts across Europe and the United States, and a common mission to promote international human rights against the threat of a neoliberal world order.

A popular refrain across ages to overcoming the crisis was a shift from the "I" to the "we." Solidarity gained importance as vulnerability among citizens mounted. Talk of fellowship and community struck me as particularly sincere and passionate. As a sixty-five-year-old widow said, she and her friends have become more conscientious about helping one another as well as offering charity to strangers. Some claimed that to the extent that they can afford it, they purchase a few extra items of food or hygiene at the supermarket, fill a basket, and leave it on the doorstep of less privileged neighbors. Said a woman who sat next to me on the bus one day,

> Glory to God, I recently noticed that people do not throw their clothes in the trash anymore . . . they wash them and then they either hang them outside . . . shoes, clothes . . . So, people take them, or they bring them to the street markets and sell them for a euro or two.

Others had begun donating clothes to residents in lower-income neighborhoods. Accompanying financial decline was a public rise in fellowship, altruism, and charity that inspired the donation of personal and household items to public markets where a jacket that might cost 500 euros in Tsimiski would be available to one in need for 5 euros. This "new social self-organization," argued a thirty-seven-year-old teacher, was a direct consequence of a "national calamity and evidence of the Greek sensibility of common humanity" in perilous times.

People spoke of feeling closer to one another and caring more about others who were suffering. I asked my companions to share with me their observation of visible changes to citizenship they attributed to the impact of the fiscal crash. Some young adults offered to tutor children whose parents could not afford the service. Performing artists staged concerts without compensation. Informants considered the potential increase of voluntary practices to be civic virtues that the crisis ignited and that continued threats of the recession intensified. Focusing on the "positive outcomes" of the crash, a forty-two-year-old civil servant emphasized "spending more face-to-face time with each other in person, and less on our cell phones and other costly devices." He also highlighted an increase in empathy and mutual support, specifically in sharing of pain and anxiety of the times with others. People "care more about who and how you are now, rather than about what you do and what you have," he clarified.

Conscious of collective suffering, people admitted to feeling empathetic toward one another. While support among family members and friends is intrinsic to Greek society, wider systems of social support proliferated as a collective response to financial insecurity (Papadaki and Kalogeraki 2017). Accordingly, participants claimed that the crisis encourages them to be "more unified as a people," and more inclined "to help my fellow man." A spiritual disposition to reach out and to help more vulnerable victims of the crash through charitable contributions of food, medicines, and clothing, informants observed, was becoming more systematic and organized. The rise of new nongovernmental organizations and volunteerism confirmed a shift toward "humanitarian citizenship." "We see that our public welfare is dying, and social welfare services are shutting down; now citizens must act," advised a member of a health awareness volunteer group. Indeed, the fiscal collapse diminished the capacity of an already dysfunctional and corrupt welfare state to provide safety nets to the masses of newly impoverished citizens, particularly children.

Philanthropic outreach from local churches also intensified. An attorney reported that a priest took the initiative to pay the utilities for some of the most unfortunate members of his congregation. Each night he also went to the local bakery to pick up previously frozen baked goods that were not sold and brought them to the church, where he distributed them to needy parishioners. Others noted that restaurant owners provided churches, schools, and nursing homes with food that was left untouched at the end of day, food that "in the past they just threw away."

To be sure, the Greek Orthodox Church is a target of criticism for its accumulation of wealth, as much by those who identify as religious as by those who consider themselves atheists or agnostics. However, as poverty became increasingly real for many families, my hosts acknowledged the benevolence by some priests toward the destitute of their congregation. Locals' references to the church as a safety net were limited to its role in providing food for the homeless and other needy families. Congregants prepared these meals in their own homes and delivered them to the church for distribution. During my time in the field, the Holy Metropolis of Thessaloniki[8] increased its supply of meals from 100 to 1,000 in a matter of weeks.

Personal modesty and restraint now are reflected in religious practices, said a theology student. "People today do not go to church as a social convention and to call attention to themselves by leaving money and lighting candles for all to see. Now many congregates may lack money for candles, but they go in to pray. What matters now is that life has meaning beyond material consumption."

Most encouraging to a vocational schoolteacher was evidence "that people now come closer together and they become creative." The crisis, he felt, was the catalyst for self-reflection, primarily on the meaning of well-being. Crisis-stricken Greeks need to reconsider the meaning of "the good life," which he distinguished from indulgences in "material pleasures." In times of crisis, he argued, Greeks must focus on "the creative potential" of young citizens who are poised to redefine the vision and direction of a new and better life for the nation. Disgusted and disgruntled with "the failure of state officials to provide a vision and direction," this educator proposed that social reforms should be left to "the citizens themselves"—those who are well-intentioned and possess the self-motivation to stabilize Greece.

Indeed, in the absence of trustworthy political representatives, my interlocutors emphasized self-reliance and solidarity not only as forms of resistance against external threat, but as proactive cohesion to rebuild their society. A self-employed scholar affirmed the notion of self-determination with the Homeric notion "Συν Αθηνά και χείρα κίνει"[9] (*Sin Athina ke khira kini*/an antiquarian expression equivalent to the English "God helps those who help themselves"). Many participants uttered variations of this proverb to convey their belief that a stronger Greece depended on individual and collective resilience to improve one's personal lot in life, and the future of the nation itself.

The Promise of Resilience

> We will get over this . . . because I have heard . . . people from our family from previous generations who have been through tragic circumstances in the past, they survived and they bounced back. So will we!
>
> —LITSA, 35, 2012

In their projections of a future, my hosts referenced Greeks' resilience in having survived worse calamities in the past. Greeks' heroic determination throughout history to salvage their country from foreign invaders was also a source of hope. "We will survive, as always," posited a retired international businessman. Elders were particularly inclined to invoke the resilience intrinsic in human nature. Some insisted that human beings must suffer through such upheavals so that they can recover and improve. An elderly woman who had lived through what she described as "terrorizing calamities" elaborated:

> Greek people have been through thousands of disasters: for 482 years, the Turks enslaved Thessaloniki. We survived two World Wars, the Civil War, and the Asia Minor catastrophe, and we withstood and recovered. I believe that we will withstand this catastrophe and recover again. Now we know better . . . we will survive as always.

Recovering from crisis, some argued, meant moving away from "a culture of parasitism" (*parasitismos*) to one of productivity and self-sufficiency. "In every obstacle, an opportunity" (*kathe ebothio yia kalo*), my hosts resolved. Recalling the Greek idiom "learning through suffering," πάθει μάθος (*pathi mathos*), older informants conveyed their conviction that Greeks must recognize that struggle and suffering build resilience, and that adversities are prerequisites to a victorious outcome. In the words of a seventy-three-year-old notary public,

> We must find the strength to suffer today so that we may enjoy tomorrow. The table may be set, and dinner may be served to us, but why would we feast on a full stomach? Should we not starve first before we indulge?

The will to survive, affirmed the retired public official, must emerge from the anguish that plagued him, and his fellow compatriots, who struggled to manage austerities. Convinced that suffering begets strength, he postulated:

> What we did not do for so many years by choice, we must now do by force! Let us go hungry, let us crawl, let us experience the pain of birth, as does the mother who bears a child who wails as it confronts the world . . . From this painful birth comes new life, joy, and laughter. Without a nightfall, without a fall into darkness, how are we to appreciate the warmth of the sun and the beauty of light at dawn?

In a similar line of thinking, a forty-one-year-old employee of the Ministry of Education shared this sentiment: "We [Greeks] are not likely to straighten out on our own [*then prokite va strosoume*]. We must be destroyed first and start over . . . perhaps then we will think sensibly [*bas ke valoume mialo*]." A mother of a discouraged young son agreed.

She felt certain that young people would become stronger because of their suffering and alienation. "The young will learn from their experience that difficulties turn into strength. Once [my son] has suffered enough, he will become determined to persevere" (*ton piani to pisma ke lei, ai sto kalo, tha ta vghalo pera*), she hoped.

"The Human [*o anthropos*][10] does not understand unless you hit him hard on the head! He has to experience shock, a big shock, in order to understand and to change [his habits]," asserted a sixty-six-year-old financial consultant. The experience of acute financial embarrassment, this man concluded, would propel one person at a time to invent alternative ways to be productive and to earn a living, which in turn would improve the economic system for all. He argued that Greece as a nation-state must become impoverished so that many more young citizens are forced to abandon their old work ethic based on corruption and instead to value innovation, creativity, and productivity. He contrasted this principle with this depiction of a precrisis lifestyle among youth.

> Young people have been accustomed to being out until 4 a.m. If they have a job, they may show up late two or three times a week. They do not face consequences. In the future, when they find a job and show up late, they must be told, "Leave!" This is how they will learn how to behave when they find a new job. They will tell themselves, "I will go to sleep at 11 p.m. so my boss will not fire me in the morning for being late."

Having internalized the Western work ethic that he learned during his professional life in the Netherlands, the retired businessman was certain that "people's financial discomfort would necessitate a change in their mindset. They will learn the value of work and of earning money legally, and this is how they will adapt." With the words attributed to the Greek lyric poet Simonides (c. 556 BC–469 BC), "Ἀνάγκα δ' οὐδὲ θεοὶ μάχονται" (*Anagka th' outhe thei makhode*/Not even the gods fight necessity), he concluded that from the pains of crisis will emerge resourceful adaptations.

Thessalonikians acknowledged universally that their country's future lay in the hands and minds of its younger citizens. Current dangers, believed a forty-year-old instructor, must propel people into "grassroots, organized and deliberate action" to halt any further deterioration of the social fabric. A few felt that the country was in dire need of a single, wise, and noble leader; "a young Greek Messiah," uttered one woman in desperation. However, most participants, young and old, insisted that recovery rested with the will of self-determined, creative citizens. As a thirty-nine-year-old librarian put it,

> All of us are now aware that no savior will come to rescue us. We went astray because we believed that others [state officials, European elites] would take care of us and would do right by us. Now we know not to believe in saviors, and we realize that we have to try to rescue ourselves in solidarity.

Having acknowledged the consequences of a reckless neoliberal system, my interlocutors turned to hindsight. The retired accountant asserted the following:

> Had I known then what I know now, I never would have complied with the madness of borrowing and living in debt. Now we can put our heads together and think critically of how to proceed. We must be prudent and introspective, evaluate what we did wrong, and begin doing the right thing. We must establish new social and institutional foundations on which to build a future. There must also be a settling of scores [*ksekatharisma loghariasmon*]. We inflated everything. Now it is time to pay! There must be better approaches to live as a society that are just and humane. This new birth will be painful, we will all suffer, but we must hurt if we are to improve.

Discussions about resilience, hope, recovery, and securing a future usually highlighted the importance of collective grassroots organization and socioeconomic development (Narotzky and Besnier 2014). All were eager to provide recommendations of how the country might not only survive the crisis but also become stronger, more productive, and stable. To that end, hosts prioritized investment in their history and their geography.

Heritage and Landscape

> Greece is the most beautiful and the most coveted piece of land in the world! And as many say, God gave us the best plot (ikopetho) on earth, and we must fight to keep it.
>
> —Angelos, 41, 2012

In April 2012, a brisk morning walk on Thessaloniki's seafront brought me face to face with two tall, older gentlemen who stood between the White Tower and the National Theater on Nikis and Megalou Alexandrou avenues.

The glistening waves of the Thermaic Gulf and the lively cityscape framed their figures in motion. One man pointed in all directions, as if unsure of their next steps. As I approached them, I heard one tell the other while pointing, "Look at the wealth that surrounds us—the sea, the sun, [Mount] Olympus there, historical monuments here, theaters all around us; these treasures are ours and here to stay." As he gazed reverentially at the natural and cultural landscape, his companion replied, "I agree, but the issue is this: How will *we* manage to hold on to these treasures?"

Acknowledgments of belonging to a globally recognized geographic territory, an affiliation with ancient Greek "lights of civilization" (*ta phota tou politsmou*), and references to historical conquests reassured locals of their perpetuity when their security as a nation was threatened, and their personal survival was uncertain. Some Thessalonikians referenced Greece as the *fons et origo* of Western civilization. Others boasted about their city as a place famous for its historical figures, ideas, and art that its many monuments and museums display. The aesthetic and sensual qualities of their homeland—the crystal blue seas that caress its coasts, the warm sunshine in which the country basks most of the year, and the culinary specialties for which the region is famous—reinforced locals' confidence in their endurance as a people. Some cited "Greece never dies" (*I Elladha pote dhen petheni*), a phrase in a Greek military march that captures a nationalist ethos of determined perpetuity.

A history of economic and political defeats and conquests reassured older participants that organized resistance against yet another foreign occupation promised recovery. Angelos's reference to Greece as the most desirable piece of land in the world depicts others' preoccupation with "losing Greece to the Germans" or "becoming Europe's farmers and cheap laborers." Some asked rhetorically, "How can Greece, the birthplace of European civilization, end up as the pawn of European integration?" Like the gentlemen on Thessaloniki's seafront who contemplated the historical and cultural significance of their homeland, locals' references to the *past*—the splendor of *their* antiquity, cultural heritage, historical consciousness, identity, and worldview—reveal their attempts to make sense of uncertainties in the *present*, and to cultivate potentialities for a *future* (Macdonald 2012: 234).

Fearful of declining social stability, citizens reconfigured and constructed their past in various ways by embracing the material culture in their midst, including heritage sites, monuments of antiquity, museums, and cityscapes. Thessalonikians pointed to their fifteen UNESCO

Heritage Sites of *tangible heritage* as a source of their imagined inextin-guishable identity.[11] Their reinvestment in the archaeological treasures and Byzantine art reflects not romantic or naïve nostalgia, but assertions of belonging through their understandings and interpretations of an-cient history and intellectual heritage. Perceived threats of societal dis-integration also inspired citizens to imbue their landscape with notions of righteousness, cosmology, and perpetuity. They condemned citizens' and politicians' neglect of the city's urban landscape, evident in the disre-pair of infrastructure and in the filth on the street. But such blight could not erase the fixed, natural features that surrounded them. "The sun will always rise, the mountains are here to stay, and the sea will always breathe life into us," asserted my friends. Pemble's account of "Mediterra-nean madness" marked by the four S's (sun, sand, sea, and sin) resonated with some study participants (Pemble 1987). Their physical and built environment, and the cultural practices and meanings that it inspires, constitute cultural property that is theirs to keep and to consume.

Loss, uncertainty, and insecurity—real and imagined—affected people's daily lives, yet their depictions of a prized landscape and a cherished national heritage inspired them with hope that recovery was plausible. As a forty-two-year-old recently unemployed and passionate bank manager put it,

> No self-pity is necessary. Greece is a very rich place, one of the richest countries in the world. Its strategic geopolitical posi-tion, its soil, and the level of education among our young make Greece a powerful country. We have not seized this power yet . . . now we can seize it.

In their eagerness to embrace the "modernization" that membership in the eurozone implied, my hosts claimed to have neglected, or subor-dinated, their classical and historical heritage. Instead, some declared, they embraced transnational messages of "being current" disseminated by media outlets, tourists, and wealthy Greek travelers. "Foolishly eager to secure membership in the club of Europeans, we forgot our civiliza-tion, our heritage, and our humanity . . . Instead, we dove face-first to import goods, services, and values from European manufacturers that exploited our vulnerability," argued a journalist of ERT, the Hellenic Broadcasting Corporation. Indeed, Greece's historically dependent rela-tionship to foreign powers, a series of financial boom, bust, and bailout cycles, and its pre-existing financial vulnerability to the eurozone debt hazards subjected its people to the inevitable economic calamity from which, a decade after the crash, they struggle to escape (Kalyvas 2015).

Threatened by a recession that many feared would annihilate Greece as a sovereign nation-state, hosts questioned their own uncritical tendency post–eurozone status to categorical subordination of Greece as a "backward, agrarian society" in favor of the industrialized West, including the United States. Attention to ancient Greek ideals, argued a forty-two-year-old civil servant, is necessary now more than ever to survive and recover from this socioeconomic calamity. "We must value and exalt our past . . . to pull ourselves together and admit that we were fooled, that we made mistakes, and that we need to change our conduct from now on," he insisted. "Repentance is not a bad thing; this is how we can change ourselves as a people and become stable again in the future," Angelos concurred. He objected to the label "nationalistic" that others attributed to him when he spoke of his "deep love for and commitment to [his] homeland." However, when he announced that "only God, as a philhellene, will create a miracle to save [Greece] from another [German] occupation," his comrades agreed. Potential "foreign engulfment" of their beloved homeland preoccupied many who feared the country's demise. Survival, they argued, requires solidarity and collective action to protect their homeland. Angelos's words reflect this popular sentiment:

> While people are disillusioned and psychologically deflated now, they love their land, they still feel that they are Hellenes, and believe that Greece will not die.

Greece's subordination to outsiders reinvigorated ethnocentric orientations and popular valorization of Greek heritage. After all, my hosts argued, Greeks conserve the intellectual ancestry of the West, the history, monuments, and artifacts needed to affirm their identity, and in which they must invest time and energy to preserve.

Determined to counter the negative stereotypes that the international media ascribed to Greeks, locals also emphasized the value of language, customs and traditions, rituals, family bonds, music, food, the fine arts for which the city is lauded, folklore, and forms of spirited, "Zorbaesque" qualities. The crisis offered an opportunity to adopt a pre-eurozone, happier way of life. Living well, my hosts claimed, included "simple Greek virtues" that transcended creature comforts. When basic needs are met, participants argued, leading a decent life (*enan aksioprepi tropo zois*) requires above all health (*pano ap' opola ighia*), a good profession (*ena kalo epangelma*), and companionship (*parea*). Companionship consisted invariably of family and friends. When these criteria are in place, and one's children are thriving, "life rolls beautifully," concluded a retired accountant.

The crisis inspired citizens' articulations of a cherished history and heritage. Investment in and consumption of domestic cultural capital might lead to revival of international respect, they argued. In the face of depleting financial resources, locals shifted their investment to promoting existing cultural assets, especially the city's monuments, museums, and universities. Loss of income reinforced attention to emotional and spiritual fulfillment, while unemployment provided leisure time to organize politically and to cultivate deeper family commitments and more meaningful social relations. A shift in locals' daily allocation of time and cultural resources in liminal times reveals a process of sociocultural changes in the hands of citizens, and characteristic of a society in flux.

Sustainable Development

> When you change your mindset, you will change your praxis as well. From now on, I won't wait to open a shoe store. I will look to open something productive. I will not live again in an informal market economy [*pareborio*].
>
> —Miltos, 55, 2012

Immediate, short-term adaptations to the economic collapse included various forms of hidden welfare—informal, nonmonetary exchanges between family members, friends, and neighbors. News about emergent consignment shops spread through the Internet and word of mouth. During a focus group with five college women, I learned that individuals were selling expensive garments and accessories for a few euros—a small fraction of their original value. My collaborators viewed this as a smart and a humanitarian response to the crisis. A barter economy also intensified, reported acquaintances who exchanged goods and services such as food items, clothes, jewelry, or school supplies with others instead of purchasing them.

A spirit of generalized reciprocity like that which prevails among family members and close friends inspired some to propose bartering as a more formal, if temporary, system of exchange alongside the cash economy. Bartering is a viable option now that people depend on each other to get through the week, said a college instructor.

Material interdependence, he argued, freed people to "focus on other, more meaningful aspects of life." He believed that this type of gift economy would elevate people's moods and direct their focus away from greed and debt to reciprocity, cooperation, and humanism. He proposed the following scenario:

> You are a professor of English. You will offer me lessons in English, and I will repair your electrical equipment. Or if you are a painter, offer someone a piece of your work, and ask that person to cultivate your vegetable garden or to repair your car. We will exchange services and labor time. You dedicate so many hours to meeting my needs, and I will dedicate the same number of hours to meet yours.

Such "steps," he suggested, would help move a fiscally downtrodden population away from "the money-driven cycle of life" and direct it to a way of life where "money is not a mechanism of oppression."

It is up to the young, participants agreed, to figure out how to survive through the crisis by seeking new opportunities for sustainable socioeconomic development, and by "looking outside of Greece for ideas and for strategies." "The young cannot afford to just sit and complain; they must become actively involved . . . invent solutions," declared a seventy-seven-year-old grandmother. Her son-in-law, an owner of an art gallery in the outskirts of the city, had sought for years to rent space in the city center but the cost was prohibitive. Two years earlier his earnings from the gallery had come to a screeching halt, so that he and his young family needed his parents' help to get by. Meanwhile, she said proudly, he pursued his dream of relocating his gallery in the city center by taking advantage of falling rents. "The young must believe that the crisis is temporary, and that they should not ignore prospects for leading the recovery; they should take advantage of this crisis in order to secure their future." Her premise resonated widely.

New Leadership

Socioeconomic development, respondents argued, depended on new and trustworthy leadership. Many spoke of the need for "an enlightened" and "cultivated" leader who would reinforce the country's membership in the European Union lawfully (*nomima*). Such a Greek leader would possess "intellect, Hellenic ideals and principles, a cultivated Western mentality in industry, and a European cultural orientation to save us from bankruptcy and societal collapse," insisted a fifty-eight-year-old surgeon who feared a forced exit from the eurozone. An art historian argued that a future, genuine democracy "must be transparent," and marked by "the separation of church and state." She advocated for political leaders who are authentic intellectuals and learned men and women, "not just people with degrees" who thrive on patronage. Whether through grassroots mobilization to replace the current Greek government, or through foreign leadership imposed by the European Union, public discourse and private responses to my inquiries reflected the following sentiment: that a new and just state was needed for there to be meaningful reforms in other social institutions, most urgently in higher education, as well as the media, the military, and law enforcement.

The dominance of what one writer called "a state class" had produced a functional deadlock. "This is a period of decay, a period in which the current system is dead, and an alternative system is unavailable," she explained in a resolutely liminal voice. Greece needs parliamentarians able and willing to represent the people. Leonidas, an idealistic young man, called for empathetic and sympathetic candidates who publicly recognize that people have problems, that they are frustrated, and that others suffer. Such candidates must also be objective and committed to treating everyone fairly. He continued:

> One must not seek a seat in parliament strictly to become a wage-earner, or motivated only by a professional position. He must love the work and think of it not as business, but as public service [*litourghima*]. Otherwise, walk away, and let someone else do this important work. Keep your seat in parliament one or two terms, but no more! Do not entangle yourself in the madness and chaos of being a career parliamentarian. And be a law-abiding citizen; if not, turn yourself in!

Thessalonikians also proposed that new political leaders must be articulate and good listeners. To rule Greece justly, leaders must acknowledge the different ideologies that permeate Greek society, including neoliberalism, socialism, and communism. They must also know how to manage the factions, how to foster reconciliation through enforcement of the middle ground (*ti mesi otho*), Leonidas preached. Unlike current political figures who seek to destroy one another, a new government must enforce policies that promote unity and fellowship.

Most critical, locals agreed overwhelmingly, is that the top priority of a new leader must be enforcement of the constitution. With the refrain "We have laws, but we don't follow them," participants expressed their exasperation at state officials who did not hold citizens accountable, and who themselves were immune to punishment for illegal transactions. Stated a forty-year-old biologist and a mother of two daughters,

> The [current] politicians must be punished, and severely. Then people will understand that the law is implemented and those who break it are reprimanded and punished by going to prison. Then aspiring political officials will be forced to implement the law to avoid imprisonment.

This informant stressed, and others concurred, that reforms of state policies and procedures are likely to be enforced only if citizens—individually and collectively—abide by the law, and demand social justice through their voting practices. The general recommendation by study participants for a new type of governance typically came in the form of this argument:

> Only if the constitution is validated, if all laws are implemented, if civilians and politicians are held accountable, and if all those who commit illegal acts are punished, will decency and prosperity prevail in the Greek mainstream.

Such sentiments preceded the debt crisis, but precarity stimulated more passionate calls for a more just government. Participants reasoned that ideal, just leadership would enforce the constitution, which would diminish patronage, increase the quality of higher education, and propel young people to pursue professional careers in the private sector. Such "national development" would be based more on merit, and less on connections. Recognizing the idealism of such proposals, my hosts made specific recommendations to develop existing industries within the context of Mediterranean tourism and globalization that held promise for recovery: tourism and agriculture, which are productive industries for domestic and international consumption.[12]

Cultural Tourism

Greece remains a tourist destination for fun, leisure, and education, and the "reinvention" and global commodification of heritage during the current crisis has never been more urgent (Tzanelli 2016). The tourist industry is one of the country's most viable economic sectors, and one that the 2004 Olympic Games in Athens only strengthened, as visits by millions of tourists from all regions of the world attest.[13] My interlocutors identified "cultural tourism" as an employment opportunity for college-educated young people, and an earning opportunity for small business owners in Thessaloniki and the surrounding region.[14] Participants cited a ready-made list of cultural tourist destinations, including its many archaeological museums, the coastal region of Chalkidiki, Mount Olympus, Mount Athos (for male visitors only), Meteora, and Pella and Vergina (the birthplace of Alexander the Great and the burial site of his father, King Philip II). "We want Thessaloniki to become globally known," said a retired businessman and world traveler. He advocated for state-funded and citizens' investment in the local tourist industry, already spearheaded by Thessaloniki's mayor at the time, Yiannis Boutaris.

Unlike Athens and the Cycladic and Ionian islands, Thessaloniki and its many heritage sites are neglected by tourists, locals believed. Greece has much more to offer than delicious food, friendly people, and sun-drenched beaches, they argued, and Thessaloniki provides all those desirable qualities, and an education in history, art, and religion. "Every tourist who heads to coastal Chalkidiki must be encouraged to visit and study Thessaloniki and the cultural sites that define the region," proposed a seventy-five-year-old retired entrepreneur. Young people should know that Greece could experience "a rebirth" through tourism and related commercial development, and solve its unemployment problem at the same time, he argued.

Another proponent of *cultural tourism* advocated for a "thematic tourism." This sixty-nine-year-old ophthalmologist saw the Greek tourist industry as needing "elevation"—enhancement that would cater more to the needs of more affluent, cultured visitors. He elaborated:

> A piece of watermelon in hand and sitting on the beach is not tourism! By thematic tourism I mean, religious tourism, medical tourism, cultural tourism, archeological tourism, tourism of gays, conference tourism . . . I don't care, but with a theme! So, tourism with a theme!

The consensus among participants across age groups was that the combination of a highly educated population of young adults and a highly valued tourist destination held promise for the country's recovery. Argued a forty-year-old owner of a small fitness center,

> There is no other country on this planet more beautiful than Greece . . . We have an amazing climate, fabulous leisure sites, and a great civilization . . . Therefore, we should develop tourism by investing in our civilization, which we had, and we threw it away to buy a Porsche Cayenne and Jeeps.

Because most young adults in Thessaloniki are college educated, speak several languages, and aspire to global integration, locals saw them as ideally suited to develop a regional tourist industry.

Economic development, whether grassroots or externally imposed, is more likely to be sustainable if innovations fit, and if they are culturally compatible and built on, pre-existing resources (Kottak 1991). Tourism that highlights the Mediterranean region's diverse civilizations, Greece's ancient sites, and the city's heritage, art, architecture, rituals, and festivals would certainly provide meaningful and perhaps even gainful work for the city's educated and creative adults. It would also boost the viability of local small family businesses, including hotels, shops, cafés, and various eateries. Heritage, landscape, and culture would be creatively packaged for consumption by Greek and foreign tourists.

Agriculture

Since entering the European Economic Community in 1981, Greece has received subsidies from the European Union's Common Agricultural Policy (CAP) to support rural development initiatives. However, politicians' tendency to exploit rural residents by exchanging CAP resources for votes, and the lack of accountability by farmers to authorities for agricultural development, created another cloud of corruption. Stories of rural residents who accepted CAP funding to upgrade their home, purchase rental properties, or indulge in expensive vacations were rampant. The tractor became a symbol of prosperity among farmers, who used it to drive to the village square and show it off, according to urbanites. Informants expressed outrage in hindsight about farmers who allegedly let their orchards of crops rot, while Greece imported food items and beverages from nearby Balkan or Mediterranean countries. Many were indignant about the absurdity of importing lemons and oranges, wine, olive oil, and nuts, while thousands of acres in the country's hinterlands remained fallow.

In 2012 a weekly organic farmer's market held on the campus of Aristotle University gained popularity as more local residents opted for "a cooperative approach" via "solidarity networks" to the rising costs of store-bought food items (Rakopoulos 2015, 2014b). "The benefits are mutual," remarked a young mother whom I met while I was selecting eggplants and okra one morning for my weekly batch of roasted vegetables (*briami*). She bragged about her ability to help struggling farmers, while she took pride in providing her family with food that is "clean and flavorful." Patrons of the university farmer's market spoke to me enthusiastically about purchasing honey, peppers, wine, even chickens from producers with whom they had established a relationship. Such transactions differed markedly from the rather tense and anxious conversations between consumers and sales personnel that I witnessed at the neighborhood supermarkets. There the focus was typically on the high-priced items that one could no longer afford. In contrast, interactions between the shoppers and farmers at the open market were pleasant and focused instead on the quality of the food item—the vibrant purple of eggplant, the honeyed, mouth-watering taste of figs, the sweet aroma of cantaloupe, and the appetizing flavor of olives.

Citizen-driven, short- and long-term innovations in the agricultural sector were another popular project proposal for economic development.[15] Locals emphasized the country's underinvestment in the production of food. They also critiqued the misguided notion that imported food "was better because it looked better," even when it cost more.[16] A popular example of grassroots efforts at the time was "the potato project," a movement that connected farmers and consumers.[17] Farmers produced thousands of pounds of potatoes and sold them in a matter of days out of the back of their truck. They brought their products directly to the consumers without intermediaries. The purpose was to meet the needs of consumers for fresh vegetables and to maximize the financial benefit of producers. By removing the profit-motivated middleman, locals viewed open markets as "an exchange of service" rather than as a "profit-driven business." Some farmers often offered their produce free of charge to customers who claimed indigence.[18]

A woman praised young people who established websites for exporting Greek products abroad. She narrated for me a scenario that she found plausible: "A young man gathers and sells oregano abroad through the mail. And when the mail carrier delivers it to the Germans, he tells them, 'I brought you an envelope with aroma.' What is inside?

Oregano!" Greeks must learn to beautify and market domestic products, she recommended. More and more young people, hosts advised, ought to export olives, olive oil, honey, and other goods. Behind all creative and sustainable agricultural development, locals noted, is the time and opportunity that the crisis affords us. "If people had access to big and easy salaries, they would not embark on such noble ways to earn money. Now they can! By doing so, they can bring capital to Greece, a country that is in desperate need of agrarian development," concluded a social worker. Others criticized owners of productive olive groves for their lack of technological and marketing savvy to brand their product, package it aesthetically, and export it abroad. Referring to thousands of unemployed young adults, the ophthalmologist said this:

> Development in Greece means creation of a brand and export of goods. Agricultural products must be branded as vertically integrated with allied industries in association with the International Organization for Standardization. Young people can produce high quality products within our own land, learn to package them beautifully, and introduce them to the international market.

Others saw the strategic location of the country, and Thessaloniki in particular, as a prospective service center. Locals imagined that industries could emerge based on the products that Greeks would produce. For example, explained an international businessman, Greeks produced olive oil that Italians then wrapped and packaged beautifully, and marketed for its "Italian flavor." He felt passionate that young Greeks must learn to launch private industries, and "even make the machines that will do the packing!" A man who received his MBA in the United States recommended that agricultural producers should fight for access to collaborate with the Greek Merchant Navy for international maritime transportation of food products between Greece and regions the world over. An agronomist advocated for investment in renewable energy, arguing that "sun and wind are Greece's natural assets" that must be harnessed.[19] Thessaloniki must become "an open city," the ophthalmologist recommended, and its port, with its proximity to the Balkans and the rest of Europe, could function again to revitalize our agricultural economy.

Many participants articulated the wisdom of linking cultural development with agricultural development by pointing to the country's presumed rich biodiversity and fertile landscapes. City-dwellers fantasized about a return to the land as a potential solution to a developing economy. A fitness center owner in a focus group commented: "Nothing is easier for us than to develop our land; throw an orange on the ground, and 100 orange trees will grow . . . Orange trees don't need water. Let us reclaim our olive trees; they do not require hard work. We can preserve our culture through our agriculture," she asserted confidently. As more people contemplated even temporary abandonment of city life and a return to the countryside, the prospect for increased food production as an adaptation to the economic downturn gained momentum even if, in 2012, it was still only a seed in the minds of these would-be farmers.

Large-scale farming in Greece is difficult due to a lack of arable land.[20] Agriculture has been limited to small family farms. This sector of the economy has depended on the labor of immigrants. Until recently, urban, college-educated Greeks denigrated farming as work for uneducated rural folk, racialized pariah groups like the Roma, and hard-working, ambitious immigrants. Raising livestock and cultivating crops, younger informants learned from their parents, is as undesirable as becoming plumbers and electricians. However, in times when public sector employment opportunities diminished and professional employment became superfluous or inaccessible, the food industry gained wide appeal and valor. Legal implementation of CAP subsidies, and accountability for production and distribution of crops and livestock products, would certainly boost the region's agricultural sector. As we will see in the epilogue, economic and social developments have multiplied in Thessaloniki and in Greece more generally.

The debt crisis challenged Thessalonikians to acknowledge the causes and prospects of their society in flux. Their collective social liminality also demanded conscious and unconscious adjustments to their daily practices and values to increase the likelihood of desirable social change and cultural continuity. State-mandated austerity measures and loss of household incomes compelled citizens to adopt conspicuous frugality and to advocate for values of moderation, humanitarianism, solidarity, civic responsibility, and ecological well-being. Public gatherings for costly food and drink decreased, while cooperative meals at home with friends and family gained momentum and value. A reciprocal exchange of useful and homemade goods and symbolic gestures replaced the exchange of expensive store-bought gifts.

Consumption of luxury goods and services in many cases almost ceased, while investment in accessible resources and personal relationships sustained quality of life and dignity. Youth and elders abandoned independent living arrangements to recreate economically more efficient, multigenerational households. More people walked, biked, and relied on public transportation. A few fled to ancestral villages or to distant lands to secure a living. Losses of material resources also coincided with gains in time, which allowed my hosts to think critically about their past and to act self-consciously to ensure their future. Thessalonikians valorized their heritage, called for social solidarity, proposed alternative socioeconomic developments, and advocated for cultural practices to revitalize their city. Characteristic of actors determined to navigate conditions of liminality, Thessalonikians' despair fluctuated with resilience. Young adults, the primary victims and potential beneficiaries of the crisis, are the focus of the next chapter. They agonized about how, and where, to express themselves as individuals, and about how to respond, as an educated and creative generation of potential change agents, so as to hasten their nation's recovery.

Notes

1. Progress (*proothos*) is the term by which participants referred to personal and national reforms, and technological, economic, and sociopolitical advancement, to be distinguished from progress as evolution (*ekseliksi*).
2. *Haratsia* is a Greek rendition of a Turkish word for an Ottoman capitation tax that the Troika imposed.
3. The phrase *Láthe biósas* (live hidden) is attributed to the Greek philosopher Epicurus (341–270 B.C.), who held that politics disturb the souls and minds of good citizens, and that people ought to protect themselves from such troubles by living away from cities and by avoiding political careers.
4. *Tsipouro* is a brandy produced by the distillation of pomace (the pulpy residue of grapes) that contains 40–45% alcohol and is a popular spirit in northern Greece. *Petimezi* is dark grape molasses that Greeks use in some desserts, including cookies and cake, as well as a topping on bread for a snack. This syrup is also the base for *retselia* (spoon sweets), a popular treat and gesture of Greek hospitality.
5. *Koulourakia* are small, crispy, buttery, orange-scented cookies that are especially popular on Easter.
6. Based on comparative ethnographic analysis of reciprocity and the exchange of gifts, Marcel Mauss (1967) demonstrated long ago that such practices build both instrumental alliances and mutually beneficial intergroup relations based on moral and humanitarian sensibilities. I observed such

emergent forms of reciprocity and exchange among individuals and families who, determined to maintain the convention of obligatory gift-giving, altered the nature of the gift to help meet the new needs and to reinforce the new values of community solidarity.

7. The number of road deaths between 2006 and 2017 decreased by 925. Since 2012 there were fewer than 1,000 fatalities per annum. See "Number of Road Traffic Fatalities in Greece from 2006 to 2017," Statista, last edited August 15, 2019, https://www.statista.com/statistics/437913/number-of-road-deaths-in-greece.

8. The Metropolis of Thessaloniki is a Greek Orthodox ecclesiastical see that belongs to the Jurisdiction of the Ecumenical Patriarchate of Constantinople, and is ministered by the Church of Greece.

9. The Greek Goddess Athena symbolizes wisdom, and literary figures depict her as the patron goddess of heroes—individuals who are of noble character and who possess strength, courage, and initiative to protect others from danger and lead them to safety.

10. The use of the term "man" (*Anthropos*) here refers to humankind or humanity.

11. The city's World Heritage Sites include monuments and churches that depict its early Christian and Byzantine period, including the churches of St. Demetrios and St. Sophia, monasteries, and Byzantine baths; fortification constructions for defense, including the White Tower, the Heptapyrgion, and the Akropolis Walls; and the Rotunda, a temple of ancient worship near today's Navarino Square.

12. About 11% of GNP is directly attributed to tourism and about 27% is attributed to direct and indirect contributions; see "Greece Tourist Arrivals," Trading Economics, last updated August 2019, https://tradingeconomics.com/greece/tourist-arrivals. Regarding Greece on the economic impact of tourism, see "Economic Impact of Global Travel and Tourism," World Travel and Tourism Council, https://www.wttc.org/-/media/files/reports/economic-impact-research/countries-2017/greece2017.pdf.

13. Tourism accounts for 18% of the country's GDP and employs nearly 1,000,000 people, or one fifth of the workforce. In 2011, the number of international tourists reached 16,000,000, a 10% increase from 2010. See "For a Sustainable Tourism Industry." Hellenic Republic-Greece in the USA, last edited October 2017, https://www.mfa.gr/usa/en/about-greece/tourism/for-sustainable-tourism-industry.html.

14. See Richards (2007).

15. See "Why are so Many Young Greeks Turning to Family?" Al Jezeera, published May 2017. https://www.aljazeera.com/indepth/features/2017/04/young-greeks-turning-farming-170417123546814.html; and "Greece's

Future: Agriculture or High-Tech?" Deutsche Welle, published March 2015. http://www.dw.com/en/greeces-future-agriculture-or-high-tech/a-18293013.

16. By 2015, alternative, greener, and sustainable agricultural movements had captured the attention of urban youth. Agricultural restructuring emphasizes greater political autonomy, popular participation, a cooperative consciousness, and a sense of community identity among farmers. Such movements also build on the so-called Mediterranean diet that the media popularized as being particularly Greek. New farmers promote the nutritional value of various food products and new crops of Protected Designated Origin in different regions throughout Greece's countryside and sea, and seek to complement new rural policies with Renewable Energy Sources. Investment in Greece's agricultural sector is evidenced by attention from scientists, cultivators, and online marketing innovators.

17. The potato movement was the brainchild of Christos Kamenides, a professor of agriculture at the Aristotle University of Thessaloniki. He designed a system of exchange from producer-to-consumer that he and his students implemented. Consumers preordered their produce, and Kamenides and his students obtained the produce from local farmers and delivered them to consumers in designated locations.

18. On April 30, 2014, farmers who often distributed packages of free food to an increasingly needy population protested legislation proposals designed to control the management of open markets.

19. See Argenti and Knight (2015).

20. See "Greece-Arable Land Percent of Land Area," Trading Economics, published July 2011, https://tradingeconomics.com/greece/arable-land-percent-of-land-area-wb-data.html.

CHAPTER 6

The Leisurely in Spite of Themselves

E arly in 2012, as austerity measures were choking households across Greece, young people saw the problem as "not a crisis of banks, but a moral crisis, a crisis of ethics." The city's youth were concerned more about their personal and generational loss of place and direction than about the eurozone policies that had brought their society to its knees. Their despair and rage at the time of this research reflects what these millennials viewed as a "betrayal" by their social institutions, including government, the economy, and education. Unlike older Thessalonikians, young adults born in the 1980s and 1990s had neither experience with, nor memory of, the previous disasters that mark their city's history. Their recollections of years past depicting a life of plenty contrast starkly with the reality of their present. This ethnography introduces a group of young, educated, ambitious Greeks of a weak state in which kinship remains a primary safety net, especially under dire economic circumstances. Through thoughtful and impassioned narratives, these urbanites enlighten those who might otherwise write them off as spoiled brats, lazy consumers, or entitled men and women of leisure. In this chapter I highlight individual and composite profiles of young adults who self-identify not only as victims, but also as potential mobilizers and architects of a "better Greece" and a "different Thessaloniki." I examine the predicaments, emotions, and responses of this segment of the Greek population that had known only peace, prosperity, and fun—until now.

Fall from Innocence

> It is as if we were born and raised in a world where every-
> thing was ours . . . all was good and beautiful . . . life would
> always be ideal!
>
> —GEORGE, 26, 2011

After Greece's 1981 entry into the EEC, and its replacement of the drachma by the euro in 2002, Thessalonikians enjoyed unprecedented rates of upward mobility, the primary beneficiaries of which were their children. As their parents reminded me, "Whatever we had, we spent it so that the kids would live well." To live well translated into consumption of goods and luxuries that for most families had previously been prohibitive. Markers of youth's rising middle- and upper-middle-class status included private lessons in academic subjects, the arts, and sports; higher education abroad; living on their own in rental properties or in a unit that parents acquired for them; recreational travel domestically and abroad; private health care; and a display of higher-end personal possessions. For the youth with whom I spoke, the former life of plenty was "normal" and "natural." By 2011–2012 that life had been replaced by personal and family vulnerability.

Many older Thessalonikians grew up enduring hardships, including wars, poverty, and loss of homeland—what one elderly woman called "real torture." Their memories are part of local or family folklore for many youth, especially the few who claimed to be descendants of refugees from Asia Minor. Some admitted that before the crisis they had tired of listening to their parents remind them repeatedly of how difficult life had been when they were coming of age compared with their children's "life of luxury." As adolescents and rising young adults, youth's focus was on the future, rather than past catastrophes and the human struggles that preceded their charmed lifestyle. Until 2009 young Greeks thought of themselves, and lived, as thriving "Europeans." The cultural cues they emulated were principally those of peers in other European countries and the United States. Immersed in a *habitus* of overall wellness, the young were oblivious to the fact that although their currency had changed, their economy had not. Nor did they fully realize that the very global forces that had fostered upward mobility for their parents were generating competitive market pressures across nation-states that would ultimately compromise, and for some eradicate, their opportunities for continued growth and development (Appadurai 2001; Giddens 2007).

Without warning, young Greeks found themselves in a state of double-liminality, a continuum of dependence between youth and adulthood: first, developmentally they were betwixt and between the status of *adult children* who lived with and depended on their parents, and the status of *social adults*—financially self-sufficient, socially independent men and women with households of their own. Second, they were betwixt and between the status of dependent *student/temporary or unpaid worker*, and the status of *professional*—gainfully employed full-time in the competitive global labor force. Thirty-four-year-old Alexander put it like this:

> We are in the middle. There are two boats. Our one foot is in one, and the other foot is in the other . . . we'll see where we will sail, or if we will drown in the sea . . . This predicament causes me more angst than anything else—this middle ground in which we exist nowhere.

Being and going nowhere, a symptom of liminality, was a prevalent and overwhelming sentiment among young people. Some waited impatiently for "light" to guide them through "the dark tunnel," while others wandered nihilistically as a category of displaced youth. However, actors in limbo inevitably change through a process that requires of them reflection, innovation, and action.

Bewilderment, ambiguity, and anxiety mark personal and societal transitions, and the experience of these young Greeks is not an exception. "I for one," remarked thirty-one-year-old Kostas, "am confused. I can't even think about what I want for my future, how I see my life . . . the crisis interferes with our maturity. Under normal circumstances I should have a career. We haven't lived as adults yet." Among young women, even more remote were previously anticipated intentions of adulthood to marry and have children (see Kazana 2018). "That's the last thing on my program," said Sophia. "I can't even take care of myself; how will I take care of children?"[1] Thessaloniki's young people attributed avoidance of having children to being "in limbo" between their pre-2009 lives as upwardly mobile adults and a future that was financially and socially indeterminate.

The Lost Generation

> My friends and I say often, that we are false persons . . . that we were born in a false world, at a false time.
>
> —MELETIS, 20, 2011

Young Thessalonikians referred regularly to themselves as "the lost generation." Members of focus groups summarized their generation's predicament as "feeling of being nowhere, of belonging to nothing." In limbo, no longer able to count on institutional resources or to determine new ones to pursue, young people were grieving the losses inherent in the crisis and theorizing accountability for the fiscal downturn that had "problematized" their life.

Graduating from college during a recession marginalizes young people economically and socially. Moreover, delayed full-time employment on a career path reduces the chances for upward mobility in the long run. Seeking and accepting any job, with or without compensation, became a daily concern for all young Thessalonikians. Some migrated abroad to pursue opportunities both within and outside the European Union. Those who stayed in Thessaloniki, and with whom I had the privilege to work, began and ended their days with questions and theories about the disintegration of their society in general and the precariousness of their families in particular. Athena's words rang true to her peers.

> I don't know what tomorrow will bring. I don't know if I will manage to find work, in spite of my higher education, in spite of all my studying. If only after thirty and forty years I could say, "Now I have studied, labored, created a family, raised my children, and now I may very well sit and live the rest of my life as such." Now I don't know to what I will awaken tomorrow; that's today's evil.

Most acute was young people's anxiety about their personal and generational predicament as the first "casualties" of their country's fiscal disaster. They share this fate with peers who are similarly neglected by labor market policies and politics the world over (Newman 2012).

This generation was socialized to expect easy access to resources, such as graduate education, professional careers, and marriage alliances with "good families"—members of the cultural and business elite. They expected to inherit property, including a house or a condominium, and income from their parents' rental properties to help support their lifestyle. A medical student whose parents' debt had "destroyed the family" cried to her best friend: "Can you imagine? My father is incapable of even giving me a house [*To phadazese aphto? O pateras mou dhen ine ikanos na mou dhosi oute ena spiti*]!" This young woman's complaint reflects her father's violation of a widely—albeit variably practiced—rule of inheritance among middle-class urban Greeks.

Parents provide a residential unit or condominium in a building at the city center, or a unit in a multistory building in which the parents and another sibling may also reside. While the legal requirement of dowry was abolished as part of the 1983 Family Law transmission of property from parents to their children as a foundation on which to build their own prosperity as adults constitutes a core cultural practice across Greece.

Reacting to the Troika policies that threatened the stability of their households, thousands of young men and women took over the streets and squares of Greece's cities to protest corruption, unemployment, and austerity measures that interrupted their development. In individual and group interviews, young Thessalonikians accused the state of generational neglect and abuse. As eighteen-year-old Zoe put it,

> The state lies to its children. He who governs looks after only himself, and a couple of others who help him acquire what he wants. No [politician] cares about our generation, about the city's youth, and about the problems our society faces.

Born and reared in Thessaloniki's upper middle class, Zoe and her peers had accepted the system as natural; they had been encouraged by family, school, and society "to succeed within it." Now, she argued, "The government does not function to serve Greece. State officials don't even try. They talk, and they talk, but they stop at words . . . they are not doing anything for society." Echoing Zoe's sentiments, "Greece is devouring its children!" insisted twenty-three-year-old Yiannis. "It is sad for such a country with such fine people, with such potential, to not invest in the talent of youth!" In reference to the referendum and bailouts, young people spoke adamantly about state officials as "living in their own world—clueless about how ordinary people live," stifling their potential and selling them to "eurozone sharks" for their own profit.

Younger participants admitted to barely understanding the making and meaning of eurozone policies, and the role that Greek officials played as mediators between Greece and the European Union. As Alexandra put it, "I can't say much about policy; I have only now learned that they [members of parliament] have eaten all our money and we are paying for it. That's it."

Despite general ignorance of political–economic technicalities, young people felt justified in blaming the adults who enculturated them to believe in their social institutions. The same politicians whom their parents and educators credited for the country's integration in the European Union and the eurozone, and family prosperity during their childhood and adolescence, they now viewed as reckless and self-serving technocrats who had set them up for defeat. Athena, twenty-six, figured that "it would be very easy for me to take two Molotov cocktails, three Molotov cocktails, four Molotov cocktails and throw them at the parliament! So that it blows up. State officials are not human!"

Young people experienced the fiscal collapse not only as a political betrayal, but as personal agony. Loss of faith, hope, and spirit marked every conversation they held with me in the wake of the financial bust. "The state," explained twenty-eight-year-old Meletis, "killed my soul, and eventually it will claim my body." Speaking on behalf of his friends, twenty-three-year-old Yiannis explained:

> The worst is that we cannot make dreams and continue to live in the style to which we were accustomed. We can't do what we want. We want to work; we want to create and to produce but Greece's market does not provide the foundation or the basis for us to do so. We have wonderful ideas, but we lack the environment in which to realize them. Greece doesn't give young people the means to develop themselves . . . to start something and to sustain it.

Meletis, who lost his job managing his father's now closed garment shop, lives with his unemployed parents. He searches the Internet for jobs in computer programming. "I say it with a heavy heart . . . they took away my right to dream. I don't have the right to create my life as I please." His trembling voice revealed his frustration at being displaced and the uncertainty about his future. Like Meletis, other educated and professionally inert young people spoke passionately about their desire to work and to become self-sufficient. "We are not lazy!" insisted Dimitris. "We just did not learn to work! No one taught us!" Dimitri clarified that by "work" he meant a professional career relative to earned college or graduate degrees.

Notions of labor or laborer, indicative of low-skilled, blue-collar, or agricultural jobs one does for low wages subject to an employer, were reserved for immigrants, not Thessaloniki's educated Greeks. Every young participant expressed anxiety about the lack of opportunities for "good work," by which they meant professional white-collar careers or positions in the public sector, which by 2012 were obsolete. Most feared that unemployment was indefinite, a perception that sometimes appeared to paralyze them. Yet in different conversations the same people expressed the notion that "something will be found," and the more hopeful stance that "we will prevail." Such a spectrum of emotions is characteristic of cultural transients.

No thought deflated my young interlocutors more than being deprived of opportunities to actualize their potential as contributing citizens of Greece—within their homeland and abroad. Socrates is twenty-seven years old and holds a master's degree in history. He is prepared and eager to pursue doctoral studies in history and anthropology. He has his eye on an academic career, preferably in Greece, but he is "willing to leave for Germany, the US, or anywhere I can work. But how can I afford to get there? I don't have the funds to leave," he agonized. He worried that a doctorate may not be an option now given his family's diminished resources. While between graduate degrees and living with his parents, Socrates struggled to find a job so that he could earn his keep. Instead, he admitted, "I wait in limbo and suffer psychologically." Subject to emotional turmoil and helplessness inherent in liminal status, he relies on meager wages from giving an occasional private tutorial in German to children, while "I still search for myself" (*akoma psakhnome*). He described his experience of crisis as "being and going nowhere at the moment."

In addition to hopelessness, others in Socrates's position feel shame and anger when people question their apparent idleness as laziness. Yiannis dreads facing relatives and responding to parents who say to him, "You are thirty years old; find something to do . . . find a way to pass some exams so that you can have a job making 600–700 euros a month." While these educated young men and women suffer the burden of their own disillusionment and indeterminacy, they find the persistent pressure from parents to achieve and succeed, now without their financial support, disorienting and gut-wrenching.

Zoe is distressed when her friends who are abroad ask her constantly, "Why are you in this situation . . . how can your people behave this way?" With the intention of one day pursuing a career abroad, Zoe worries that she and her peers will suffer personal discrimination because of Greece's institutional failures. Tasos defends himself. "Foreigners may criticize us; some refer to Thessaloniki as *phrapedoupoli* [the city of frappé]. That's a stereotype. If there were jobs available, I, for one, would be working!"

Young, Educated, and Searching

> Now my generation is pessimistic . . . we don't believe in
> anything.
>
> —Thanasis, 27, 2011

The young people who participated in this study spent hours each day comparing the "chaotic present" with their previous lives. Two years ago, Mihalis "was accustomed to living well—not wealthy, but fully," he said. "I had my job, as sales manager in my father's shop, and I was getting by OK. Now nobody shops for clothes; these circumstances have displaced me from life." Troubling to young adults has been not only the lack of opportunities to earn a living, but also the loss of resources to continue their education. Dimitris agonized that "the bust prohibits me from having a job and pursuing my graduate degree!" They all lamented the devaluation and underutilization of their educational and professional credentials.

Did all these educated young people expect to secure a professional position after graduation? Had it occurred to any of them that a graduate degree does not guarantee a career in one's own country, let alone one's city? As they were growing up, these young people imagined that they might one day: (1) work for a parent or relative in private industry; (2) find work in public service through family or political connections; and (3) for those of higher means, migrate to Athens, other countries in Europe, or the United States for study or work. The following monologue by a cab driver illustrates this point.

> In Greece jobs do not exist unless you have connections . . . take my son's godfather for example, who lives in a small town outside of Patra. He told me the other day that his son passed the Panhellenic examinations and wants to go to [the University of] Patra to become an engineer. I said to him, "Excuse me, but are you an engineer? Am I an engineer? Is your brother or your brother-in-law an engineer? Do you know any engineers? No! Then how will Grigoraki become an engineer?"

By 2012, Greek youth had become thoroughly disillusioned with the dismal life chances they saw on the horizon. Mocking her parents' generation, Erini said, "Every Greek mother's yearning [*kaimos*] a few years back was, 'My child, complete your high school, complete your college, do about five graduate degrees, get a doctorate and become a great scientist' [*epistimonas*]." Another graduate student recalled testing his mother by telling her that following high school he intended to become a plumber, only to hear her scream, "Shame, shame, shame [*dropi*]!"

Many college graduates blamed university faculty for mythical and counterproductive mentoring that led them to believe in higher education as the road to socioeconomic mobility (Bourdieu 1984). "None of the college graduates is working in their major area of study. Not one!" remarked Persephone. "We are all victims of broken promises," declared a twenty-three-year-old man who dreamed of a career in Greece's Diplomatic Service. He elaborated:

> There was a time when our society was in great shape. We got into a school, and we were promised placement and work. Our school's president said it. At the reception they welcomed us new students, and they said all kinds of bright things . . . and for a while we lived the experience. We came, rented our houses, we furnished them . . . we were economically comfortable. And we had hope!

Teachers encouraged Spyros to train as a computer programmer, promising that a job in that field was guaranteed. After he finished his training and fulfilled his military duty, he returned to Thessaloniki seeking work as a programmer. To his dismay, prospective employers informed him that "as an Internet person you can find a job only in an Internet café."

Graduates who failed to secure a job in their field relied on pocket money (*hartziliki*) they earned by giving private lessons to children (*ta idhietera*) in foreign language or music. Others offered tutorials (*frodistiria*) in various school subjects.[2] These economic strategies certainly did not suffice. As these teachers indicated, "With the private lessons you make better money, but you don't have insurance, while with tutorials you have insurance, but the money is terrible." Every young college graduate had at some time earned spending money by giving private lessons to children of the wealthy. Predictably, opportunities for private lessons decreased as parents began to cut back on what they now perceived as luxuries. The owner of a dry-cleaning establishment asked me, "How do I tell my eleven-year-old little girl that I can no longer afford private lessons in English [as a second language]?" "And without English, what will she be able to do? Where will she go?" Multilingual competency is certainly a status symbol in Greece. But proficiency in

European languages is also a pragmatic strategy if one is to maximize her or his chances to work in the global market, including the tourism industry in Greece.

Although his closest friend had a job, Aris reported that out of his "social circle and college friends I've had since high school, seven out of ten are unemployed and relying on their parents." Aris, who earned a college degree in physical fitness, holds two jobs—as a personal coach in a private fitness center, and as a swimming coach in Panorama, the affluent suburb of Thessaloniki. His second employer owed him 3,000 euros, which he eventually wrote off as "lost." He explained that given the precarious economic system,

> I try to work as much as possible, in case I lose one job, I will still have the other one so that I may survive. If a third came along, I would take it! Given the cuts in my wages, I have to work two jobs to earn what previously I earned from one.

Maria has a master's degree in history, but now works as a secretary in the biomedical industry. She admits that while she did not expect to find a professional position in her field, she was discouraged when she was offered a job only as a clerk. She also felt humiliated that despite her two master's degrees and proficiency in English and French, she secured her job through a political connection. "I was not even worthy to be a secretary on my own merits," she bemoaned, "I got the job through a contact." Predictably, those young people whose parents had lost their jobs, and whose grandparents' pension had been reduced, expressed higher levels of fear and anxiety. As twenty-seven-year-old Adonis put it, "Businesses are closing every day, and people are getting hungry slowly but surely, and some risk not surviving at all." In fact, reports of individuals who had taken their own lives preoccupied these youth, who interjected them in their narratives of threat and fear about the future of Greece and its people.[3]

Although displacement from the labor force left young people scared and depressed, it also inspired them to search—not only for any opportunities to earn money, but also to soul-search. Virtually all admitted to engaging in self-reflection and self-examination to an unprecedented degree. I heard the phrase, "I'm still searching [for myself]" from men and women in their late twenties and thirties who a year or two earlier had had "direction," "purpose," or at the very least, "a plan." Consistent with postdisaster communities struggling with psychosocial adjustment and recovery, these men and women were asking questions about how to determine or invent better, more suitable, and more humanistic life directions. While grieving the loss of a former life, young people had the privilege of time to ponder, imagine, organize, and create alternatives. Chiefly because of their middle-class status and continued support from parents, they could still engage in an intellectual and emotional examination of self, nation, and the world.

The Futility of Higher Education

> We are not interested in jobs, we are interested in careers!
> That's why we pursued higher education.
>
> —Alex, 31, 2012

Greeks prize education. From a young age, children learn that "education is the only possession that no one can take from you." This continues to hold true today. Young Greeks have viewed a university education as the "way to move from agricultural areas to the city and its opportunities for social advancement." As Kostas explained, "Culturally, higher education is the way to upward mobility, the basic pylon of development." Kostas's reference to "development" indicates progress across sectors—from agriculture, rural, or peasant ways of life to those associated with the prestige of an urban, and urbane, professional class of city residents (Friedl 1964). Implied in his remark is a hierarchy of cultures in which all matters urban are superior, compared to a rural existence. For most young Thessalonikians, the former status conjures up images of sophistication, progress, higher education, and cosmopolitanism. Kostas's point is that for children born and reared in villages, or those who are first-generation urbanites (born to peasant migrants to the city), access to the ranks of urban citizenry requires college and graduate degrees.

Development, in the minds of young people, amounts to an "urban, cultured way of life," which they associate with advanced degrees, lucrative careers, production and consumption of fine arts, worldliness, and a rich community and family life. While they recognize the intrinsic value of higher education, young Greeks and their parents also anticipated instrumental returns from their investment of time and resources. As Dora, thirty-three years of age, declared,

> My parents taught me that you can lose everything, but not your education. They warned me that we may lose everything [else] in life—and finally this all came true! I want to believe that I will never lose my education, but I want to contribute through it somewhere, to use it . . . otherwise my education and I are going to waste.

Offspring of university-educated, professional parents were especially disgruntled about their inability to secure their life's work, as well as to fulfill their parents' expectations. First-generation college graduates expected that the "piece of paper" (university diploma) would guarantee "a comfortable life." Instead, they find that their education, at least during this time of transition, had only prepared them for "opportunistic waiting"—a life of leisure in spite of themselves (Prothmann 2019).

Men and women described themselves as having ambition, an appetite for success, and inspiration and skills without opportunities to exercise their wishes to produce and contribute. Like the ambitious young men of urban Ethiopia, Thessaloniki's educated and unemployed young adults struggled to reconcile the national emphasis on higher education and the lack of opportunity structures for professional work and social mobility (Mains 2011). Erini depicted a national narrative with these words:

> We learn foreign languages, computer sciences, mathematics—and we are plenty developed and at a high level educationally. We have capable, qualified people, good scientists, very educated young people, but the system in which we live cannot absorb us and give us what we have earned. Consequently, we lose these people to other countries . . . the Greek brains are leaving.

Unconscionable to the young educated elite is being forced to accept work unrelated to their years of professional training. Thirty-one-year-old Alex described his anger, shared with his friends who also hold doctorates, when they have to consider any "irrelevant job . . . imagine, after years of higher education [you] end up with earnings of 400 euros a month!" Alex resents a state that encourages its young people to invest so much in obtaining advanced degrees when there are no professional positions available. He argued forcefully that the state and corporate elites should be ready and able to provide "equivalent rewards" in the form of jobs for high achievers in academia and the professions.

The "state and corporate elites" of whom Alex and his peers speak pay too little, if any, attention to the young people in local communities who are struggling to secure their economic futures. To be sure, even if elites did develop policies promoting gainful employment for college-educated young professionals, such opportunities probably would not be equally available in cities and towns throughout Greece. Greeks now question the mindset of sending every high school graduate to college and encouraging all young people to believe that a university education guarantees a bright future of meaningful and lucrative professions—in their hometown. These disillusioned young people and their parents are finding out otherwise, and in the worst way.

Continuum of Dependence

> It is not natural for thirty–thirty-one-year-old men and women to live with their parents. They ought to be living alone, to be tested in life. The crisis does not allow us to mature.
>
> —Dora, 31, 2012

Like their counterparts in other countries, including the United States, Italy, Spain, Portugal, and Japan, the choice to remain at home for those who had not yet lived on their own was young people's first and immediate response to the economic crisis (Newman 2012). As the fiscal downturn permeated households, most young adults who had left home—either to pursue postsecondary studies or to increase their self-reliance by working—returned to live with their parents and commute to college or work. Men and women in different social networks reported that most of their friends, whose parents were no longer able to subsidize their independent living, had given up their apartments and returned home. They emphasized that peers had either lost their jobs, were underpaid, or worked without pay. At thirty-three years of age and with a master's degree in forestry, Tasia works full-time for an energy renewal company, an industry on which Greece relies for its economic development. Alas, she complained, "From Christmas to Easter they gave me little money—about 200 euros total." She works overtime, ten to twelve hours a day, yet she has not been paid for this work in more than a year.[4] Working for decreased wages, or without getting paid at all, was common in 2012. Workers without wages were not volunteers, but individuals who prebust had jobs that they continued to hold, but without compensation.

While those in their early twenties were disillusioned about any prospect for self-reliance, men and women in their late twenties and early thirties, having already tasted relative autonomy, regressed to earlier stages in the continuum of dependence on their parents. Regardless of the variation in individuals' career and educational trajectories, they shared an undesirable life-course condition: a return to childhood. College students regretted the loss of their anticipated opportunities to become self-sufficient and satisfy their parents' expectations. Most had been prepared to pursue graduate studies, while working in a field related to their professional interests and living on their own. Instead, no longer able to afford independence and with career plans shattered, they returned home, uncertain, as they contemplated "which of so many closed doors" they might manage to open, if ever.

"The ideal option," said Aris, a first-generation college student, "is when your parents have a studio apartment they can no longer rent, and tell you, 'Go live there.'" The option lost its appeal when, by 2012, young and old alike deemed living alone to be a luxury when so many young people continued to rely on parents to meet their basic needs, including utilities and food.

"To tell you the truth," explained Aris, "Most of my friends and cousins in their late twenties who lived in the city center left Thessaloniki and now live in the villages with their parents." Young people with relatives or family homes in villages entertained the possibility of returning to the land. However, when they spoke about "cultivating grandpa's vineyard and olive groves," it was more a fantasy than a realistic possibility.

While everyone acknowledged that a return to intergenerational cohabitation makes economic sense, Thessaloniki's "boomerang kids" were experiencing cognitive dissonance regarding their new "in-house adulthood" (Newman 2012: 63–79). They were rejoining their nuclear families of orientation not as the adults they had come to believe they were, but in the structural position of dependent children. Erini, who returned to live with her parents after a decade of living on her own, struggled to erect and maintain boundaries between her private life and the life she shares with her parents and younger sister.

> To this day I feel as if I just graduated from high school and I'm seeking to take my next step. I am a graduate student, and I have not lived my own life. I am not independent of my family—not financially, not socially, not at all. I have not yet stood on my own feet; therefore, I am still a child.

Dora admits that she relied on her parents and appreciated their support while she lived on her own in the city center pursuing her studies.

However, now she finds the fact that she and her many friends in their thirties live with their parents "unacceptable." Forced to move back home, she feels that the combination of her parents' attention and control wear her down.

Maria's parents are retired civil servants—her father a former military officer, and her mother a former social worker with good pensions. They have always provided her with a "comfortable life." At thirty-one, and having reached "the bottom financially," Maria claims that despite her graduate diplomas, without her parents help, "I could not live." "I expected to live better than my parents, not worse," she cried. As Thessaloniki's young citizens demonstrate, reliance on family during adulthood has changed from luxury to necessity. They name their parents as their only source of support, asserting that one cannot depend on anyone else—that there is no other solution to the problem of displaced young professionals. In fact, the dwindling resources and now-restricted capacity of kinship alliances to function as the standard safety net for individuals in personal crisis may be the most emotionally debilitating effect of the economic crisis.

Returning adult children recognize the privilege of having a home to return to, and they credit their parents for the fact that "at least we're not starving." However, they also acknowledge the generational incompatibility in what Newman calls today's "accordion family" (2012). While they share the state of "delayed departure" with other economically displaced young people who find shelter in their natal homes, they resemble neither Italy's so-called mamma's boys nor Japan's "parasite singles" (Newman and Aptekar 2007). The Greek in-home adult children with whom I worked bemoaned living with their parents—a routine they found distressful, often conflict-ridden, and inevitably intrusive. They admitted to "going crazy while living with parents," but resigned themselves to the fact that this was the only option and, therefore, had to be tolerated. But, Maria asks, "At what cost?" Annoyed with her domestic arrangement, she complained,

> There are times when I lock myself in my room and my mom knocks on the door and says, "Open, I need to get something . . . what are you doing in there?" I tell her, "I am thirty years old and I deserve to have 5 square meters of my own, completely my own, without you coming in!" I don't want her to clean my stuff, to dust . . . I tell her, "I don't want it! I prefer to have [my room] dirty, to be swallowed by dirt instead of you cleaning it." My mother may think that she is doing me good, but I feel like she pressures me. Psychologically that constricts me.

For their part, parents also spoke of having to adjust to the return of adult children. Not only did they have to tend to their needs, they also had to learn to tolerate their sons' or daughters' sleepovers, dating patterns, and grooming rituals. One mother noted specifically that she resented having to cook for a family again after she and her husband had become accustomed to light evenings meals "like a salad, yogurt, or fruit."

At twenty-eight years of age, Leonidas was employed full-time as a pharmaceutical representative and was a part-time graduate student pursuing an MBA. Without hesitation to my question about his living arrangement, he replied, "I live with my parents, of course . . . due to university expenses . . . I simply cannot afford to rent my own house presently." He differentiated his status from his unemployed friends who also live at home; he considered himself "financially independent" because he was able to cover his "personal expenses."

> I am one of the fortunate ones in my peer group because I have a job in the pharmaceutical market. Most of my friends depend entirely on their parents, that is, parents or relatives give them money . . . My profile is economically independent . . . at least now.

This young man distinguishes himself from his peers as fortunate for having a "very good career," and disposable income. Meanwhile, by living with parents who fully supported his household needs, Leonidas shared with his peers the cultural pattern of unconditional parental support for life. Like his friends, he finds himself in *a continuum of dependence* on his parents. Like all the men and women in their twenties and thirties with whom I spoke, Leonidas conceptualizes financial independence from parents and siblings as relative, not absolute. With conviction in his voice he asserted, "We Greeks have this . . . parents are always there for their children." The concern that parents and children have today as they fumble their way through abrupt systemic transitions in kinship roles and responsibilities is the likelihood of role reversal. Will today's youth be in a position to be there unconditionally for their parents?

To Leave or Not to Leave

> This is a turning point for Greece. We don't see any plans for the future. In a very sadistic way, the crisis is forcing us to be globalized and to seek work far from here.
>
> —KOSTAS, 31, 2012

Young Thessalonikians are in love with their city. They speak about Thessaloniki as a personal, precious possession from which they don't want to part. Tzeni, a college graduate in her mid-twenties, adores Thessaloniki, but has decided to search "elsewhere for a better life." "I don't want to leave Greece; Greece is rejecting me [*I Elladha me dhiokhni*]," she said defensively. Most young adults insisted that leaving Greece would be an involuntary option. Twenty-eight year-old Liza reported that her friends were gradually leaving Greece—for other EU member states, the United States, or Australia—"Not by choice, she clarified, "but because of the crisis." Liza laments that "the children of Greece, the country of promise for refugees just two decades ago, are now the refugees in search of security and safety in other, more promising lands."

"Flight from a catastrophe" depicts the sentiment of six college women who pondered their postgraduate prospects during a focus group interview. They all looked outside Greece for "rescue." A couple of them fantasized about "going to America." Others wondered if their destiny was in Germany or England. Dina, a sophomore majoring in psychology, had corresponded with a professor at New York University about a potential research internship; "I will not get paid, but I will learn psychology!" She anticipated that the unpaid internship would ultimately turn into admission to a PhD program with funding. Her boyfriend, an accomplished chef, found a job through the Internet in Holland; he was prepared (ambivalently) to leave his country and his girlfriend.

Having watched her father's engineering firm close due to lack of clients, and others on the verge of bankruptcy, Georgia no longer looked to Greece to actualize her professional goals. "I look abroad, for further studies and for work." During her undergraduate and graduate studies in engineering, she anticipated finding a job in Thessaloniki working with her father, or as an associate in another engineering or architectural firm. Now, unemployed and living with her parents, she is exploring alternative paths: "I *prefer* to combine my work with a research position at a university anywhere in the world." Even her parents, who prefer to have her build a family of her own and live and work near them, encouraged her to leave.

Others with degrees in the technical and computational sciences, including Kostas and his brother, Elias, both unemployed and living with their parents, seek opportunities in "Arabic lands." As Kostas so aptly put it, "In a very sadistic way, the crisis is forcing us to be globalized and to seek work far from here." Driving those who are determined to practice their profession wherever they can find the opportunity is a search for what many called "dignified work." Others, who have relatives or friends abroad, contemplated leaving Greece for any job, however removed from their professional training. Thirty-two-year-old Vassilis, resigned to whatever "fate" has in store for him, concluded: "Even if I have to wash dishes, I will go where I can survive. Here, I don't even have the option to be a dishwasher." Vassilis was unusual in admitting a degree of desperation and a determination to secure his destiny, even if it meant stepping outside his comfort zone.

Maria's decision to leave or to stay in Greece rests on prospects for a productive career and retirement benefits. "My primary concern if I stay in Greece is whether or not I will live to receive a pension. When I reach a certain age I want to say, now that I have worked so many years, and I have contributed to society, I can count on getting a pension as my parents do." Uncertainty, while intrinsic to liminality, caused inordinate distress among all Thessalonikians. They imagined that coping with the crisis would be easier if they "knew something, anything . . . Without knowing what to expect, we cannot protect ourselves." For many young Greeks, the uncertainty of staying in Greece was harder to tolerate than the uncertainty that comes from investing in opportunities abroad (Labrianidis 2011).

Getting By and Going Through Crisis

> As you can see all the cafés are packed. People may have problems, but they will go out and drink a coffee, a beer, or a glass of wine with their companions. I see going out as a pillow, to exhale a bit . . . to stay home and put my head down and worry will not get me anywhere. I prefer to go out with a close friend to drink a cup of coffee, however minor, because that helps me! It is like therapy!
>
> —STEPHANOS, 28, 2012

The global debt crisis has had detrimental effects on the physical and mental health of citizens the world over. Most Thessalonikians with whom I worked, including the young participants, admitted to high levels of distress, including bouts of anxiety and depression. However, they all reported to have found solace from existing, informal systems of support, namely friends and family. As Ioanna explained, "I don't know anyone who sees a psychotherapist. We feel the depression intensely and frequently . . . sometimes for me it lasts for more than ten consecutive days." While the need for psychotherapy was reportedly at record levels, for most participants such treatment was financially prohibitive or culturally incongruous.

Some viewed psychotherapy as a luxury they could no longer afford. Athena asked, "Who has 30, 40, 100 euros to pay someone to listen to you for an hour? My psychotherapists are my friends, and naturally my parents." Hirschon heard the same sentiment from one of her informants, who told her, "We don't need counselors and psychotherapists; we've got friends and family" (quoted in Stewart 2014). Others considered any type of psychological or psychiatric therapy a source of stigma. "Here, if you go to a psychotherapist, they will consider you crazy," insisted Ioanna. Consultations with the more affordable clinical social workers were also an alien concept to this group of middle-class youth. As Athena said, "We never go to social workers. Here the social service agencies are for the very poor." In fact, in my interviews with social workers, I learned that even individuals from "good families" were seeking help with food, housing, and depression.

Young adults who claimed crisis-related distress denied reliance on mood-altering medications. Many smoked cigarettes and drank modestly, doing so more to improve spirits than to "get wasted." To be sure, everyone acknowledged that the sudden decrease in recreational funds had curbed their consumption of food and drinks in public venues, especially pricey distilled beverages at favorite seaside bars. However, based on interviews, my own observations, and focus group discussions, men and women expressed a personal and cultural disdain for reliance on drugs in general (whether illegal or prescribed) as a source of relief from crisis-induced mental and emotional suffering. The following refrain depicts this group's stance on controlled substances: "Depression now is very common; we are all suffering, but I don't know anyone who takes antidepressants. My own circle of friends does not take such things, and, generally, if we have a good job, we are well."

Aris and his peers cope by paying more attention to their physical health. He reported that people have cut back on overeating and eating out, and now go to the gym more often. His clients prefer to spend 50 euros a month to go to the fitness center regularly, rather than 4 to 5 euros every day for coffee or wine. "Working out in fitness centers is not a popular practice in Greek culture," observed Aris. He seeks to promote physical exercise among his friends "as a normal practice during these troubled times." After all, he argued, "I find it more economical, and it is an antidepressant because it is a matter of managing hormones." Athena, also a personal trainer, reported that even her dedicated, regular clients have cut back on personal, "face-to-face" training sessions, but they continue to exercise occasionally as a way to cope with fiscal hardship.

Sociality Is Therapy

My informants also invested in the standard Greek remedy for all ills: ritual public sociality. Young Thessalonikians discussed their primary sense of self and well-being as rooted in what many referred to as *parea*. They valued their daily gatherings of close friends and relatives to pass time, share political ideas, and divulge personal experiences and emotions. I observed young adults discuss with one another—at times tearfully—crisis-related internal conflicts, family discord, unrequited romances, and broken engagements. As Vaso pointed out, the ancient Greek principle *ta en iko mi en thimo*, which means "family matters do not belong in public," is no longer absolute. Perceiving the crisis as more systemic than a personal failure, my hosts shared their financial circumstances more openly, albeit still vaguely or cryptically.

Increasingly, people spoke publicly, for example while strolling on the seafront or riding the bus, about their household in near financial ruin. Conversations were animated and passionate. Even sitting in a café away from a group of other patrons, I could hear their tales of woe and their mutual consolations. Friends listened and empathized. They provided comfort through commiseration, advising and counseling for those who had the floor at any given time. Affectionate hugs and kisses, already standard greetings, were present in abundance. Most remarkable were deliberate, laughter-inducing anecdotes, puns, and teasing that members of these groups exchanged incessantly to improve one another's affect, even temporarily (Bakalaki 2016). It worked!

Adonis attributes his "sanity in the midst of chaos" to going out with friends. He explains, "Going out is logical in our cultural orientation. I cannot be alone. I need to go out with another person, to talk, to pass the time more pleasantly. What's the point of staying home?"

As Stewart notes, "In Greece, to be alone is pitiable, or else an ascetic religious choice, not an everyday value" (2014: 14). "Sociality is the only certainty and pleasant outlet left," Dora concurred. "We don't sit at home draped in black and creating a depressive climate. Being out with friends is integral to Greek society, whether one lives in a mountain village, an island, or a city." Maria echoed her sentiments.

> I don't know why Greeks like to go out so much. I don't know if it is cultural, that is, a traditional Greek habit. Going out and socializing are strategic survival measures for us that change our lives . . . we are improving the quality of our life.

Indeed, Greeks consider the notion of being alone nonsensical, whereas they argue that socializing in public with friends (and family) daily is essential to life, particularly when doing so may signify "collective defiance" against economic hardship (Knight 2015a: 127–131). Indeed, communal, playful sociability in public "third places," including cafés and *tavernas*, offered participants across age groups breaks of fellowship and joy during an otherwise distressful period (Oldenburg 1999).

Companionship, always accompanied with food and drink, is a core value and cultural practice that Greeks associate with a "beautiful life." However, in times of crisis, it has also proved to be an effective and accessible ameliorant. Coffee, for example, as a daily, secular, and public ritual, is part and parcel of Greek life. During the crisis it has also become a source of healing, and for many, the most affordable social and recreational outlet (see figure 6.1). As Spyros put it, "Pardon me, but there is no way that I will not drink a coffee out . . . If we did not even have that, life would be intolerable." As if she were enculturating me to local customs, Ioulia explained, "It's not the coffee we crave; I can have coffee at home. It's the being out!" (*Ine to ekso!*) Drinking coffee among Greeks is less about seeking another quick caffeine buzz, and much more about "socializing leisurely," "passing the time" with friends and, most critically, "talking to feel better" (see Cowan 1991).

During a three-hour long interview with Stephanos, a twenty-eight-year-old-doctoral student, and after three coffees, he received a call from his friend Stavros, who asked him to accompany him to an outing. We both agreed to have Stavros join us at the Byzantine Museum Café, where I, for one, was coffeed-out. Stavros began his conversation with me by ordering a cup of coffee for himself and for Stephanos. As our pleasantries turned into a lively conversation about the crisis, I invited both men to have lunch with me. Two hours later, and at the completion of an impromptu, unstructured interview with Stavros, the three of us strolled out of the restaurant ready, on my part, for a nap. Without missing a beat, Stephanos turned to Stavros and asked, "Shall we go for coffee?" He was

FIGURE **6.1 Youth at a café.**
Source: Photo by Kathryn Kozaitis.

serious, but we all dissolved in laughter. A habit that these men would otherwise have taken for granted became a topic that the three of us cotheorized as a mainstream cultural practice, particularly in its function as one of the period's most accessible acts of leisure and anxiety-reduction.

Small Concessions in Big Changes

During their social and recreational activities in which I participated, including birthday and name-day celebrations, dinner parties, and street festivals, young people spoke about a subject that before the fiscal collapse had been taboo: lack of money. Conversation about the economy, politics, education, family dynamics, or romantic relationships often began and ended with concerns about "getting through the month." Conversations focused on the lack of money not only to meet daily expenses, but to sustain one's social identity. As Sotiris put it,

> Because I don't have money, I feel that I don't have value. I never felt this way before, because there was always something to do, some way to work and earn something. Now without anticipating it, I am deeply troubled by being without a job or money.

The precrisis pattern of "I like it, I buy it," has become "I like it, but I don't need it." College-age men in a focus group interview on the subject identified "not having money to sustain a decent living" as the major concern of their generation. Dimitris related that he and his friends talk about how to meet "basic needs: luxuries are dead—trips, going out every night, buying clothes and shoes, finished!" he claimed. Among basic needs this young man counted books, and expenses related to securing alternative paths to work and life beyond Greece. He stated emphatically, "Now we save money for books, and just to get through the day. Even for fees, taxes, a transportation card, printed copies of our applications [to universities abroad] the money is not enough!" The young men emphasized that even though they were not hungry yet, self-imposed measures of frugality, previously a foreign practice, now constituted an orienting principle of daily life.

Everyone reported "cutting luxuries" and "counting euros" to adapt. Some spoke of relying on 10 euros to make it through the day, while others attempted to get through a week without spending any money— an unthinkable act for these consumers just months earlier. This was a shared experience: "Now we always manage our expenses, and put aside what we can to avoid hitting bottom. We are learning to economize," Maria said. Economizing also meant investing in alternative sociality: gradually reducing the days of going out for entertainment and saving the money by staying in. As Dora put it,

> I see how my friends and I cope by changing our behavior about sociality. When it comes to getting together now, we pause to consider everyone's financial situation, and speak discreetly about it. Because we may not know who may be struggling more than others, we say, "Shall we go out?" But why should we go out? We can find amusement at home!

Fiscal embarrassment gave rise to more communal sensibilities. Dora's response reveals both an economic strategy—staying in costs less than going out—and a heightened empathetic and ethical sensitivity toward peers who might be worse off.

My young hosts referenced staying in more as the first concession to fiscal constraints. Twenty-three-year-old Arete rationalized the shift from going out to staying in most succinctly:

> We hardly go out [for expensive meals and drinks] anymore. But I am trying to understand if it is only a matter of money— of course this is a reason, but I, and some of my friends, think that another reason is that [going out] got to be a bit boring.

Changes in behavior are easier when we can justify them rationally by pointing to benefits. Participants reasoned that going out to the same places even every week, to see the same people and do the same things, was losing its appeal. "Better to stay at home to view a film, or a series on television," Effie told me. She reasoned, "You enjoy going out more when you do it only once a month."

Others justified entertaining at home by comparing costs "of going out with staying in." Christina explained:

> We all want to go out with friends on Saturdays for drinks, but instead of going to the waterfront and paying 12 euros, which is crazy, you will drink on your own balcony. Incidentally, the view from my balcony is the same [as that from the bars on the waterfront]. So, you pick your mint from the flower pot, and you will drink there . . . you will set out a beautiful tablecloth on the balcony, and mine is a large and beautiful balcony . . . and you call your friends there to visit you. You provide snacks, and you spend your time like that . . . and you have your speakers (music), you have all that which is super! Why not do this at home? You'll enjoy it more!

Fiscal constraints have altered their value system about what they consider to be having a good time. Going out for a drink or two on the weekend, rather than several times a week for several drinks, suffices. Everyone confirmed that "instead of eating out every Saturday and Sunday like before, now we may eat out every ten days or once a month." Instead of two or three coffees at an outing, they will "sip slowly for hours" a frappe or a cappuccino. Many chose to forgo cocktails for a glass of wine or a beer. "Before the crisis," explained Vera, "My companions and I began almost every day with coffee in the afternoon, drinks in the evening, a meal at a taverna later, and then out to a club for socializing and dancing. All that is past now."

Not quite. As far as I could tell by looking out at the city from my balcony, the nightlife in Thessaloniki, certainly on weekends, remained lively and vibrant. While a rare site, I witnessed young people, including teenagers, walking and laughing on the street, clearly after having partied until dawn. In fact, clubbing continued to be a weekend recreational outlet for some, but they all controlled their consumption of food and drink in public venues. The difference, my young friends said, is that we may pass the time, talk, and dance, but we avoid spending money. Some joked about patronizing bars where friends worked where they were guaranteed a free drink (*kerasma*). Others were happy to be out among friends, listening to their music of choice, and nibbling on appetizers "to justify keeping the table."

Increasingly, I noticed that groups of young people gathered at one another's home for a meal that the host's mother prepared. Eftichia noted that the crisis was altering the meaning and activities of "social entertainment."

> Before we used to get together in public almost daily, but now we rarely go out; and no one is offended. Given that everyone is in similar circumstances, no one misunderstands; there is a commonality [*sinohi*] in this. We move from house to house rather than go out.

Without necessarily knowing it, some were adopting the American pot-luck dinner, a practice that made economic sense during the crisis.

Eftichia has found new meaning in entertaining at home by grilling in her little garden. She invites friends to dinner on Sundays, an event that pleases her and one she can afford. This is also her way of sustaining social relations with friends who may hope for an invitation. Her approach:

> You buy from the supermarket and you make a wonderful meal at home that will not cost as much as it would cost to go to a restaurant. Some people prefer to come and see you. Others may want to go out as a group, but if they pay 15 euros for a meal, the rest of the week they will be financially strained. So, you opt to invite them to your house delicately, to drink wine, to drink coffee, while avoiding all the hassle.

Tina also prefers to open her home to her friends. "My friends came last Saturday night, and I was so happy to have prepared various appetizers, with beers in the refrigerator . . . It was super!"

Others, sensitive about burdening their guests with an obligatory gift or contribution to a meal, think twice even about entertaining at home. Dora explained. "If I invite him, he will have to bring something . . . how can I put him in that predicament? What if he can't afford to bring any-thing? Better to leave him out. And then you do nothing." In fact, many admitted having to negotiate their home get-togethers. Sometimes, they felt that such gatherings needed to be kept secret lest they hurt the feelings of someone who "should have been there, but may not have been able to contribute and to participate."

Throughout the year, I observed that a resolutely new empathic sensibility was guiding sociality: being mindful that there might be members of one's inner circle who could not afford an invitation to one's home, let alone an excursion to the city center for a meal or to a club even once a month. Moreover, young adults demonstrated that crisis—that liminal period of "being nowhere"—was transforming them into more discriminating consumers of market-driven products and ideals, and into more critical, self-determined, and conscientious citizens.

Prospects for Solidarity and Collective Action

> The truth is that our society was awakened. Before [the fiscal bust] student activism existed as a luxury, more so rhetoric, while now it is a question of praxis.
>
> —CHRISTOS, 31, 2012

Foremost on the list of concerns among young Thessalonikians were notions that Greece and its citizens suffered from "an ethical crisis." At stake were not only material comforts, social stability, and national sovereignty, but the very essence of who the country's young are now and who they might become. They imagined themselves as a generation of young, middle-class, and educated adults eager to be contributing architects of a developing Greece, and responsible citizens of the world. The crisis mobilized them to imagine and create self-defined roles as agents of reform.

Disasters spur sociocultural changes and continuities. People, practices, beliefs, and values are in constant, cyclical motion, enabling a society to change in order to sustain itself. People in transition are displaced from habits of a seemingly stable past, as they cope with a destabilizing present. Integral to this process are personal and collective imaginaries—perceptions of identity, community, and belonging in futures yet unknown. In 2011–2012, even as young Thessalonikians were succumbing to a state of confusion and disorientation, they always pondered potential, more abiding forms of revitalization and the role that they, as self-conscious agents of social reforms, might play during the crisis. Dora believed that "it is up to the young to do something to make things better. We have to learn to live differently."

Young people's response was not so much to end the crisis as to apply its lessons to realize what many saw as "a more responsible, modest, and congenial way of life." Tina believes that "from all this [chaos], something good will prevail . . . something that we don't know yet."

Tina was one among the few whom the fiscal downturn had yet to assault personally. "However," she remarked, "the system must change to work more justly for everyone." She argued that the public sector must undergo radical transformation if productivity and responsibility, rather than "neglect and apathy," are to govern.

While politics has always been a topic of conversation among Greeks, discussions traditionally focused on what "they"—the politicians and policymakers—have done, are doing, and will or will not do. In contrast, conversations among young, middle-class Greeks at the height of austerity were about themselves as a potentially unified, politically minded body of global citizens, distinct from conventional political parties. As Alex remarked,

> We have begun to speak politically, but at the same time, there
> is a new consciousness of a common base. We sit and talk about
> "what to do" together, regardless of party affiliation. Solidarity
> is being created.

Instead of merely talking about *politics*, youth spoke more often about *policies*. Young people reported that conventional political talk consisted of opinions that they shared "as a way to relax and entertain one another." Now, they insisted, "each one supports a cause with much more strength and power. We tend to get into arguments now." Loukas put it this way:

> The crisis has freed us to imagine what could happen, how can
> or could our society be different. But in this black future where
> we have nothing, there is simultaneously a parallel activism
> where we think, "How would our society be different?" And
> we begin to discuss, "Is our society ready for such a change,
> for a transformation?" But not necessarily with a communist
> orthodox phraseology . . . but wondering how our society can
> be different . . . After such pressures, we accept that something
> better may be created. Because indeed our past was not ideal;
> it was problematic.

Participants expressed anxiety about politics that "could have ugly repercussions like the nationalism, racism, and xenophobia that gave rise to the neo-Nazi party, Golden Dawn." More akin to what these young social agents seek is what they call "a new solidarity." Now, they argued, young neoliberals and leftists alike share one concern: "What are we going to do?" They claim that the crisis has "matured" them to shift from philosophizing about the political system to thinking more pragmatically about how to make it work not just for the few, but also for society at large. Now, declared Kostas, "It is a matter of building!"

While the future remained uncertain, some felt invigorated by the prospect that change is possible through new articulations of civic responsibility and global citizenship. Vera, an MBA educated in London who manages her family's seafront resort in Chalchidiki, informed me that she and her friends are thinking that they should become examples of what Greece's new citizens should be. She pondered, "If each of us becomes an example by doing something that represents all of us, then maybe we can help Greece. Otherwise, nothing will change." Erini also finds hope in "this struggle," which she believes is required for one to acknowledge and respond to social unrest. In her words, "When you have a problem and you say, 'I have a problem and I can't do anything about it,' you will never overcome it. When you recognize the problem and convince yourself that you must overcome it, then you will find the way to transcend it. It will happen at a social level."

Erini rests her hope for recovery on her premise that "Greeks, as a race [ratsa], as an ethnos, as an ancestral group [ghenos], once we decide [what to do], we are capable of many things." She contrasted "a sensibility of relaxation" that she associated with Greeks, and particularly Thessalonikians, to the "programmatized German" who follows the rules that he is given. "If you remove a German from his program, he may not be able to change direction or find a solution. The Greek, because he lives every day with problems and is disorganized, will always find a creative way to adapt." She furthermore theorized that "perhaps as a result of finding ourselves in the society in which we now live, we become more flexible. After many difficult circumstances, we can recover. We may find solutions more readily."

Although sudden downward mobility affects segments of a population differentially, the shock, loss, search for accountability, and recovery efforts are universal. We witnessed resurgence in national unity among Americans across class, religious, and ethnic lines following the September 11 terrorist attacks. In September 2011 the eurozone debt crisis, which most Greeks defined as a "form of terrorism," stirred interclass linkages, as all Greeks experienced a threat to national survival. Through 2012 and beyond, I noted that young citizens were exploring a new transnational solidarity and taking agentive steps toward social reforms. Tina's words represent her peers:

> From crisis circumstances, good things are bound to emerge. When you are well—financially, socially, culturally—you don't have any problems, and you are not preoccupied with anything basic, or anyone else. Now you see, after a difficult period that we all share, that people are starting to draw close to one another. You understand another's need because you have the same needs; you become a bit more humane and you see things more clearly.

Indeed, deeper levels of consciousness and clarity emerged along with shock, ambiguity, and indeterminacy. Young Thessalonikians discovered painfully that crisis brings death to some ways of life, strengthens others, and generates new ones. The crisis gave rise to creative and affirmative ethical orientations along with practical and adaptive decisions and actions.

At the onset of the financial disaster in early 2010, Greece's educated youth were consumed with shock, fear, and uncertainly. While material austerities constrained their personal lives, they spoke most passionately about an "ethical crisis" they felt plagued them as a generation. Their collective disorientation and paralysis, which I observed in 2011–2012, gradually gave way to critical reflection and assessment. Central to their conversations with me and with one another were narratives of displacement and victimization on the one hand, and the prospect for change through collective agency and social reform on the other. These sentiments remained front and center in their minds throughout 2012. However, a discourse of critical thinking, self-determination, and political awakening now qualified their narratives of loss, displacement, and rebirth. Propelled by a personal struggle to survive, many reported a shift in their behavioral patterns, including reduced and more discriminating material consumption and more modest, cooperative forms of sociality. With a new awareness of social and ethical responsibilities, they could better offer sympathy, empathy, and support to their peers, especially those who were struggling most financially and psychologically. As do all survivors in transition following natural and political disasters, young Thessalonikians harnessed existing cultural resources, such as their middle-class status, education, social media, and parental support, to make sense of the crisis and live through it. Also characteristic of adaptive actors in sociocultural transition, they proposed mobilization of new resources, including political solidarity, volunteerism, and immigration to move away from social liminality and toward emergent states of relative certainty, security, and meaning. In the epilogue we will revisit their transformation, and examine the moral, political, economic, and social outcomes of their efforts toward recovery and renewal.

Notes

1. Research participants named "inability to afford" children as the primary reason for avoiding marriage and building a family, a developmental milestone that they considered to be normative before the crisis. Unemployment and austerity measures in Greece correlates positively with a 15% drop in rates of fertility in the past four years, mirroring a 25% drop in the country's GDP since the onset of the crisis. See "Greece's Birthrate Falls as Austerity Measures Hit Healthcare," The Guardian, published September 2013, https://www.theguardian.com/world/2013/sep/18/greece-birthrate-austerity-measures-healthcare.

2. On the premise that public education in Greece is of very poor quality, prohibiting most high school graduates from passing college entrance exams, teachers offer private lessons for a fee. Parents who can afford additional help for their children hire private tutors in specific subjects who usually come to the student's home to offer individualized instruction in academic subjects or in the fine arts.

3. In 2011, 40% more Greeks committed suicide in the first five months of that year compared with the number who took their own life one year earlier. Crisis-driven rates of suicide continued to rise in 2012 and 2013. See "Increasingly in Europe, Suicides 'by Economic Crisis,'" New York Times, published April 2012, https://www.nytimes.com/2012/04/15/world/europe/increasingly-in-europe-suicides-by-economic-crisis.html. On May 8, 2014, a fifty-seven-year-old man committed suicide by hanging himself on a tree near his vacation house in Chalkidiki. His wife reported that her husband was "a victim of the crisis" after austerity measures cost him his life savings.

4. Maria's employer claimed legal protection through Article 99 for not paying her until the industry recovers. According to Article 99 of the Bankruptcy Code, effective the third quarter of 2011, debtors receive sufficient protections and flexibility until they are able to repay their debts, while creditors gain time for sufficient recourse to retrieve their money. Such provisions benefit corporations that have financial interests in Greece and have defaulted on their obligations.

CHAPTER 7

Theory of Crisis as Liminality

This work examines emotional, cognitive, and behavioral responses among Thessalonikians to the Great Recession of 2008, and to the 2009 European debt crisis that exposed Greece's structural vulnerability to fiscal collapse. How did these middle-class urbanites respond to an economic tsunami that ruptured life as they knew it? How did ordinary citizens, accustomed to gainful employment and accessible wealth, reconcile an unanticipated loss of work and money and a gain in the abundance of leisure and time? In this chapter, I summarize and theorize my findings about this community's experience of the Greek debt crisis through the lens of social liminality: a people's collective practices, values, and meanings during a transitional, precarious, and revelatory period between an abrupt break of established structures and uncertain future outcomes. At the center of crisis theory are liminal actors—elite and ordinary citizens who feel, think, and act to cope, adapt, and effect social reforms. Grounded in ethnographic interviews, my analysis reveals participants' *feelings* of despair, fear, and hope; *deliberations* about the roots and causes of the meltdown; and *acts* of resilience, solidarity, and recovery. Consideration of the Greek crisis as a symptom of a rapidly changing, precarious, uncertain global economy and a debt-ridden world illuminates one urban community's vulnerability and response to financial calamity.

Local Vulnerability to a Global Disaster

The inception, geography, and history of modern Greece relegate it to "crypto-colonialism," the economic and political margins of the West, and to the periphery of the capitalist world system (Faubion 1993; Herzfeld 2002). The vulnerability of the modern Greek state to global transformations, including the Great Recession of 2008, subjected its citizens to a political–economic disaster for which they were unprepared. Intellectual debates about Greece's current crisis as evidence of its "underdog" status vis-à-vis the developed and modern North Atlantic states illuminate the country's long and multifaceted dependence on external powers (Triandafyllidou, Gropas, and Kouki 2013). Such theoretical accounts of modernity contrast an industrial, market-based, and progress-directed social order with technologically developing traditional societies (Giddens 1991). However, Greece's demographic complexity and sociocultural hybridity defy binary contrasts such as East versus West, oriental versus continental, industrial versus agrarian, and traditional versus modern. Analysis of the current Greek debt crisis points to the conjuncture of (1) global and impersonal market forces, (2) an opportunistic, ill-executed European project, and (3) personalistic socioeconomic practices within Greek society.

Mass Access to Global Capital

Sudden shifts in global market conditions, such as the stock market crash of 1929, the collapse of Eastern European communism (1989–1981), and the Great Recession of 2007–2009 destabilize sovereign states and threaten the well-being of communities. Fiscal policies and practices of global markets drive regional and state economies, which in turn influence the social realities of individuals and households (Wolf 2010; Wallerstein 2004; Wallerstein, Lemert, and Rojas 2013). Shifts in neoliberal market conditions propelled the eurozone debt crisis, destabilized the more vulnerable segments of its member states, and undermined Mediterranean economies in general. Greece's access to subsidies from the EU and loans from predatory lending agencies fueled three decades of unsustainable nation-wide prosperity in these domains: a burgeoning public sector, a boost in the country's construction industry, and high rates of enrollment in institutions of higher education in Greece and abroad. European integration and a new age of credit supported Greece's economy and Thessaloniki's professional class. A buoyance of private entrepreneurs, principally in the fields of medicine, law, engineering, and architecture, as well as visual, literary, and performance artists, magnified Thessaloniki's image as a city of cultural production (Bourdieu 1994).

Decades of easy access to subsidies and bank loans turned the Greek masses into avid consumers of material culture. Thessaloniki's working and lower middle classes also partook in this unprecedented abundance of resources. A rising middle class of *culture builders* (Frykman and Lofgren 1987) emerged. They joined local elites, including descendants of Thessaloniki's old families, in the conspicuous consumption of products and sensibilities imported from northern Europe. Rising spending by civil servants and professionals boosted the financial and social status of the local merchants who fed, dressed, and entertained consumers on demand. The tastes, aromas, sights, and sounds of a bustling cosmopolitan city became a captivating milieu in which locals indulged and to which tourists, within and outside the boundaries of Greece, traveled to amuse themselves.

An increase in the social budget, public expenditures, and income transfers intensified in the 1980s, fueling the rise of middle classes who competed for even greater access to state resources, including generous cash benefits and pensions (Petmesidou 1991). It is no wonder that visitors to Greece during the 1980s through the first decade of the twenty-first century were astonished at the conspicuous prosperity of an underindustrialized, developing country on the margins of the global economy. On my visits to Greece during this period, I questioned the wealth and generosity of local Greeks compared with the more moderate economic success and thriftiness of Greek emigrants to the United States. "Greece is a poor country with rich people,"[1] acknowledged my friends. A more universal response to my query then was, "With Andrea [Papandreou], all Greeks solved their economic problem! He gave [money], and we took it!"[2]

Greece's historical, economic, and political linkages to fluctuating global markets, combined with corrupt social and cultural practices within its institutions, turned perceived prosperity into a real catastrophe overnight. A thirty-year period of economic and political integration in the global economy transformed Greeks from a people for whom debt was a source of disgrace into accomplices in a fraudulent financial system. Enjoying their apparent unprecedented prosperity, the newly indebted embraced an upwardly mobile lifestyle. While some of my hosts admitted to not recognizing or anticipating the inevitable financial and moral trap of debt, others sought loans on the assumption that gainful employment was guaranteed: "I will work to repay my debt," they all surmised at the time.

Indeed, most people may have embraced unwittingly the "financial benefits" and "social advances" that membership in the eurozone offered. Convinced that financial security was indefinite, members of the working and middle classes exploited access to subsidies, loans, and other profit-making maneuvers to become property owners and to propel their children to the privileged classes (Zhang 2010. As new, "miniature capitalists," including rentiers, middle-class professionals embraced what Graeber calls "crisis of inclusion"— reliance on debt and increased discretionary spending to become homeowners and to raise their standard of living (Graeber 2014: 374–379). Urbanites embraced and displayed a sense of acquired Europeanness, even as their country's infrastructure and social institutions weakened in the process.

Europeanization and Its Costs

Global economic and political forces do not drive themselves; their creators do. Against the backdrop of historical shifts, neoliberal ideologies, and political–economic conditions—all determinants of social change—are human beings. These "producers of globalization" invent cultural myths, create institutional policies, and enact practices that over time, morph into global cultural orientations (Antoniades 2010). They exploit resources at their disposal to influence how others within and beyond their sphere of influence feel, think, and behave. Ruling elites, including international policymakers, financiers, and administrators, possess the resources, power, and influence to orchestrate the conjuncture of structures, ideologies, and relations of exchange to direct sociocultural change and to make history.

Driving the inevitable crash of 2008 was a fury of transactions among international financial experts, politicians, and bureaucrats who created and ran a global economic system that would benefit creditors at the cost of borrowers (Graeber 2014: 16–18). From microinteractions and interdependencies among elites and ordinary citizens linked in relations of power and systems of exchange, emerge ideologies that translate into and manifest as macro-level sociocultural changes (Barth 1967; Giddens 1984). Greece's integration into the European Union, and its subsequent membership in the eurozone, demonstrate the agentive power and influence of actors to conceive, design, and implement structures that constitute, and are constituted by, patterns of cultural change and continuity.

Greece's formal Europeanization impressed most of its citizens as a shift toward *modernity*—as both economic development and socio-cultural progress (Giddens 1990). In the 1990s and through the early 2000s Europe was an essential, albeit hegemonic partner in an alleged *modernization* of Greece.[3] Both elites and middle-class Greeks adopted and promoted a pro-European ideology and transnational sensibility that became pervasive (Hannerz 1996). Older informants recalled the exhilaration with which the masses accepted their right to a European passport. Younger research participants were oblivious to an identity and worldview that did not include "European" in its configuration.

Europe as a supra-state fell short of its promise to protect its histori-cally hierarchal and demographically diverse societies (Giddens 2007; Graeber 2014: 109–119). Indeed, EU policies led to humanitarian cri-ses from which citizens of economically weaker member states, notably Greeks, continue to suffer. Such defining features of neoliberal econo-mies as industry, specialization, competition, efficiency, and technology were and are at best dismal, if not altogether absent in Greece's political economy. The Greek state's *dependence* for resources upon wealthier European states ensured unsustainability of its prosperity, and exacer-bated its *underdevelopment* (Mouzelis 1978).

Creation of the euro expanded the gap in wealth and power be-tween northern European and Mediterranean countries. Predictably, the Greek state's vulnerable position in the global market, neither devel-oped the country economically nor guaranteed a sustainable quality of life among its citizens. Since Greece entered the eurozone, the state bor-rowed, spent, and consumed without limits, blinding its citizenry with a false sense of prosperity. My hosts experienced the economic crash as a "shock," even as, in hindsight, they insisted that "something had to give; sooner or later the bubble had to burst."

Negotiating exchanges, treaties, and subsidiaries are middlemen who represent to global stakeholders the presumed interests of member states and their communities. In doing so, such brokers gain easier ac-cess to resources, and increase their power and influence. As patrons and architects of social institutions, Greek elites thrived during the pre–debt crisis. As middlemen between eurozone administrators and the Greek masses, Greek officials distributed EU resources with ques-tionable measures of accountability. Through fiscal interventions in households, institutions, and industries, those in power altered inter-personal transactions, social practices, and value orientations among a large segment of Greece's citizenry to favor exploitation for profit as a mainstream eurozone practice.

Transnational elites then used their power to impose austerity pack-ages, while the security of Greek households declined by the day. Greek parliamentarians approved austerity plans in exchange for bailout aid from the European Central Bank and the International Monetary Fund, while Greek families struggled to stay warm and sane through the win-ter. While financiers downgraded Greece's debt to junk bond status, Greek parliamentarians' cuts in public spending enraged citizens who struggled to make ends meet. Meanwhile, in consultation with Greek officials, Troika leaders called for the privatization of government as-sets and the state's restructuring of debt to galvanize Greece's economic productivity and development. Such top-down interventions led to un-employment, reinforced Greece's dependence on foreign capital, and jeopardized its social welfare.

Eurocratic control reinforced citizens' feelings that a form of neocolonialism—another foreign occupation of sorts now descended upon their country, and that their own representatives were playing a prominent role in their subjugation to foreign creditors. As the coun-try's credit ratings declined in 2011 public services vanished, and reports of poverty, crime, and suicides filled the airways. Correspondingly, the public's trust in their representatives plummeted. Citizens saw their politicians and other elites as opportunistic middlemen between the Greek masses and Europe's rulers. In their role as brokers, state officials wielded their power and influence through negotiations with eurozone administrators in their favor, and at the ultimate cost of their constit-uents (Gellner and Waterbury 1977; Roniger 2004). For example, the infamous Memorandum of Understanding (*Mnimonio Katanoisis*) that eurozone and Greek state officials signed required cuts in pensions and salaries of government employees at a time when unemployment rates were rising, and emotional, mental, and physical health was declining.

In 2012, then-Prime Minister Antonis Samaras negotiated with the global political partners and creditors to ensure that Greece remained part of the European project. Greek leaders pledged to curb corruption, including that in the country's malfunctioning tax administration. The "rescue packages" that promised to sustain the Greek state subjected ordinary people to an all-encompassing crisis. Unmistakable in the private financial struggles and the public moral protests was the human side of debt. Meanwhile, Greek officials welcomed Troika leaders who visited Greece to monitor the implementation of EU mandates, with the threat that bailout payments could be halted if Greece failed to comply.

Of Greece's Patrons, Clients, and Thieves

The cultural hegemony of political elites relies on the "consent" of the masses, for whom compliance becomes "common sense" (Gramsci 1971). While corrupt elites build corrupt social structures, corrupt individuals engage in corrupt acts and reinforce corrupt cultural systems. In the minds of many citizens, the Greek state represents a collective patron, a father of the nation who failed in his duties to protect his children and, in the process, jeopardized his family. However, as acting subjects, ordinary citizens participated in, and reportedly have accepted, partial responsibility for their personal and domestic economic embarrassment. Individual acts of ineligible borrowing, patronage, and consumption of imported brand products fueled an increase in middle-class households, while a national culture of fiscal disorder was brewing. Contributing to perceptions and aspirations of prosperity were rising rates of disposable personal income during the 1990s financial boom, only to leave thousands of inexperienced investors feeling betrayed and defeated (Graeber 2014).

Ordinary Greeks exploited opportunities for upward mobility that their political representatives and business elites, in compliance with their eurozone patrons, constructed and guarded. Widespread financial indiscretions, including money laundering, abuse of office, tax evasion, and bribery jeopardized the country's systems of health, education, and welfare. Corruption as ideology and as practice in profit-seeking, such as fraudulent building permits, and historic conservation projects, afflicts the Greek masses because their representatives promote and reward it (Herzfeld 2015). As so many insisted, "That's how the system works!" "We are all thieves," claimed a restaurant owner. "The politicians steal from us, and we steal from them and from one another; that's how the system worked here." Including themselves in this category, others argued passionately that "not all Greeks evade taxes" or engage in corrupt transactions. And yet those who do pay their share of taxes may not fare any better with respect to an equitable distribution of state resources than those who mock the state and its representatives (Guano 2010).

Living in Limbo

Historical disruptions to social order destabilize communities, generate liminality, and foreground agentive social change. Those who manage to survive abrupt, human-made disasters adapt through shrewd and affective adjustments, characteristic of a life in limbo (Oliver-Smith 1996; Hoffman and Oliver-Smith 2002). During risk-laden societal transitions people's emotional states oscillate between despair and hope, while their cognitive capacities compel them to search for meaning and understanding of their circumstances (Frykman 2012). In the wake of disasters, including economic and political collapse, social hierarchies "become luxuries," and people tend to cultivate "a rough-and-ready communism" (Graeber 2014: 96). In times of crisis a "baseline communism" emerges, a "spirit of solidarity" expands, conviviality and sociality increase, and "the need to share" with others dominates social relations (Graeber 98–99).

Equipped with innate agency, actors in societal liminality interpret, manage, and unite to restore order (Horvath, Thomassen, and Wydra 2015). Through their creative and experimental responses to unanticipated and threatening conditions, people adjust their routine practices and thoughts, and in doing so sow the seeds of larger social and cultural transformations (Barth 1967). The collapse of Greece's state economy upended the lives of ordinary citizens, including those of my research collaborators. Analysis of life in crisis as social liminality reveals participants' emotional states, their economic strategies and forms of sociability, and their intellectual and ethical principles of sociocultural change and continuity.

Internal States of Crisis

During times of abrupt societal disintegration people's feelings are raw, passionate, and persistent. Emotions constitute a fundamental ingredient of crisis, as they contain both healing properties and strategic revelations. Participants' affective testimonies in Chapter 3 show how the financial collapse influenced their choices, practices, and spirits. Two years into the debt crisis, men and women, across the age groups, spoke passionately about the fits of anger, guilt, and fear that consumed their every day. Such states of shock, dislocation, and uncertainty are inherent in postcrash liminality. Yet in conversations about the despair that they associated with job loss, cuts in pensions, and the inability to pay monthly utilities, my hosts also expressed such sentiments as relief, exhilaration, intentionality, and hope.

A resurgence of nationalism emerged. Angry and suspicious locals feared threats to their nation by "an invisible enemy." Some insisted that a "European economic invasion" threatened Greece, while others pondered the onset of WWIII—another German occupation, and other signs of national obliteration. The same people with whom I had celebrated life in the summer of 2009 now worried about impending social disorder and a takeover of their government. No longer were my old and new friends concerned about the problem that had preoccupied them two years earlier: the presence of postsocialist immigrants who were "changing the face of Thessaloniki," or the new foreigners from East Asia and Africa who occupied the city center. Instead, my hosts spoke about the crisis as a form of "terrorism" that engendered feelings of loss, confusion, and fear.

Insecurity and uncertainty reign during periods of social liminality. The collective angst that I witnessed arose from the devastating effects of austerity on their economic standard of living, and also reflected the indignation and humiliation that befell Greeks as individuals and as a nation. Former routines of going to the office, to class, grocery shopping, or out to dinner with friends morphed into contingencies. A visit to the doctor, or to one's attorney, a child's private music lessons, and homecare for elderly parents now required calculations of priority, affordability, and meaning. Threatened by loss of control over how much and to what ends they should invest depleting funds, such as household utilities, property taxes, or a daughter's college tuition abroad, middle-class Greeks found themselves constrained by "radical" limitations to self-actualization as proper urbanites.

Financial distress manifested as both discord and support within households. For example, domestic disputes escalated following the unemployment of one or more adults in a household, while the rise in taxes rekindled family feuds regarding inheritance and property rights. Men often became targets of blame for domestic finances gone wrong, typically due to a husband's "playing stock market lotto"—engaging in small trade activity on the Greek stock market, investments or personal expenditures without his wife's consent or his adult children's knowledge. As austerity intensified, testimonies of marital estrangement increased, while parental guilt for inability to meet children's needs prevailed. Bittersweet separations of families when members migrated abroad in search of work rose by the day.

Crisis time calls for unconventional measures to increase the likelihood of survival. Family break-ups through emigration impressed participants as a necessary but radical way of surviving financial embarrassment. The impact of the debt crisis on families had a ripple effect. When one household suffered financially, other families in the same kinship network empathized with their loved ones, or they extended their own diminishing resources to help more vulnerable relatives. Women, in particular, turned to one another for emotional support, and when feasible provided material resources such as paying an unemployed father's electric bill, or hosting a birthday party for a godchild whose parents were financially worse off. Others carpooled to share transportation expenses with siblings and neighbors. Some shared medications with relatives, including those who suffered from chronic conditions such as diabetes, cancer, and depression.

Extended family members might provide groceries to an adult daughter's home, or drop off a cooked meal to an unemployed and orphaned nephew. Such charitable acts reflected as much a moral obligation and duty to "care for one's own" as they did unconditional love and sympathy. As household incomes were falling for most and evaporating altogether for others, the family became the only safety net on which participants could rely for emotional sustenance. Empathy, support, altruism, and intensification of emotional bonds within nuclear and extended families signified liminal times for everyone, however differentially. Amid the instability, uncertainty, and ambiguity of outcomes that characterize living in limbo, new and decidedly clear revelations emerged about the value of family as the primary source of emotional, moral, and often material support.

Noteworthy is the empathy and compassion that individuals demonstrated when they discussed with me the difficulties of not only relatives and friends, but fellow Greeks in general. Social crises expose the fluidity of social hierarchies, as citizens within and across strata experience dislocation and embrace "increased communality" (Graeber 2014: 99–100). In response to threatening conditions during liminal times, exhibitions of *communitas* are common and adaptive for populations that maintain firmer social hierarchies in times of societal stability. For example, wealthier owners of condominiums empathized and "hurt" for their poorer tenants who were unable to pay the rent, income on which landlords relied to support their own families. Reduction of the rent by 50 to 70 percent, reasoned some property owners, is more humane than evicting "our own people." Precarious living conditions and anxieties about an unknown future relaxed social hierarchies and united Thessalonikians into a community of shared displacement, angst, and resilience. Testimonials by individuals of living in limbo highlighted the emergence of communitas and general reciprocity in material and emotional support among close friends, neighbors, and colleagues.[4]

Empathy became the unspoken, but demonstrated sentiment of the time, as people invented ways to comfort one another through small acts of altruism and large gestures of compassion. Young adults began to share with a best friend what little money they did have to enjoy one weekend night out in the city together rather than two evenings without a favorite companion. College students shared books and other supplies with peers who lacked funds to copy a paper or complete an application for funding to study abroad. Women swapped clothes and accessories with friends to freshen and diversify their wardrobes when purchasing new items became financially prohibitive and, as so many noted, revealing a shift in values, "sheer foolishness." Musicians performed and teachers tutored, pro bono. Physicians and attorneys adopted a sliding scale that they adjusted to their patients' and clients' ability to pay for services.

Farmers and discreet shoppers left bags of food for the needy on street corners, while neighborhood grocers threw an extra potato or a bruised cantaloupe into one's plastic bag. Such displays of "communism" constitute not only *economic* cooperation, exchange, and reciprocity, argues Graeber; rather, these are also *moral* principles that reflect "mutuality" and interdependence among a community of equals (2014: 100–103). People whose lives are in limbo provide and accept solutions to problems that may be practical and rational in times of crisis, but not necessarily preferable or conventional during times of social stability.

Out of crises are born rituals that provide liminal actors with opportunities to express new beliefs that are both comforting and conducive to resourceful adaptations. For example, everyone suspended their former practices of carefree spending and consuming food and fun out on the town throughout the week. Instead, participants ritualized cooking at home for one another, illustrating both conspicuous frugality and the adoption of more conscientious and healthier nutritional habits. Even instrumental relations in business and commercial exchanges appeared to soften as strangers comforted one another by commiserating about the crisis, and by affirming recovery through words of wisdom, courage, and hope. Participants imagined, even assumed, that the crisis-driven distresses were temporary symptoms of a transition (*metavasi*); however, they also noted that the crisis, both fiscal and moral, had forced them to suspend what in hindsight they deemed to be self-destructive practices. Social liminality favors both critique of popular habits and values, and the construction of new rituals, perspectives, and beliefs.

Young adults agonized about a dismal economy that had displaced them; they searched for any opportunity to be employed, even without compensation. The numbers of credentialed young adults who continued to work because they preferred even part-time productivity to complete idleness rose by the day, even as months passed while they waited for wages that never came. Unmarried men and women surely grieved their crushed career aspirations, while they dismissed any expectations they might have had to marry and have children. They insisted that as dependent adults, bringing children into such a weak social structure was "irrational." This was a time of diminishing material resources that threatened citizens' financial security, while a coincidental inflow of empathy, sympathy, and mutuality strengthened their social stability.

Deliberations of Crisis

Liminal periods generate self-examination and collective introspection of conduct and values among members of a community. This is a time of leisurely contemplation that yields deeper, more critical understandings of customary realities that preceded rupture to the social fabric. In times of societal unraveling "the unquestioned grasp of life is loosened," and people are particularly inclined to ask "radical questions" about socioeconomic and political conundrums that threaten their survival (Thomassen 2009: 47). Locals' own questions of "why" and "how" related to the financial meltdown of the Greek economy generated insights that may be grouped under categories such as globalization, corruption, and vulnerability. Analysis of interview and focus group data reveals that participants' understandings of the debt crisis varied chiefly across age groups, as did the weight they placed on various roots and causes.

All participants considered Greece's incorporation within a global capitalist system to be a plausible explanation for their country's financial meltdown. Refrains such as "the crisis is not Greek, it's global" indicate the perspective of an urban educated class of Greeks, some of whom are critical social observers and familiar with formal research analyses of global transactions. Most others follow various media sources— some more discriminating than others—on international events, including the fluctuation of global markets. Newspapers, websites, and television broadcasts aroused the curiosity of everyone and left some people confused and disoriented. Consciousness of Greece's global political–economic profile rose exponentially following the eurozone crash. Crisis time—a time out of normality—demanded and facilitated deliberations about worldview and assessments about self and a nation in transition throughout Greece, while I solicited and chronicled them among Thessalonikians.

Societal liminality can generate a rise in social consciousness and critique of systems and power-holders. Such ruminations unfold during a period of epochal change, including the 2007–2008 recession (Sakwa 2015; Graeber 2014). Concomitant with local explanations of the crisis as a symptom of globalization emerged a consensus that Greece's debt is rooted in a system of *patronage*—a set of fiscal policies, practices, and moralities among actors across local, state, regional, and international levels who collaborate and manage financial transactions that favor the well-connected and protect the privileged (Pardo 2004). The now-revealed deceptive figures who had gained Greece its membership in the eurozone engrossed my hosts, who passionately condemned their representatives and their foreign allies. Of interest to this analysis is the omnipresence of its critique and condemnation once the corrupt debt system crashed, and the indebted emerged to assess the damages.

As established structures crumble, customary practices, norms, and moralities give way to new standards and values, while a future once taken for granted, dissipates. Liminal actors look inward for answers; they question their beliefs, decisions, and actions of the past, and they ponder possibilities for change in anticipation of a future (Horvath, Thomassen, and Wydra 2009; 2015). Most heartrending and illuminating were participants' accounts of *vulnerability* to a government steeped in patronage and a large public sector economy—two social institutions on which they, as middle-class urbanites, depend for survival and prosperity. Embedded in these structures is public education, and a university system that those both within and outside Greek academia deemed ineffective.

Participants of all ages agreed that Greeks are "controlled" by their state officials, whom all perceive as principal perpetrators of the Greek crisis. However, an overwhelming majority also saw themselves as accomplices of opportunistic politicians in perpetuating a vulnerable economy. While several informants made a point of excluding themselves from such practices as cronyism, nepotism, tax evasion, and bribery, everyone with whom I spoke admitted passive complacency with the system that "forces" citizens to behave illegally "to get things done." The schism between the Greek state and the nation is not new; the unrelenting mass evaluation, assessment, and judgment of it by ordinary citizens is a national pastime. However, in times of social disorder and crisis, such discussions are interspersed with declarations of dismantling the political system at its root, and building instead one that reflects futuristic goals of socioeconomic development that promotes meritocracy and social justice.

Experiencing generalized anxiety, and while stretching their diminishing euros to meet household expenses and repay debts, my hosts demonstrated relentless efforts to determine the external and internal roots and causes of the debt crisis so that they might conquer it. Contemplation of the causes and effects of the financial catastrophe, they noted wisely, was critical to the country's sustainable economic development. The fervor with which Thessalonikians interrogated one another about their predicament and theorized their recovery reveals an urgency in self-understanding characteristic of liminal actors during crisis time. Discourses about blame and accountability helped to cool the rage that plagued my informants and to counter their disorientation and confusion. The popular refrain "We, too, are accountable" represents the voice of a community jolted into contemplation, self-critique, and self-determination, even as most of them were struggling to find a way out through intentional changes in their daily practices and the values that reinforced them.

This cognitive investment in theorizing the crisis yielded conclusions about the need "to change the Greek mentality." Such a shift, argued young and old alike, must "move us away from competitive individualism to social solidarity, and from dependence on state-control to a civil society." These revelations indicate only a tentative adoption of neoliberal principles among Greeks. Participants of all ages agreed that grassroots change is "the only way out" of the crisis. My hosts advocated that a new ethic of civic responsibility must guide institutional reforms and that mainstream cultural practices must change to reflect new normative ethics, including justice, fairness, and civic responsibility. However, discussions about implementation of such ideological transformations fell to the young. Elders, and those with adult children, argued that the young must assume responsibility for the country's recovery, and that their own role would be to support their efforts.

The young adults, particularly those for whom emigration was unlikely, were united in their conviction to lead recovery efforts through civic engagement, transnational solidarity movements, and voluntarism.

The Will to Praxis

Periods of liminality stimulate the human brain to respond. Driving adaptive responses to unanticipated distress is resilience, an innate human capacity to recover, and even to benefit from adversity. Behavioral responses in times of crisis include "increased arousal, alertness, vigilance, improved cognition, and focused attention"—coping mechanisms that increase the likelihood of survival (Chrousos 1998; quoted in Konner 2007: 305). Thessalonikians acknowledged that while they struggled financially and suffered emotionally, their experience of crisis was not limited or dominated by decline and gloom. While uncertainty preoccupied them, helplessness, or "stuckedness," did not (Hage 2009. Indeed, living in limbo awakened their sense of resilience, mobility, and generativity toward renewal.

Analysis of narratives indicates that despite—or perhaps because of—the ruptures to routine and customary ways of life, these men and women gained awareness of their collective resilience not to simply endure the crisis, but to call for change. Participants spoke passionately about the urgency for conventional, internally directed, and extroverted solidarity, the need for building a more civil society, and the prospect of innovative and sustainable socioeconomic development. For most participants these indicators of a new mindset remained abstract, and framed as "musts," "hope," and "intent." However, as we will see in the epilogue, grassroots mobilization and volunteerism emerged as evidence of a new civic consciousness and citizen-driven sociocultural reforms. Such formative and transformative practices signify citizens' proactive responses to rebuild society that a breakdown in the social order stimulated and impelled (Horvath et al. 2015: 1–8).

Recalling the words of poet and novelist Antonis Samarakis, "as long as there are concerned people, there is hope," a young resident of Thessaloniki asserted at the height of austerity season: "Today there exists only one exit from danger: it is youth. As long as youth are concerned, there is hope." Indeed, discussions of recovery among participants of all ages often featured the word "must" (*prepi*), suggesting new responsibilities that young Thessalonikians embraced in order to ensure their own survival as a generation, and to repair their society. Informants sprinkled their narratives of a new political consciousness with declarative statements such as "We must change our mindset; we must promote solidarity; we must control our consumption patterns; we must learn to be productive; we must learn to cultivate our grandparents' land; we must invest in energy sources; we must become politically active; we must become externally directed; we must embrace volunteerism." These musts manifested initially as a philosophical framework—organized conceptions of how Greeks ought to live during and beyond crisis. Such assertions reveal that during the "shocking," "confusing" and "paralyzing" phase of crisis a new transnational solidarity intensified, and imagined, "practical" engagements that might lead to recovery emanated. Severe financial constraints of their nation, fostered new ideologies of collaboration, voluntarism, and humanitarianism.

New notions of formal education and work highlighted the "need to learn to work collaboratively and in partnerships" across national boundaries. Aspiring professionals emphasized the value of teamwork for the well-being of all, in place of profit-driven individualism—of "standing on the corpses of others in order to win," as a young teacher exclaimed. Out of solicited perspectives of Greece's future arose such social critiques by men and women who, precrisis, had claimed compliance with the status quo. Crushed by what they viewed as "betrayal" by their parents, professors, and politicians, young adults admonished their older counterparts for "building wealth on the backs of others" and for "manipulating one another for personal benefit."

Dismal opportunities for professional development in their homeland—indeed lack of any opportunities for earning a decent living at the time—inspired in study participants critical and thoughtful commitments to international solidarity as a strategy for survival, and as an ideology for national sustainability. These young people imagined a "new Greece" built on unaccustomed moralities such as the collective good, "a society whose education teaches it to work collectively [omadhika], promotion of solidarity and mutual support across state boundaries, and investment in better services in health and education." They advocated that doctors, attorneys, teachers, and policemen all should work not as "businessmen who chase profit," but as conscientious ministers of society (litourghi). Young people urged the adoption of a new ethical orientation: the new mission ought to be "I am in this position not to get a better salary, but to serve people," as one young clerk put it. "The only road to a positive metamorphosis of our society," he concluded, "rests with a new, moral education."

In their narratives of crisis, young adults expressed interest in productive and joyful engagements in *communitas* with other peers "in flow" across class and national boundaries of Greece and Mediterranean Europe (Turner 2012). Young Thessalonikians renounced raw material consumption as a value and as a practice of "a precrash Greece." Instead, life in social liminality, where money was at a premium and time to think and feel and care was in abundance, inspired in them a new, self-conscious pursuit: "spiritual, aesthetic, sensual, and social prosperity of being and belonging to a future." The shift to a "shared ideology of togetherness" stems from the "dysphoria" to which their political system subjected them. As one young volunteer explained, "The former mentality dissolved/destroyed us, and we now turn to volunteerism and to collective action as a change of attitude."

For these young adults, solidarity translated into new behavioral patterns of life—acting on behalf of all citizens. Evident in their narratives of recovery is their articulated, critical view of the former structures that collapsed, and the broader structures they wished to build. Grassroots, voluntary, collective action to revitalize the city was a start. Thessalonikians were forced to play a new game, one that fuels social transformations of the city. These urbanites adapted both by questioning and resisting established structures (Ortner 2006) and by creating new networks of allegiances (Graeber 2014). In the process, acts and principles of resilience appear to have taken root, generating new microstructures and practices that over time are likely to lead to macrolevel societal transformations (Barth 1967).

One such "urban experiment" of planned change is an initiative that its founder and editor of the magazine *Parallaxi*, Yiorgos Toulas, dubbed "A Different Thessaloniki" (Thessaloniki Allios). The centerpiece of this initiative is "West Side Story," the revitalization of the city's neglected western neighborhood populated by poor Greeks, economic immigrants, undocumented workers, and other disfranchised individuals. Initiated in the spring of 2010, just months after households across Thessaloniki were feeling the crisis in their homes and wallets, West Side Story targets the city's western bank as a priority in urban revitalization efforts. This grassroots initiative promotes the city's "civic culture" through stylized representations and textures. Attention to local heritage and revitalization of the natural landscape illustrates the generative dimensions of crisis in the hands of ordinary citizens.

A new civic-mindedness and voluntary collective action led to a cleaner boardwalk, a greener public space, promotion of food festivals, and talk about new and creative economies. Public walls previously had been covered with graffiti, indicative of an angry or neglected city in decline. They now became canvases of hope for street artists to paint life-affirming images inspired by historical events and cultural representations that depict Thessaloniki in the last century.[5] Even abstract notions of the production and distribution of cultural goods and services impressed Thessaloniki's mobilized youth to use their creative energies and synergy to foster community development.

In 2012, while Greece was in the throes of agonizing financial struggles, Thessalonikians were celebrating their centennial of having reclaimed the city from the Ottomans in 1912. Meanwhile, Thessaloniki's youth, while devastated by the economic decline of their families, were also preparing to host thousands of their European peers in celebration of their city's title as the 2014 Youth Capital of Europe. Collective responses across Greece to the country's perilous conditions included political demonstrations, violent protests, and passive rage (Theodossopoulos 2013). Paralleling such forms of resistance were constructive and collective engagements by groups of Thessaloniki's young and old alike to construct new social structures and cultural realities. These liminal actors emerged as agents of international solidarity movements, determined to counter economic displacement by creating new networks and activities of being and belonging within, and outside, of Greece.

The combination of threat and hope mobilized Thessaloniki's youth to historically unprecedented forms of collective action to showcase their city to the world and, in doing so, demonstrate a sense of *life politics*—generational consciousness as politically and culturally proactive citizens of Greece, of Europe, and the world (Giddens 1991). Driving their efforts, in their words, are options of creativity, participation, free expression, and solidarity with a "common purpose." Activists saw their mission as architects of a new national paradigm—one of "extroversion" (*eksostrephia*). They perceived this investment in their city as a shift "from the *I* to the *We*," from the personal to the political, and from the national to a global landscape of identity and belonging. Integral to this economic and moral reorientation is an emphasis on Internet linkages, information technology, diversity and multiculturalism, collaboration with international peers, transnational networks of skilled, project-oriented initiatives, generational accountability, and "respect for all." Their collective action is already evident in the reshaping of the city's infrastructure and image. The crisis-born "re-enchanting" of politics generated a cultural logic of praxis in the present that informs grassroots initiatives by actors poised for, and aspiring to, a future through new economic and community developments (Zournazi 2002: 274).

We might be tempted to situate Thessaloniki's young activists among Richard Florida's "creative class"—the intellectuals, scientists, artists, entrepreneurs, and other highly skilled, technologically savvy, credentialed professionals who dominate the labor force through creativity, innovation, and economic growth (Florida 2012). However, Florida's "knowledge-based workers" are gainfully employed and embedded in state-supported industries, including top-down gentrification. In contrast, the young citizens who are rebuilding Thessaloniki are state-driven economic fatalities. Their humanistic values, egalitarian sensibilities, and interests in a socially responsible lifestyle are more in accord with Ray and Anderson's "cultural creatives" (2000). If neoliberalism led to the material displacement of Mediterranean youth, it has also inspired the spirit and will to act as self-conscious and newly conscientious citizens of the world. Through face-to-face contact, organized events, and Internet-based mobilization across Europe's south, volunteers embrace the crisis as a welcome catalyst to easing economic and political unrest through shared values that drive social and cultural reforms.

Celebrations of history and heritage symbolized and affirmed the very identities that neoliberal market logic and the economic collapse threatened to extinguish (Herzfeld 2009). Awareness of their newly realized resilience manifests in an aesthetic gentrification of the built environment that beautify and sensualize the urban milieu, and civic engagements that imbue it with democratic responsibility. In the process, locals promote their city's current cultural, and cultured capital, a move they hope will sustain Thessaloniki on the European map for centuries to come. Thessaloniki is a "city in transition," declared the popular mayor, Yiannis Boutaris. The colorful slogan that marked the 2012 centennial celebrations appears in banners gracing the walls of city hall and other public spaces. It reads: "We Celebrate, We Participate, We Look Ahead." In the wake of economic collapse my interlocutors spoke of loss, fear, rage, confusion, uncertainty, depression, and suicide. Yet despite all of those concerns, and as current initiatives indicate, such sentiments co-occurred with a new cultural orientation of participation, synergism, creativity, inspiration, joy, laughter, courage, innovation, integration, fun, vitality, and praxis.

Analysis of public discourses and private narratives of crisis that research participants shared with me reveals a community and society in limbo. From unanticipated societal disintegration emerged sociocultural patterns of change and continuity. The impact of the 2008 global recession and the 2009 eurozone debt crisis on the Greek nation-state demonstrates that historical and global relations of money and power ultimately transform the social and cultural life of states and communities. In the interregnum, people are subjected to unanticipated and threatening disruptions to their normal life and conventional values. Through incremental and gradual adjustments to how and in what they invest their leisure time and resources, liminal individuals and groups change their daily circumstances to cope and to adapt. Systemic ruptures also foster a heightened, critical consciousness among displaced actors, who may respond proactively to preserve cherished aspects of their culture.

The recession left its mark on a grim cityscape scarred by barren shops, closed family-owned stores, abandoned offices, and vacant apartment buildings. Meanwhile, social life on the streets, squares, parks, and waterfront remained vibrant as ever, and public gatherings at art venues and cultural events rose. Emotional ties and interpersonal relations intensified as people united in struggle and in hope. New ethics and morals surfaced, promoting attention to civic duty and human welfare. Commensality filled homes with life, while public spaces and places surged with conviviality. "What crisis?" tourists might ask at the sight of this lively city. A closer, ethnographic look revealed a community in peril, agonizing about the bust and its impact on personal finances, even as they ruminated about strategies to overcome. They strengthened kinship bonds; cultivated fictive, chosen kin; affirmed personal and social relations; and engaged in acts of renewal, large and small. Featured in the epilogue of this work are examples of these transformations.

Notes

1. Greece's gross domestic product per capita is approximately 23,000 US dollars, below the pre–Great Recession 30,000 USD in 2007. The rate of unemployment in Greece was 7.30% in 2008, reached nearly 28% by 2013, and in February 2019 it was 18.5%, and fell to 16.9 by July 2019. See "Greece Unemployment Rate," Trading Economics, accessed November 15, 2019, https://tradingeconomics.com/greece/unemployment-rate.

2. Andreas Papandreou's expenditure program (1981–1990) raised the purchasing power and standard of living among Greeks, while the country suffered from a lack of economic revenue that led to rapidly rising rates of public debt.

3. See Rostow (1952; 1960) on stages of modernization. In their deliberations as to the roots and causes of the crisis, participants tended to ascribe to Greece features of Rostow's "traditional stage," and rationalize the country's integration into the European Union as marking what Rostow refers to as "cultural change stage."

4. See Sawyer (2001) for a discussion on theories of emergence in sociology.

5. See Harvey (2000).

Resilience and Praxis

I have maintained contact with Thessaloniki and its residents through phone calls and the Internet, brief visits to Greece in November 2013 and February 2015, follow-up ethnographic data by a graduate assistant during summers 2013–2019, and published literature on the Greek crisis and related questions. Most Greeks still endure the consequences of the 2008 global recession and the financial meltdown that followed, while others, such as bankers and consignment shopkeepers, may have benefited from the crisis (Agelopoulos 2016). While many families in Thessaloniki continue to struggle financially, and individuals migrate or emigrate to secure survival, the city has turned decidedly more optimistic. There has been a noticeable shift away from despair toward resilience—encompassing reforms in institutional and bureaucratic practices and policies, heightened awareness of other affected communities throughout Greece and southern Europe, and local, grassroots community mobilizations (Barrios 2016). Local government agencies and nongovernmental organizations support revitalization initiatives. Middle-aged parents and retirees offer unwavering support of young adults' efforts to not only overcome but to benefit from the crisis through social movements in cultural developments. Thessalonikians' articulations of their city's value, national pride, and transnational solidarity now dominate discourses of recovery.

Fight, Flight, and Fix

Resistance to state-imposed austerities and perceived assaults on national integrity ignited social unrest, a rise in extremism, protests and demonstrations by the thousands, and a generalized distrust of formal institutions and their representatives. Discourses and symbols of resistance that dominated mass media and interpersonal communications years ago also persist, even as proactive measures of coping and civic engagement proliferate (Hatzidaki and Goutsos 2017). Anti-austerity slogans and graffiti signaled mass opposition to dependence on the European Union in 2012 (Knight 2015b). New slogans and graffiti of resilience and renewal now grace the city's public spaces. However, such demonstrations of resistance and hope coincided with a rising number of local people fleeing Greece in search of economic opportunities abroad.

Most likely to emigrate were young adults. In 2011–2012, speculation about leaving Greece for more promising career paths and accommodating societies was popular among single adults and parents of young children. More than 500,000 Greeks emigrated to Germany, Australia, Great Britain, Canada, and the United States, as well as to the United Arab Emirates, particularly to Dubai and Abu Dhabi, cities that some participants had enjoyed as tourists in better economic times. Participants point principally to "push factors" to justify their exodus from Greece, including lack of jobs and resources on which to build new industries, and the sharp decline in trust of government officials. The public sector, accounting for about 40 percent of GDP, which for generations financed the social mobility of households, has crumbled.[1]

A weak state had pushed hundreds of thousands of young, predominantly male, rural workers out of Greece in the early 1900s, primarily to the United States, Australia, Canada, and Brazil. A second wave of families during 1960–1972 fled the military Junta (1967–1974), pursuing upward mobility through hard manual labor in the factories of the United States and Northern Europe. Of the third wave of emigrants that coincided with the 2009 crash of the Greek state economy, most are young, multilingual, college-educated professionals who are trained for intellectual and creative labor (Triandafyllidou and Gropas 2014; Labrianidis and Vogiatzis 2013). For them, opportunity to secure a position anywhere, even as a starting point, is worthy of pursuit. Participants in this recent third wave of emigration made it clear to me that leaving Greece for countries outside Europe is an adaptation, not a volition. The emotional cost of leaving parents, siblings, even children is a high price to pay, but a necessary one. Whether they hold professional credentials or a high school degree, these new emigrants are driven to work hard in order to ensure their survival and contribute to the well-being of their family.

Indeed, emigrants with young children or frail parents insisted that the search for any job abroad was a sacrifice for the well-being of family—to provide and protect loved ones left behind. Some contemplated a permanent move, vowing to "throw a black stone behind" [*tha rikso mavri petra piso mou*], a popular expression meaning one will never set foot in a place again. Others saw emigration as a temporary relocation in a more promising work environment that could yield experience, skills, and expertise that would be useful in developing the Greek economy upon their return. Such a return orientation seemed to ease anxiety among some of my consultants, who dreaded uprooting themselves. Others, like immigrants in previous waves, spun fantasies about annual returns to Greece for holidays and summer vacations, and the ultimate return to the family home during the third age following retirement.

The young adults who worked with me prioritized advanced studies, further professional specialization, and career-oriented pursuits as pull factors. Accepted by a competitive doctoral program in England, one young woman left to find her destiny "without looking back," even as she struggled to support herself with graduate assistantships and whatever money her parents sent to her. She completed her doctorate, married an Englishman, and speaks of Thessaloniki as a holiday destination. Another young woman "managed to escape" by pursuing a college degree, and subsequently a graduate degree, in the United States. While she cherishes her opportunity for professional development in the States, she struggles financially and relies on student assistantships, subsidized housing from family friends, and small installments of money that her parents and sister send her. A return to Greece is "not even a thought," she insists, while she agonizes about what prospects might be in store for her to continue living, studying, or working in the United States without a permanent visa.

Precarity and uncertainty continue to haunt this young woman, who is neither legally employable in the United States nor a candidate for any gainful employment in Greece. Her friends in Thessaloniki, she reports, advise that she "should not come back!" These two women, and others who fled Greece after their participation in the study, continue a life in limbo as they await a more formal socioeconomic integration into their host society. However, having escaped a still vulnerable Greece, they now anticipate a future that holds some promise. The will to flee Greece among young adults in 2019 is as strong as it was in 2012. In the meantime, those for whom Thessaloniki remains their only home have taken their future, and the future of their city, into their own hands.

Engaged Citizenship

Some Thessalonikians for whom emigration was either financially or emotionally prohibitive vowed to take on the challenge of the country's recovery through humanitarian public initiatives, voluntary organizations, collaborations with local NGOs, and grassroots solidarity movements. Others have dedicated themselves to inventing creative solutions to make ends meet through community currencies and alternative economies. The shift in ideational orientations from hope to action and from self-interest to civic duty that young adults proclaimed in 2011 remains evident in alternatives to austerity—new mobilization movements and a cultural dignity by which thousands of young adults in Thessaloniki define their purpose today (see Bear and Knight 2017). Follow-up ethnographic documentation in Thessaloniki during consecutive summers from 2013 to 2018 reveals that locals are engaged in a variety of grassroots solidarity movements.[2] With support from the mayor's office for urban development and an increasing proliferation of NGOs in the Municipality of Thessaloniki, young adults, and increasingly more middle-aged citizens, have come to embrace voluntarism as a mainstream practice and a new governing ethos. Bouziouri and Pigkou-Repousi (2014) note that participation in solidarity movements between 2010 and 2012 increased by 44 percent (quoted in Gemenetzi 2017).

The city's progressive mayor, Yiannis Boutaris, elected in 2010, vowed to implement social reforms and to transform Thessaloniki into a thriving, sustainable capital and tourist destination in which business, citizenship, and culture intersect. Such a city, he advocated, must demonstrate the inclusion of its multiple strands of heritage, such as Roman, Ottoman, and Jewish, and its embrace of human differences, attention to human rights, and extroversion—that is, a transnational and global worldview. While debt crushed residents' dreams of continued, upward mobility, the city's investment in human capital has elevated their spirits toward philanthropy and civic responsibility.

Church members, volunteers, and employees of local NGOs tended to the city's indigent residents and the increasing number of homeless individuals and refugees needing shelter in the winter.[3] Although the economic displacement of youth threatened the city's future, the precarious conditions also produced thousands of individuals for whom non-waged labor took on meaning as personal and civic pursuits. The city's anticipation of two global events—the 2012 centennial of Thessaloniki to Greek sovereignty and union within the modern Greek state, and its title as the 2014 European Youth Capital—propelled and reinforced a commitment to civic engagement among youth. Volunteerism and civic engagement gained in value as the responsibility of a generation determined to assert itself.

Mega-events mobilize hosts, attract tourists, invite media attention, and are transformative (Müller 2015). My hosts learned this lesson in 1997 when Thessaloniki earned the title European Capital of Culture. While the fiscal constraints of 2012 compromised the overall mood of Thessalonikians, the city's centennial celebrations were already in effect when I was there in 2011. Anticipation of the city's recognition as the 2014 Youth Capital of Europe also had captured the imagination of everyone, who viewed both events as markers of resilience and impetus for regeneration (Smith 2012). The local government's plan to improve the city's infrastructure was underway in 2011. As figure E1 illustrates, revitalization included expanding pedestrian zones in the city center, widening roads between the center and old town, and expanding green spaces and cultural venues.

Critical to urban development was the expansion of the city's underground rapid-transit system, even as financial constraints and archaeological considerations, including Roman and early Christian and Byzantine discoveries during construction, challenged its progress. The financial collapse constrained the advancement of sustainable urban development that preceded it, and the public infrastructure of metropolitan Thessaloniki remains underdeveloped and in need of financial resources (Gemenetzi 2017). However, political and ethical investment in the city's built environment across stakeholders dominates even in the face of crippling austerity (Bear 2015). The revitalization of the eastern seaside promenade, the centerpiece of the city's facelift, was completed in January 2014. Local architects with whom I spoke praised this accomplishment, which the Hellenic Institute of Architecture formally recognized as the best public project in Greece within a five-year period.

FIGURE E.1 Aghia Sophias Avenue, now a new pedestrian zone.
Source: Photo by Aikaterini Grigoriadou.

During my stay in 2012, informants referenced Boutaris's plans to enhance Thessaloniki's tourist industry, a proven yet underdeveloped economic strategy. Preserving the city's cosmopolitan history figured prominently in his platform. Thessaloniki's multinational and multireligious past must be revived, he argued, most importantly its Ottoman and Jewish presence. Boutaris, who was short-listed for the title "World Mayor 2014," famously wore the Star of David on his lapel as an act of solidarity with Jews within and beyond Thessaloniki. Reportedly he has reached out to Israeli authorities to encourage tourism from Israel and to Turkish authorities to cultivate interest in tours of Thessaloniki, home of biological and cultural ancestors to contemporary Jews and Turks.

The momentum that centennial celebrations stirred in 2012 continued into 2014.[4] Global recognition of Thessaloniki as a Youth Capital, and the thousands of European visitors that it would attract, mobilized efforts to revitalize the city's built environment and cultural venues. Collective engagement appeared to overshadow the collective shame that plagued Greeks in the aftermath of the 2009 economic meltdown. International solidarity emerged as a competing, corrective ideology alongside the conventional self- and family-centered orientations. A transnational *extroversion*—"looking beyond Greece for direction," as one informant put it—rose as both a strategic and a moral adaptation to the country's newly exposed vulnerability. This new form of *extroverted solidarity*, while stimulated by external threat, embraces outsiders—sympathetic, young co-cosmopolitans in struggle against proponents of the neoliberal order that subjugates them.

On May 1, 2014, the city erected a monument on the campus of Aristotle University and the former grounds of the historic Jewish cemetery to commemorate Thessaloniki's Jews, whom the German Occupation persecuted. With Boutaris's support and funding from the German government and the Niarchos Foundation, Thessalonikians further acknowledged their city's history with plans to erect a six-story Holocaust Memorial Museum and Education Center (currently in progress and to be completed in 2020) on property near the railway station, from which in 1943 approximately 51,000 Jews were deported to Nazi death camps. The mayor also visited Istanbul to establish cultural alliances with Turkish counterparts and to promote tourism to Thessaloniki as their ancestral homeland. Boutaris, who is under attack by Greek far-right extremists, plans to preserve the city's Ottoman heritage by building a museum of Islamic art, and by requesting support from the Greek Ministry of Culture to renovate five Ottoman structures, including mosques and baths, to attract tourists from Turkey and beyond. Boutaris also visited Germany, seeking recommendations to enhance the city's aesthetic qualities, and he promoted gay rights by his support of gay pride parades.

Although economic constraints remain, acts and symbols of civic consciousness demonstrate collective resilience. While Thessaloniki's remaining young citizens dread continued economic and social insecurity, they are investing their time and talents in productive social labor even without material compensation. In the process, they are rebuilding meaningful identities and relationships as underpaid or unremunerated intellectual, social, and cultural workers. For example, in 2014, young volunteers asserted that the moral turn from individualism to a "shared ideology of togetherness" stems from the "sudden and rapid decline" of their economy, and the "dysphoria" to which their state subjected them as a generation. Residents across age grades and educational levels are conscious of their *territorial capital*, the city's topography and its aesthetic assets, which they seek to preserve as part of their "inerasable identity" (Edwards 1998: 242; Perucca 2014). Thessaloniki's strategic geography at the crossroads of East and West, its seafront, its historic upper townscapes and city center, and its fifteen UNESCO Heritage Sites inspire locals' investment in building tourism. International and domestic tourists help support local businesses and provide employment opportunities. The city's educated, multilingual, and unemployed young adults are ideally poised to serve as tour guides (Guano 2015).

The initiative known as West Side Story exemplifies this civic turn. It targets the city's western bank as the priority in grassroots urban revitalization efforts. In 2014 volunteers declared, "through participation and new, creative energies, we are mapping the western entrance of the city, and through praxis and public dialogue we expose the problems, the possibilities, and principally, the city's prospects for it future." Proud to be revitalizing the underresourced, neglected, and *hidden* area at the margins of the city center, a group of volunteers, in collaboration with government agencies, NGOs, and in consultation with local residents, now showcase the industries, peoples, and stories that reveal the city's past to domestic and international tourists.

In 2015, participants in the West Side Story initiative led walking tours and promoted concerts, theatrical productions, street performances, and photographic exhibits that were free to the public. Other activities included a theatrical documentary coproduced by the Magazine Parallaxi and the National Theater of Northern Greece titled "At the Other Bank." This referred to the part of Thessaloniki that for decades wealthier residents "otherized" as less than the more affluent city center. Bright images depict historical moments of Thessaloniki in the twentieth century, including independence from the Ottomans and the forced deportation of the Jews. Other images publicize the fiftieth anniversary of the Thessaloniki International Film Festival, a cherished fixture of urban life and national cinema (Papadimitriou 2016; Toby 2012). The organizers of the West Side initiative, in response to requests from local residents, report that they give color and life to the formerly bleak industrial neighborhood, including refurbishing a previously dilapidated school. Driving their efforts, in their words, are notions of creativity, participation, free expression, and solidarity with a common purpose.

Integral to these youth-driven movements is an emphasis on "diversity and multiculturalism, collaboration with international peers, transnational consciousness, generational accountability, and respect for all people." While top-down gentrification favors wealthier urban-ites, grass-roots revitalization focuses on community building by and for economically more marginalized residents. Participants seek to im-prove the quality of their own lives and, in the process, earn a living by applying their cultural knowledge and interpersonal skills. These chang-es in values and actions shift their attention away from idle personal indulgence toward what they now perceive as creativity, innovation, and "urgent productivity toward a common good." With their new, humani-tarian values tested and their skills honed, Thessaloniki's residents are poised for yet another opportunity for personal, professional, and eco-nomic development in accord with local NGOs. On September 2017, the members of the European Pride Organization chose Thessaloniki to host EuroPride 2020, another major event in which the municipality and local citizens are now investing.

Rise in NGOs and Civil Society

NGOs, themselves a byproduct of global neoliberalism, serve a com-pensatory function in late capitalist societies with a weak, or in Greece's case, gutted welfare state. By their "legitimacy" as a solution to struc-tural adjustment that slashes social services and safety nets, NGOs fill an economic niche for a displaced, typically educated, middle-class la-bor force (Schuller 2009). Local and international NGOs advocate hu-man rights, social equity, and grassroots social reforms, values that an unemployed class of professional wage earners and volunteers readily embrace (Kamat 2004).

NGO workers expose social inequities and meet human needs that the neoliberal state neglects, and which Greece can no longer afford to meet. However, by their privatization of the public good, NGOs rein-force a civil society that minimizes the state's role in fostering democracy (Kamat 2004: 157; 164). These organizations receive funding from glob-al institutions and private donors that situate them at the center of global neoliberalism. Meanwhile, social reforms become the responsibility of ordinary citizens, including volunteers. By promoting human rights as their life's work, underpaid or unpaid workers benefit from what they view as personal growth and professional development. Such ideologies distinguish the websites of voluntary organizations that target youth groups who are eager to make a difference in the lives of the needy, even as they reinforce the neoliberal project (Biehn 2014: 77; Harvey 2000).

The increasingly popular framing among Greek youth of their state's meltdown as a humanitarian crisis has intensified grassroots volunteerism and fueled an increase in local nongovernmental organizations.[5] Charged with the noble mission of ameliorating local social disorders and helping communities marginalized by the debt crisis, volunteers construct solutions through collective action. Voluntarism, some argued, has not been a core value of modern Greek society. Care work has been the domain of family and friends—a kind of voluntary, principally women-centered, labor that is directed inwardly and personally through generalized reciprocity, rather than outwardly and publicly through charity. Moreover, during the three decades preceding the debt crisis, Greeks' sensitization to social inequities had diminished as they embraced the prosperity that accompanied European integration. Today's emphasis on "civil society" reflects at once an impotent Greek state, the decrease in family resources, and the corresponding proliferation of NGOs (Clarke, Huliaras, and Sotiropoulos 2015).

A history of dependence on governmental resources and reliance on familial support in times of need has not favored volunteerism as a conventional form of public aid. However, given the sharp and continuing decline in state-supported services, a new reliance on private contributions and social support has proliferated throughout Greece. Examples include soup kitchens and the open and discreet distribution of food, clothing, and free medical services (Papadaki and Kalogeraki 2017). In Thessaloniki talented young adults volunteer as tutors, dance instructors, and performers, such as the ensemble Orfean Harmony, as acts of resilience to counteract the effects and conditions of poverty (Grigoriadou 2018). Municipal employees collaborate with NGOs to help the indigent and homeless find shelter during the winter. Volunteers have also intervened in drug rehabilitation programs. Mayor Boutaris has urged sympathetic citizens to collaborate with NGOs, such as Programs of Development, Social Support and Medical Cooperation (PRAKSIS), and Médecins du Monde (Doctors of the World), as well as churches, to provide food, clothing, and other forms of care to residents of senior citizen facilities.

While displacing them from the formal labor market, neoliberal restructuring and "excess time" has encouraged young Greeks to think and act as more self-conscious and ethically conscientious citizens (Muehlebach 2012). Thessaloniki's leisurely-in-spite-of-themselves, with still-strong bodies and minds, embrace the neoliberal precepts of individualism and benevolence, self-reliance, and collective well-being. Analysis of ethnographic interviews conducted in 2014 and 2015 indicates that these young adults have found purpose and meaning in work that they imbue with such values as fellowship, altruism, collaboration, and brotherhood. They project a new, postcollapse ethos of global moral citizenship of, by, and for a new generation of Greek Europeans.[6]

Countering Europeanization from above is the United Societies of Balkans (USB), a nongovernmental organization founded in 2008 by a group of Thessalonikians. It includes participants from other European countries and seeks to "create a better future for all Europeans."[7] USB relies principally on participants in the European Voluntary Services (EVS), a European Youth Mobility Program that engages volunteers from various countries, seventeen to thirty years of age, who work collectively to reinforce Europeanization through humanitarian strategies.[8] Volunteers engage in a variety of public service activities in a country within and outside the European Union for ten to twelve months. Orientation to and membership in USB, claim its members, requires adoption and promotion of such ideals as intersocietal solidarity, civic leadership, and teamwork to inform collective praxis for the common good.

EVS volunteers design projects that in their view promote social justice, multicultural equity, and human rights on behalf of vulnerable populations, including immigrants, refugees, and LGBT communities. In opposition to the 2012 rise of Golden Dawn,[9] USB volunteers launched Media Against Xenophobia (MAX) and the Week Against Racism (WAR). To publicize their work widely, these men and women receive and provide training in new media. In June 2015, USB participants reported that working with peers across national and linguistic borders increased their appreciation for cultural diversity, their mutual understanding and empathy, and their self-awareness as prospective agents of recovery and citizens of a healthier Europe, and a more unified world.

Graduates of the EVS Program receive a Youthpass Certificate, which acknowledges their work in European Voluntary Services. This credential recognizes their participation in workshops, projects, and community services as "humanitarian agents of change for the common good," and lists the marketable skills that they gained in the process. Such skills include communication in a foreign language, basic competence in science and technology, digital competence, social and civic competence, initiative and entrepreneurship, and cultural awareness and expression. Facilitators encourage graduates of the program to include their certificate of successful volunteer work in their dossiers or career portfolios as they seek gainful employment, as well as in applications to undergraduate and graduate programs that they hope will ultimately lead to paid employment.

These international NGOs instill in young volunteers the belief that they can improve social conditions by being active, responsible citizens (Biehn 2014). To be sure, many volunteers recognize that their good intentions are not only altruistic and instrumental. There is also an exploitative side to volunteerism (Forte 2014). In the words of one young Thessalonikian, "I was a volunteer, but I do not believe that youth will solve the problems by volunteering. The state exploits [young volunteers], who perform the work of the state. We need [economic] development." Indeed, the rise in the "unwaged labor regime that thrives under neoliberal conditions" (Muehlebach 2012: 7) reflects the predicament of youth who face an uncertain future, even as they work to transform their resilience into praxis toward sustainable sociocultural reforms.

Self-Preservation and Cultural Continuity

Principles of preservation, resilience, and agency that *individual* hosts emphasized in 2011–2012 emerged in subsequent years as *collective* responses to economic decline and austerity. A new cultural orientation depicts Thessaloniki as a *forward-looking, inclusive, innovative,* and *enterprising* city that its crisis-enculturated architects—local government employees and private citizens—are determined to revitalize and market for local and international consumption. Streets, squares, and other public spaces are cleaner, and the city now boasts innovative and experimental urban community gardens. Voluntary social and educational services abound. There are plans to renovate the international airport. Construction of the new thirteen-station metro system will increase public transportation and reduce the number of automobiles in an already congested urban center. It will also enhance the city's promotion of its cultural heritage in that this infrastructural development has unearthed historical artifacts that will be displayed in public spaces. The Pavlos Melas military base has been transformed into a metropolitan park.

On March 30, 2017, the municipality of Thessaloniki released its *Resilience Strategy* as one of 100 Resilient Cities (100RC), a global initiative that the Rockefeller Foundation funds to help "cities around the world become more resilient to the physical, social and economic challenges

FIGURE **E.2 "Resilient Thessaloniki," 2017 flyer.**
Source: Photo by Aikaterini Grigoriadou.

that are a growing part of the 21st century (see figure E2)."[10] Thessalon-iki's activists conducted (and later published) a preliminary resilience assessment to determine how to create, in the words of Mayor Boutaris, the leader of this movement, "a thriving, resourceful, and equitable city that ensures the safety and well-being of our citizens, strengthens our local economy, and protects our natural resources."[11] Given its "compet-itive advantages," including its institutions of higher education, its port, climate, and vibrancy, Thessaloniki is well poised to invest in an upward trajectory of resourceful initiatives (Gemenetzi 2017: 96).

Three years after its selection as a member of the 100RC network, and with the participation of more than forty organizations and two thousand local citizens, a comprehensive agenda of social reforms is in the works. Under the umbrella "Resilient Thessaloniki," locals promote and engage in a variety of projects. For example, the Resilient Thes-saloniki Tour, designed as a mystery game in June 2017, exposes tour-ists to the city's ancient and historical points of interest. Tour guides describe current goals and strategies and their "vision for a resilient future";[12] they also charm visitors with the city's youthful culture and fine arts, enlighten them about the multicultural heritages that have shaped contemporary Thessaloniki (Macedonian, Christian, Muslim, and Jewish, as well as refugees from Asia Minor and immigrants from the Balkans) and direct them to gastronomic options for which the city is famous.[13]

Discourses about solidarity, renewal, and creative revitalization (whether of the built environment, human rights initiatives, or food, music, and film festivals) co-exist with, and now dominate, the once more common discourses of shock, loss, precarity, and annihilation. Through behavioral adjustments, thought experiments, and ideational shifts, survivors of the economic warfare have put fear aside and hope at the forefront. Collective resilience competes with mass helplessness; urban renewal trumps devastation of community and households, and social chaos gives way to increasing public clarity. In their narratives of crisis, and within the same interview, my hosts wove sentiments of shock, rage, and discontent with proclamations of relief, hope, and resilience. Their deliberations included self-critiques and demands for a new civic-mindedness and collective action. Older participants shared their recommendations for economic development and recovery, including new political leadership, cultural tourism, and agricultural development. Younger adults listened and went to work on recovering from the global economic depression and rebuilding a locally oriented, yet internationally integrated sustainable city.

Analyses of crisis tend to focus on disruption, destabilization, and decline. Yet societal crises can also foster material, social, and moral reconstruction and cultural preservation. As this work demonstrates, those who survive a societal collapse often become agents of collective revitalization and social reintegration. Crises may prompt their survivors to replace maladaptive sociocultural patterns with new configurations of the cultural continuities through which human communities maintain and reproduce themselves. The youth of Thessaloniki marked their revitalization efforts with the slogan (in English), "It's time!" This phrase describes mobilization and collective action to renew the urban environment by investing in existing cultural and material resources, including—and especially—young people themselves. In this work I have argued that such responses do not constitute absolute resistance against the crisis. Rather, they are processual engagements toward societal revitalization that crisis as liminality—in its impact on people's psychological and cognitive awakenings—generates and reinforces.

This ethnographic account of one urban community of middle- and upper-middle-class Greeks in the aftermath of the 2009 economic collapse demonstrates that *crisis as liminality* is a process of change that constitutes and is constituted by loss, continuity, and the rebirth of people, materials, traditions, rituals, beliefs, and ideals. Any shock to a social system, including an economic bust, impels a societal shift. Transitions from predictability to uncertainty induce fear and anxiety among those whose way of life the shock destroys. Such a crisis also initiates a process of emotional and cognitive healing that fosters recovery, and in turn accelerates societal renewal. The possibility of renewal following such a disaster rests on the power and intersection of three human proclivities: self-preservation, resilience, and agency. Arising simultaneously among individuals who are surviving a national tragedy, these propensities meld into a collective intelligence that allows people to harness existing resources to drive sociocultural transformation. Such is the state of affairs in Thessaloniki today. The tragic circumstances that the fiscal crash caused in 2009 are reconceptualized as valuable lessons that in 2019 form the impetus for their more enlightened, and participatory citizenship.

Notes

1. See "The World Factbook," Central Intelligence Agency, last edited January 2017, https://www.cia.gov/library/publications/the-world-factbook/geos/print_gr.html.

2. Analysis of evidentiary sociocultural reforms in Thessaloniki during consecutive summers 2013–2017 is based on ethnographic documentation by Aikaterini Grigoriadou. Grigoriadou, a native of Thessaloniki, was one of my primary consultants during the year-long study in the field. She subsequently served as my undergraduate student assistant (2012–2016) and as my graduate research assistant (2016–2018).

3. See Cabot (2014) for an account of the refugee crisis in Greece.

4. See "The European Youth Capital," European Youth Forum, last edited November 2018, https://www.youthforum.org/youthcapital.

5. Thess-Diktyo, the network of more than sixty nongovernmental voluntary organizations in Thessaloniki, was established in 2011 to coordinate activities designed to enhance civic consciousness and to mobilize social reform initiatives and access to health, education, and welfare.

6. For example, see the Shedia stin Poli (City Raft), an INGO founded in 1999 dedicated to the cultural and aesthetic revitalization of Thessaloniki

and its underprivileged youth. See "The Concept of Volunteering," Shedia stin Poli (City Raft), last edited May 2016, https://www.sxediastinpoli.gr/ethelontismos/ennoia-ethelontismou.

7. Analysis is based on ethnographic data that Grigoriadou collected during her placement as a research intern with USB during the summer of 2015. My goal in directing this project was to document through an unstructured interview guide, which I designed for follow-up research, the recovery efforts among the city's youth who, while still insecure and dejected, and still contemplating fleeing Greece for school or work, were determined to engage as active architects of a culturally enriched and aesthetically pleasing urban milieu. The sample of participants included 208 men and 218 women seventeen to thirty years of age.

8. See "European Youth Portal," Europa, published January 2016, https://europa.eu/youth/volunteering/evs-organisation_en.

9. The Golden Dawn focused its campaign on concerns about anti-immigration and anti-globalization.

10. See "About Us," 100 Resilient Cities, published July 2015, http://www.100resilientcities.org/about-us/#section-2. On its Centennial in 2013, the Rockefeller Foundation initiated its 100RC mission with thirty-two cities and by 2016 a total of 100 cities became participants of this global network. 100RC is a conglomerate of international governments, INGOs, the private sector, and private citizens who promote innovative leadership, change, global partnerships, and diverse stakeholders.

11. See "Preliminary Resilience Assessment-Thessaloniki:" Issuu Inc., published July 2016, https://issuu.com/resiliencethessaloniki/docs/pra_thessaloniki_en_a4.

12. See "Resilient Thessaloniki Tour, Re:Publica, last edited November 2017." https://re-publica.com/en/eu17/session/resilient-thessaloniki-tour.

13. See "Greece is Thessaloniki," published October 2017, http://www.greece-is.com/greece-thessaloniki-2017-2018/.

NOTE ON TRANSLITERATION

....

Non–Greek speakers may follow the phonetic roman transliteration to pronounce Greek terms and phrases. Certain Greek words and proper names are familiar in English.

Vowels and Diphthongs

α = ah	as in *frolic* or the first syllable in *doctor*
ε = e	as in *red*
ι, η = i	as in *me*
υ = i	as in *me* (pronounced as/f/or/v/in diphthongs αυ, ευ)
ει = i	as in *me*
οι = i	as in *me*
αι = e	as in *bed*
αϊ = ahy	as in *dye*
ου = ou	as in/o/in *move*
ο, ω = o	as in/o/in *door*

Consonants and Diphthongs

β = v	as in *value*
γ = gh	as in *why* or *year*
γγ – ng	as in *get*
γκ – gk	as in *good*
δ = dh	as in *this*

ζ = z	as in *zerox*
θ = th	as in *thought*
κ = k	as in *kite* or *king*
λ = l	as in *love*
μ = m	as in *mom*
μπ = b	as in *boy*
ν = n	as in *never*
ντ = d	as in *door*
ξ = ks	as in *fox*
π = p	as in *proper*
ρ = r	as in *road*
σ, ς (final) = s	as in *sun*
τ = t	as in *time*
τσ = ts	as in *pizza*
τζ = dz	as in *kids* or *pods*
φ = ph	as in *fun*
χ = kh	as in *here* (before ee sounds) or *Bach* (before ah sounds)
ψ = ps	as in *sepsis*

GLOSSARY

....

aftoghnosia αυτογνωσία   self-knowledge
aksioprepia αξιοπρέπεια   dignity
allilengyi αλληλεγγύη   solidarity
allilovoithia αλληλοβοήθεια   mutual assistance
anaktisi ανάκτηση   resilience or recovery
anisikhia ανησυχία   worry
anthropia ανθρωπιά   humanistic qualities and humane conduct
anthropos άνθρωπος   human
apelpisia απελπισία   despair
apesiodhoksia απαισιοδοξία   pessimism
aposvolomeni αποσβολώμενοι   despondent
atikhos άτυχος   unlucky
bakhalo μπάχαλο   chaotic mess
davadzis νταβατζής   pimp
dhiaphthora διαφθορά   corruption
dhiakopodhania διακοποδάνεια   vacation loans
dhiakopes διακοπές   holiday break, vacation
dhiefkolinsi διευκόλυνση   facility
dropi ντροπή   shame
dzaba τζάμπα   free
eksostrephis εξωστρεφείς   extroverted
Elladha Ελλάδα   Greece
elpidha ελπίδα   hope
enikiazete ενοικιάζεται   for rent
eortodhania εορτοδάνεια   holiday loans

epistimonas επιστήμονας   scientist, scholar
ethelodhismos εθελοντισμός   volunteerism
evghenia ευγένεια   civility, politeness
gheneodhoria γενναιοδωρία   generosity
ghenos γένος   ancestral group
ipokhreomeni υποχρεωμένοι   indebted
ithiki aftonomia ηθική αυτονομία   moral autonomy
ithiki ipostiriksi ηθική υποστήριξη   moral support
kaimos καημός   yearning/longing
katathlipsi κατάθλιψη   depression
kalozoia καλοζωία   the good life
kephi κέφι   fun or good spirits
kerasma κέρασμα   treating one to drink or food
khalara χαλαρά   relaxed
katakhrisi κατάχρηση   waste of resources
kharatsia χαράτσια   newly implemented taxes
khardziliki χαρτζιλίκι   pocket money
khreomeni χρεωμένοι   in debt
kibariliki κιμπαριλίκι   slang for nobility
kinotita κοινότητα   a community
koroido κορόιδο   sucker
krisi κρίση   crisis
kseni ξένοι   foreigners
ladhoma λάδωμα   metaphorical greasing palms for favors/bribery
lamoghia λαμόγια   corrupt persons
litotita λιτότητα   austerity or frugality
litourghima λειτούργημα   public service
litourghi λειτουργοί   conscientious ministers of society
lovitoures λοβιτούρες   fraudulent activities
metania μετάνοια   repentance
metavasi μετάβαση   transition
mezedhakia μεζεδάκια   appetizers
mezedhopolio μεζεδοπωλείο   snack bar, taverna
miza μίζα   form of bribery to secure resources
nomima νόμιμα   lawfully
omadhika ομαδικά   collectively
ouzeri ουζερί   ouzo-bar, snack bar
parea παρέα   companionship or group of friends
pareborio παρεμπόριο   informal market economy
partakidhes παρτάκηδες   self-serving

pedhia παιδεία   education

phakelaki φακελάκι   "little envelope," form of bribery

philotimo φιλότιμο   love for and attention to honor

philoksenia φιλοξενία   literally, "love of foreigners"; metaphorically, hospitality

phouska φούσκα   bubble

phrapes φραπές   iced, whipped, instant coffee

phrapedoupoli φραπεδούπολη   slang for Thessaloniki, city of frappé

phrodistiria φροντιστήρια   for-pay schools to supplement public education

phtokhomana φτωχομάνα   mother of the poor; refers to Thessaloniki

polis πόλις   city

polite πωλείται   for sale

politismos πολιτισμός   civilization

poniria πονηριά   cunning

proodhos πρόοδος   progress

rouspheti ρουσφέτι   form of bribery

sibonia συμπόνοια   compassion

sibrotevousa συμπρωτεύουσα   co-capital

taverna ταβέρνα   small, family-owned restaurant

ta kone τα κονέ   connections

Thessalonikis Θεσσαλονικείς   Thessalonikians

Thiva Θήβα   Thebes

triti ilikia τρίτη ηλικία   third phase of the life course

volema βόλεμα   personal accommodation

BIBLIOGRAPHY

Agelopoulos, Georgios. 2000. "Political Practices and Multiculturalism: The Case of Salonica." In *Macedonia: The Politics of Identity and Difference*, edited by Jane K. Cowan, 140–155. London: Pluto Press.

Agelopoulos, Georgios. 2008. "Multiple Times, Places and Cultures: Aspects of Modernity in Thessalonica." In *Thessaloniki on the Verge: The City as a Process of Change*, edited by Gregoris Kafkalas, Lois Labrianidis, and Nikos Papadimos, 199–216. Athens: Kritiki Publishers (in Greek).

Agelopoulos, Georgios. 2016. "Ex Nihilo Nihil Fit: On the Greek Crisis." *Hot Spots, Cultural Anthropology* website. https://culanth.org/fieldsights/863-ex-nihilo-nihil-fit-on-the-greek-crisis.

Alexander, Jeffrey C., Ron Eyerman, Bernhard Giesen, Neil J. Smelser, and Piotr Sztompka, eds. 2004. *Cultural Trauma and Collective Identity*. Berkeley: University of California Press.

Allen, Peter. 1979. "Internal Migration and the Changing Dowry in Modern Greece." *Indiana Social Studies Quarterly* 32 (Spring): 142–156.

Anderson, Ben. 2015. "What Kind of Thing Is Resilience?" *Politics* 35, no. 1: 60–66.

Anderson, Elijah. 2012. *The Cosmopolitan Canopy: Race and Civility in Everyday Life*. New York: Norton.

Antonakakis, Nikolaos, and Alan Collins. 2014. "The Impact of Fiscal Austerity on Suicide: On the Empirics of a Modern Greek Tragedy." *Social Science and Medicine* 112(C): 39–50.

Antoniades, Andreas. 2010. *Producing Globalisation: The Politics of Discourse and Institutions in Greece and Ireland*. Manchester: Manchester University Press.

Antonucci, L., M. Hamilton, and S. Roberts, eds. 2014. *Young People and Social Policy in Europe: Dealing with Risk, Inequality and Precarity in Times of Crisis.* Basingstoke: Palgrave Macmillan.

Appadurai, Arjun. 2001. *Globalization.* Durham, NC: Duke University Press.

Appadurai, Arjun. 2006. *Fear of Small Numbers: An Essay on the Geography of Anger.* Durham, NC: Duke University Press.

Argenti, Nicholas, and Daniel M. Knight. 2015. "Sun, Wind, and the Rebirth of Extractive Economies: Renewable Energy Investment and Metanarratives of Crisis in Greece." *Journal of the Royal Anthropological Institute* 21, no. 4: 781–802.

Babcock-Abrahams, Barbara. 1975. "A Tolerated Margin of Mess: The Trickster and His Tales Reconsidered." *Journal of the Folklore Institute* 11, no. 3: 147–186.

Bakalaki, Alexandra. 2016. "Funny." Hot Spots, *Cultural Anthropology.* https://culanth.org/fieldsights/855-funny.

Barrios, Roberto E. 2016. "Resilience: A Commentary from the Vantage Point of Anthropology." *Annals of Anthropological Practice* 40, no. 1: 28–38.

Barth, Fredrik. 1967. "On the Study of Social Change." *American Anthropologist* 69, no. 6: 661–669.

Basta, Maria, Alexandros Vgontzas, Anastasia Kastanaki, Manolis Michalodimitrakis, Katerina Kanaki, Katerina Koutra, Maria Anastasaki, and Panagiotis Simos. 2018. "Suicide Rates in Crete, Greece during the Economic Crisis: The Effect of Age, Gender, Unemployment and Mental Health Service Provision. *BMC Psychiatry* 18(1): 1–4.

Bear, Laura. 2015. *Navigating Austerity: Currents of Debt along a South Asian River.* Stanford, CA: Stanford University Press.

Bear, Laura, and Daniel M. Knight. 2017. "Alternatives to Austerity." *Anthropology Today* 33, no. 5: 1–2.

Bernard, Russell H. 2018 [1999]. *Social Research Methods: Qualitative and Quantitative Approaches.* Lanham, MD: Rowman & Littlefield.

Biehn, Tristan. 2014. "Who Needs Me Most? New Imperialist Ideologies in Youth-Centered Volunteer Abroad Programs." In *Good Intentions: Norms and Practices of Imperial Humanitarianism*, Volume 4, edited by Maximilian C. Forte, 77–87. Montreal: Alert Press.

Bitzenis, A., N. Karagiannis, and J. Marangos. 2015. *Europe in Crisis: Problems, Challenges, and Alternative Perspectives.* New York: Palgrave.

Bloch, Ernst. 1986. *The Principle of Hope.* Translated by Neville Plaice, Stephen Plaice, and Paul Knight. Cambridge, MA: MIT Press.

Boas, Taylor C., and Jordan Gans-Morse. 2009. "Neoliberalism: From New Liberal Philosophy to Anti-Liberal Slogan." *Studies in Comparative International Development* 44, no. 2: 137–161.

Bourdieu, Pierre. 1977. *Outline of a Theory of Practice*. Translated by Richard Nice. Cambridge: Cambridge University Press.

Bourdieu, Pierre. 1984. *Distinction. A Social Critique of the Judgment of Taste*. Translated by Richard Nice. Cambridge, MA: Harvard University Press.

Bourdieu, Pierre. 1994. *The Field of Cultural Production*. New York: Columbia University Press.

Bouziouri Martha and Pigkou-Repousi Myrto. 2014. "Structures and practices of social Solidarity in the Urban Web: New Aspects of Citizenship in Athens During the Crisis [in Greek]." *Scientific Projects 2014*. John S. Latsis Public Benefit Foundation. https://www.latsis-foundation.org/eng accessed September 20, 2019.

Bremer, Björn, and Guillem Vidal. 2018. "From Boom to Bust: A Comparative Analysis of Greece and Spain under Austerity." In *Living Under Austerity: Greek Society in Crisis*, edited by Evdoxios Doxidis and Aimee Placas, 113–140. New York: Berghahn Books.

Bryant, Rebecca. 2016. "On Critical Times: Return, Repetition, and the Uncanny Present." *History and Anthropology* 27, no. 1: 19–31.

Button, Gregory. 2010. *Disaster Culture: Knowledge and Uncertainty in the Wake of Human and Environmental Catastrophe*. Walnut Creek, CA: Left Coast Press, Inc.

Cabot, Heath. 2014. *On the Doorstep of Europe: Asylum and Citizenship in Greece*. Philadelphia: University of Pennsylvania Press.

Campbell, John. 1964. *Honour, Family and Patronage: A Study of the Institutions and Moral Values in a Greek Mountain Community*. Oxford: Oxford University Press.

Cappellini, B., A. Marilli, and E. Parsons. 2014. "The Hidden Work of Coping: Gender and the Micro-politics of Household Consumption in Times of Austerity." *Journal of Marketing Management* 30, no. 15/16: 1597–1624.

Chakrabarty Dipesh, Homi K. Bhabha, Sheldon Pollock, and Carol A. Breckenridge. 2002. *Cosmopolitanism*. Durham, NC: Duke University Press.

Chomsky, Noam. 1999. *Profit Over People: Neoliberalism and Global Order*. New York: Seven Stories Press.

Chrousos, George. P. 1998. "Stressors, Stress, and Neuroendocrine Integration of the Adaptive Response." The 1997 Hans Selye Memorial Lecture. *Annals of the New York Academy of Sciences* 30(851): 311–335.

Clarke, Jennifer, Asteris Huliaras, and Dimitri A. Sotiropoulos, eds. 2015. *Austerity and the Third Sector in Greece: Civil Society at the European Frontline*. New York: Ashgate Publishing.

Clifford, James. 1992. "Traveling Cultures." In *Cultural Studies*, edited by Lawrent Grossberg, Cary Nelson, and Paula A. Treichler, 96–116. London. Routledge.

Coutu, P. 2002. "How Resilience Works." *Harvard Business Review* 80, no. 5: 46–50.

Cowan, Jane K. 1991. "Going out for Coffee? Contesting the Grounds of Gendered Pleasures in Everyday Socialibility." In *Contested Identities: Gender and Kinship in Modern Greece*, edited by Peter Loizos and Evthymios Papataxiarchis, 180–202. Princeton, NJ: Princeton University Press.

Cretney, Raven. 2014. "Resilience for Whom? Emerging Critical Geographies of Socio-ecological Resilience." *Geography Compass* 8, no. 9: 627–640.

Dalakoglou, Dimitris and Georgios Agelopoulos. 2017. *Critical Times in Greece: Anthropological Engagements with the Crisis*. London: Routledge.

Dimen, Muriel, and Ernestine Friedl eds. 1976. *Regional Variation in Modern Greece and Cyprus: Toward a Perspective on the Ethnography of Greece, 268:1-465*. New York: Annals of the New York Academy of Sciences.

Doxiadis, Evdoxios. 2018. "The 'Illegitimacy' of Foreign Loans: Greece, the Great Powers and Foreign Debt in the Long Nineteenth Century." In *Living Under Austerity: Greek Society in Crisis*, edited by Evdoxios Doxiadis and Aiee Placas, 15–45. New York: Berghahn Books.

Doxiadis, Evdoxios, and Aimee Placas. 2018. *Living Under Austerity: Greek Society in Crisis*. New York: Berghahn Books.

Driessen, Henk. 2005. "Mediterranean Port Cities: Cosmopolitanism Reconsidered." *History and Anthropology* 16, no. 1: 129–141.

Dubisch, Jill. 1986. *Gender and Power in Rural Greece*. Princeton, NJ: Princeton University Press.

Dubisch, Jill. 1991. "Gender, Kinship, and Religion: 'Reconstructing' the Anthropology of Greece." In *Contested Identities: Gender and Kinship in Modern Greece*, edited by Peter Loizos and Evthymios Papataxiarchis, 29–46. Princeton, NJ: Princeton University Press.

Dubisch, Jill. 1995. *In a Different Place: Pilgrimage, Gender, and Politics of a Greek Island Shrine*. Princeton, NJ: Princeton University Press.

Du Boulay, Juliet. 1974. *Portrait of a Greek Mountain Village*. New York: Oxford University Press.

Du Boulay, Juliet. 1983. "The Meaning of Dowry: Changing Values in Rural Greece." *Journal of Modern Greek Studies* 1, no. 1: 243–270.

Dzenovska, Dace. 2018. "Emptiness and its Future: Staying and Leaving Tactics of Life in Latvia." *Focaal: Journal of Global and Historical Anthropology* 2018, no. 80: 16–29.

Eckardt, Frank, and Javier Sanchez, eds. 2015. *City of Crisis: The Multiple Contestation of Southern European Cities*. Bielefeld: Verlag.

Economou, Marina, M. Madianos, L. E. Peppou, A. Patelakis, and C. N. Stefanis. 2013. "Major Depression in the Era of Economic Crisis: A Replication of a Cross-Sectional Study across Greece." *Journal of Affect Disorders* 145, no. 3: 308–314.

Edwards, Jeanette. 1998. "The Need for a Bit of History: Place and Past in English Identity." In Locality and Belonging, edited by N. Lovell, 147–167. London: Routledge.

Ehrenreich, Barbara. 1989. *Fear of Falling: The Inner Life of the Middle Class.* New York: Harper Perennial.

Elder, Glen Jr. 1974. *Children of the Great Depression: Social Change in Life Experience.* Chicago: University of Chicago Press.

Ellinas, Antonis A. 2013. "The Rise of Golden Dawn: The New Face of the Far Right in Greece." *South European Society and Politics* 18, no. 4: 543–565.

Erikson, Kai T. 1994. *A New Species of Trouble: Explorations in Disaster, Trauma, and Community.* New York: Norton.

Fainstein, Susan. 2015. "Resilience and Justice." *International Journal of Urban and Regional Research* 39, no. 1: 157–167.

Faubion, James D. 1993. *Modern Greek Lessons: A Primer in Historical Constructivism.* Princeton, NJ: Princeton University Press.

Florida, Richard. 2012 [2002]. *The Rise of the Creative Class, Revisited: Tenth Anniversary Edition.* New York: Basic Books.

Floros, Christos and Ioannis Chatziantoniou, eds. 2017. *The Greek Debt Crisis: In Quest of Growth in Times of Austerity.* New York: Palgrave Macmillan.

Forte, Maximilian C., ed. 2014. *Good Intentions: Norms and Practices of Imperial Humanitarianism.* Montreal: Alert Press.

Foster, George M. 1965. "Peasant Society and the Image of Limited Good." *American Anthropologist* 67, no. 2: 293–315.

Fountoulakis, Konstantinos N. 2014. "Suicide Rates and the Economic Crisis in Europe." *Journal of Psychiatry and Neurological Sciences* 27, no. 1: 1–5.

Freeman, Carla. 2007. The "Reputation" of Neoliberalism. *American Ethnologist* 34(2): 252–267.

Freeman, Carla. 2014. *Entrepreneurial Selves: Neoliberal Respectability and the Making of a Caribbean Middle Class.* Durham, NC: Duke University Press.

Friedl, Ernestine. 1962. *Vasilika: A Village in Modern Greece.* New York: Holt, Rinehart & Winston.

Friedl, Ernestine. 1964. "Lagging Emulation in Post-Peasant Society." *American Anthropologist* 66, no. 3: 569–586.

Frykman, Jonas, and Orvar Lofgren. 1987. *Culture Builders: A Historical Anthropology of Middle-Class Life.* Translated by Alan Crozier. New Brunswick: NJ: Rutgers University Press.

Frykman, Maja P. 2012. "An Anthropology of War and Recovery: Lived War Experiences." In *A Companion to the Anthropology of Europe,* edited by Ullrich Kockel, Mairead Nic Craith, and Jonas Frykman, 253–274. Chichester: Wiley-Blackwell.

Gallant, Thomas. 2016 [2001]. *Modern Greece: From the War of Independence to the Present*. Oxford: Oxford University Press.

Ganti, Tejaswini. 2014. "Neoliberalism." *Annual Review of Anthropology* 43, no. 1: 89–104.

Gellner, Ernest, and John Waterbury, eds. 1977. *Patrons and Clients in Mediterranean Societies*. London: Duckworth.

Gemenetzi, Georgia. 2017. "Thessaloniki: The Changing Geography of the City and the Role of Spatial Planning." *Cities* 64(April): 88–97.

Gennep, Arnold Van. 1960 [1909]. *The Rites of Passage*. Translated by Monica Vizedom and Gabrielle L. Caffee. Chicago: University of Chicago Press.

Giddens, Anthony. 1984. *The Constitution of Society: Outline of the Theory of Structuration*. Cambridge: Polity Press.

Giddens, Anthony. 1990. *The Consequences of Modernity*. Stanford, CA: Stanford University Press.

Giddens, Anthony. 1991. *Modernity and Self-Identity: Self and Society in the Later Modern Age*. Redwood City, CA: Stanford University Press.

Giddens, Anthony. 2007. *Europe in the Global Age*. Cambridge: Polity Press.

Giesen, Bernhard. 2015. "Inbetweeness and Ambivalence." In *Breaking Boundaries: Varieties of Liminality*, edited by Agnes Horvath, Bjorn Thoassen, and Harald Wydra, 61–71. New York: Berghahn Books.

Goddard, Victoria A., Joseph R. Llobera, and Cris Shore. 1994. *The Anthropology of Europe: Identities and Boundaries in Conflict*. Oxford: Berghahn Books.

Goldstein, Amy. 2017. *Janesville: An American Story*. New York: Simon & Schuster.

Gounaris, Basil C. 2008. "Bonds Made Power: Clientelism, Nationalism, and Party Strategies in Greek Macedonia (1900–1950)." In *Networks of Power in Modern Greece*, edited by M. Mazower, 109–128. Oxford: Oxford University Press.

Graeber, David. 2014. *Debt*. Brooklyn, NY: Melville House Publishing.

Gramsci, Antonio. 1971. *Selections from the Prison Notebooks*. Edited and translated by Quintin Hoare and Geoffrey Novell-Smith. London: Lawrence and Wishart.

Grigoriadou, Aikaterini. 2018. "Orfean Harmony: An Ensemble's Creation Of Ancient Greek Music As Ode To The Resilience Of Modern Greece." *MA Thesis*, Georgia State University, https://scholarworks.gsu.edu/anthro_theses/132.

Guano, Emanuela. 2010. "Taxpayers, Thieves, and the State: Fiscal Citizenship in Contemporary Italy." *Ethnos* 75, no. 4: 377–401.

Guano, Emanuela. 2015. "Touring the Hidden City: Walking Tour Guides in Postindustrial Genoa." *City and Society* 27, no. 2: 160–182.

Guano, Emanuela. 2017. *Creative Urbanity: An Italian Middle Class in the Shade of Revitalization*. Philadelphia: University of Pennsylvania Press.

Habermas, Jürgen. 1989. *The Structural Transformation of the Public Sphere: An Inquiry into a Category of Bourgeois Society*. Translated by Thomas Burger and Frederick Lawrence. Cambridge, MA: The MIT Press.

Hadjimichalis, Costis. 2011. "Uneven Geographical Development and Socio-spatial Justice and Solidarity: European Regions after the 2009 Financial Crisis." *European Urban and Regional Studies* 18, no. 3: 254–274.

Hage, Ghassan 2009. "Waiting Out the Crisis: On Stuckedness and Governmentality." In *Waiting*, edited by Ghassan Hage, 97–106. Carlton, VIC: Melbourne University Press.

Haller, Dieter, and Cris Shore, eds. 2005. *Corruption: Anthropological Perspectives*. London: Pluto Press.

Hannerz, Ulf. 1996. *Transnational Connections: Culture, People, Places*. London: Routledge.

Hannerz, Ulf. 2004. "Cosmopolitanism." In *A Companion to the Anthropology of Politics*, edited by David Nugent and Joan Vincent, 69–85. Oxford: Blackwell.

Hanink, Johanna. 2017. *The Classical Debt: Greek Antiquity in an Era of Austerity*. Cambridge, MA: Harvard University Press.

Hart, Laurie K. 1992. *Time, Religion, and Social Experience in Rural Greece*. Lanham, MD: Rowman & Littlefield.

Hart, Laurie K. 2008. "Culture, Civilization and Demarcations in the Northwest Border of Greece." *American Ethnologist* 26, no. 1: 196–220.

Harvey, David. 2000. *Spaces of Hope*. Berkeley: University of California Press.

Harvey, David. 2005. *A Brief History of Neoliberalism*. New York: Oxford University Press.

Hastaoglou-Martinidis, Vilma. 1998. "A Mediterranean City in Transition:Thessaloniki Between the Two World Wars." *Scientitific Journal Facta Universitatis* (March): 493–507. https://pdfs.semanticscholar.org/dd73/e7ef8dd9821c8f80def94e9d9b916e279b4c.pdf.

Hatzidaki, Ourania, and Dionysis Goutsos, eds. 2017. *Greece in Crisis: Combining Critical Discourse and Corpus Linguistics Perspectives*. Amsterdam/Philadelphia: John Benjamins Publishing Company.

Hatziprokopiou, Panos A. 2006. *Globalisation, Migration and Socio-economic Change in Contemporary Greece: Processes of Social Incorporation of Balkan Immigrants in Thessaloniki*. Amsterdam: Amsterdam University Press.

Hatziprokopiou, Panos A. 2012. "Haunted by the Past and the Ambivalences of the Present: Immigration and Thessalonikica's Second Path to Cosmopolitanism." In *Post-Cosmopolitan Cities: Explorations of Urban Coexistence*, edited by Caroline Humphrey and Vera Skvirskaja, 194–216. New York: Berghahn Books.

Heiman, Rachel, Mark Liechty, and Carla Freeman. 2012. "Introduction: Charting an Anthropology of the Middle Classes." In *The Global Middle Classes: Theorizing Through Ethnography*, edited by Rachel Heiman, Carla Freeman, and Mark Liechty, 1–30. Santa Fe, NM: School for Advanced Research Press.

Herzfeld, Michael. 1982. *Ours Once More: Folklore, Ideology and the Making of Modern Greece*. Austin: University of Texas Press.

Herzfeld, Michael. 1985. *The Poetics of Manhood: Contest and Identity in a Cretan Mountain Village*. Princeton, NJ: Princeton University Press.

Herzfeld, Michael. 1991. *A Place in History: Social and Monumental Time in a Cretan Town*. Princeton, NJ: Princeton University Press.

Herzfeld, Michael. 1992. *The Social Production of Indifference: Exploring the Symbolic Roots of Western Bureaucracy*. Oxford: Berg Publishers.

Herzfeld, Michael. 1999 [1987]. *Anthropology through the Looking-Glass: Critical Ethnography in the Margins of Europe*. Cambridge: Cambridge University Press.

Herzfeld, Michael. 2002. "The Absent Presence: Discourses of Crypto-Colonialism." *South Atlantic Quarterly* 101, no. 4: 900–926.

Herzfeld, Michael. 2005. *Cultural Intimacy: Social Poetics in the Nation State*. 2nd ed. New York: Routledge.

Herzfeld, Michael. 2009. *Evicted from Eternity: The Restructuring of Modern Rome*. Chicago: University of Chicago Press.

Herzfeld, Michael. 2015. "Heritage and Corruption: The Two Faces of the Nation-State." *International Journal of Heritage Studies* 21, no. 6: 531–544.

Herzfeld, Michael. 2016a. "The Hypocrisy of European Moralism: Greece and the Politics of Cultural Aggression—Part 1." *Anthropology Today* 32, no. 1: 10–13.

Herzfeld, Michael. 2016b. "The Hypocrisy of European Moralism: Greece and the Politics of Cultural Aggression—Part 2." *Anthropology Today* 32, no. 2: 10–13.

Hirschon, Renee. 1998 [1989]. *Heirs of the Greek Catastrophe: The Social Life of Asia Minor Refugees in Piraeus*. Oxford: Berghahn Books.

Ho, Karen. 2009. *Liquidated: An Ethnography of Wall Street*. Durham, NC: Duke University Press.

Hoffman, Susanna M. 2016. "The Question of Culture Continuity and Change after Disaster." *Annals of Anthropological Practice* 40, no. 1: 39–51.

Hoffman, Susanna M., and Anthony Oliver-Smith. 2002. *Catastrophe and Culture: The Anthropology of Disaster*. Santa Fe, NM: School for Advanced Research Press.

Holton, R. J. 1987. "The Idea of Crisis in Modern Society." *British Journal of Sociology* 38, no. 4: 502–520.

Horvath, Agnes, Bjørn Thomassen, and Harald Wydra. 2009. "Introduction: Liminality and Cultures of Change." *International Political Anthropology* 2, no. 1: 3–4.

Horvath, Agnes, Bjørn Thomassen, and Harald Wydra. 2015. *Breaking Boundaries: Varieties of Liminality*. New York: Berghahn Books.

Hynes, William J. 1997. "Inconclusive Inconclusions: Tricksters as Metaplayers and Revealers." In *Mythical Trickster Figures*, edited by William J. Hynes and William G. Doty, 202–217. Tuscaloosa: University of Alabama Press.

Inda, Jonatan Xavier and Renato Rosaldo, eds. 2008. *The Anthropology of Globalization: A Reader* (2nd ed.). Malden, MA: Blackwell Publishing.

Joseph, Jonathan. 2013. "Resilience as Embedded Neoliberalism: A Governmentality Approach." *International Policies, Practices, and Discourses* 1, no. 1: 35–52.

Kafkalas, Gregoris, Lois Lambrianidis, and Nikos Papamihos, eds. 2008. *Thessaloniki on the Verge: The City as Process of Changes*. Athens: Kritiki Publishers (in Greek).

Kallianiotis, Ioannis N. 2013. "Privatization in Greece and its Negative Effects on the Nation's Social Welfare (Expropriation of the National Wealth)." *Journal of Business and Economic Studies* 19, no. 1: 1–23.

Kalyvas, Stathis N. 2015. *Modern Greece: What Everyone Needs to Know*. New York: Oxford University Press.

Kamaras, Antonis. 2008. "The Relationship of Athens-Thessaloniki in the Context of Market Reforms." In *Thessaloniki on the Edge: The City as a Process of Changes*, edited by G. Kafkalas, L. Labrianidis, and N. Papamihos, 361–390. Athens: Kritiki Publishers.

Kamat, Sangeeta. 2004. "The Privatization of Public Interest: Theorizing NGO Discourse in a Neoliberal Era." *Review of International Political Economy* 11, no. 1: 155–176.

Katsiardi-Hering, Olga. 2011. "City-ports in the Eastern and Central Mediterranean from the Mid-sixteenth to the Nineteenth Century: Urban and Social Aspects." *Mediterranean Historical Review* 26, no. 2: 151–170.

Kazana, Ioulia. 2018. "Women in Crisis? How Young Greek Women Navigate 'Emerging Adulthood' following the Effects of the 2008 Economic Crisis." PhD diss., University of Surrey. http://epubs.surrey.ac.uk/849594/.

Kazantzakis, Nikos. 1960. The Saviors of God: Spiritual Exercises. Translated by Kimon Friar. New York, NY: Simon and Schuster.

Kirtsoglou, Elizabeth. 2013. "The Dark Ages of the Golden Dawn: Anthropological Analysis and Responsibility in the Twilight Zone of the Greek Crisis." *Suomen Antropologi Journal of the Finnish Anthropological Society* 38(1): 104–108.

Kirtsoglou, Elisabeth, and Dimitrios Theodossopoulos. 2010. "Intimacies of Anti-Globalization: Imagining Unhappy Others as Oneself in Greece." In *United in Discontent: Local Responses to Cosmopolitanism and Globalization*, edited by Dimitrios Theodossopoulos and Elisabeth Kirtsoglou, 83–102. Oxford: Berghahn Books.

Knight, Daniel M. 2012a. "Cultural Proximity: Crisis, Time and Social Memory in Central Greece." *History and Anthropology* 23, no. 3: 349–374.

Knight, Daniel M. 2012b. "Turn of the Screw: Narratives of History and Economy in the Greek Crisis." *Journal of Mediterranean Studies* 21, no. 1: 53–76.

Knight, Daniel M. 2015a. *History, Time, and Economic Crisis in Central Greece.* New York: Palgrave Macmillan.

Knight, Daniel M. 2015b. "Wit and Greece's Economic Crisis: Ironic Slogans, Food, and Antiausterity Sentiments." *American Ethnologist* 42, no. 2: 230–246.

Knight, Daniel M., and Charles Stewart. 2016. "Ethnographies of Austerity: Temporality, Crisis and Affect in Southern Europe." *History and Anthropology* 27, no. 1: 1–18.

Koliopoulos, John S., and Thanos M. Veremis. 2002. *Greece: A Modern Sequel.* New York, NY: New York University Press.

Koliopoulos, John S., and Thanos M. Veremis. 2010. *Modern Greece: A History Since 1821.* Oxford: Wiley.

Konner, Melvin. 2007. "Trauma, Adaptation, and Resilience: A Cross-Cultural and Evolutionary Perspective." In *Understanding Trauma: Integrating Biological, Clinical, and Cultural Perspectives*, edited by Laurence J. Kirmayer, Robert Lemelson, and Mark Barad, 300–337. Cambridge: Cambridge University Press.

Koselleck, Reinhart. 2006. "Crisis." *Journal of the History of Ideas* 67, no. 2: 357–400.

Kosmatopoulos, Nikolaos. 2014. "Crisis Works." *Social Anthropology: The Journal of the European Association of Social Anthropologists* 22(4): 479–486.

Kottak, Conrad P. 1991. "When People Don't Come First: Some Lessons from Completed Projects." In *Putting People First: Sociological Variables in Rural Development*, 2nd edition, edited by M. Cernea, 429–464. New York: Oxford University Press.

Kourtesis, Artemis. 2008. "Creative Cities and Thessaloniki." In *Thessaloniki on the Edge: The City as a Process of Changes*, edited by G. Kafkalas, L. Labrianidis, and N. Papamihos, 265–293. Athens: Kritiki Publishers.

Koutsou, Stavriani, Maria Patsalidou, and Athanasios Rajot. 2014. "Young Farmers' Social Capital in Greece: Trust Levels and Collective Action." *Journal of Rural Studies* 34(April): 204–211.

Kozaitis, Kathryn A. 1997. "Strangers among Strangers: Social Organization among the Roma of Athens, Greece." *Urban Anthropology and Studies of Cultural Systems and World Economic Development* 26, no. 2: 165–199.

Kozaitis, Kathryn A. 2002. "Embrace of Shelter: Cultural Hybridism among the Roma of Athens, Greece." In *Ethnologia, Special issue on The Roma of Greece*, 137–168. Athens: Ethnological Society of Greece.

Labrianidis, Lois. 2011. *Investing in Leaving: The Greek Case of International Migration of Professionals in the Globalization Era*. Athens: Kritiki.

Labrianidis, Lois, and Nikos Vogiatzis. 2013. "Highly Skilled Migration: What Differentiates the 'Brains' who are Drained from Those Who Return in the Case of Greece." *Population, Space and Place* 19, no. 5: 427–486.

Lahad, Mooli, Ran Cohen, Stratos Fanaras, Dimitry Leykin, and Penny Apostolopoulou. 2016. "Resiliency and Adjustment in Times of Crisis, the Case of the Greek Economic Crisis from a Psycho-social and Community Perspective." *Social Indicators Research: An International and Interdisciplinary Journal for Quality-of-life Measurement* 135, no. 1: 333–356.

Loftsdóttir, Kristín, Andrea L. Smith, and Brigitte Hipfl, eds., 2017. *Messy Europe: Crisis, Race, and Nation-State in a Postcolonial World*. New York, NY: Berghahn.

Loftsdóttir, Kristín and L. Jensen. 2014. "Introduction." In *Crisis in the Nordic Nations and Beyond*, edited by K. Lofdóttir and L. Jensen, 1–8. Surrey: Ashgate.

Loizos, P. 1977. *Politics and Patronage in a Cypriot Village*. Oxford: Blackwell.

Loizos, Peter, and Evthymios Papataxiarchis, eds. 1991. *Contested Identities: Gender and Kinship in Modern Greece*. Princeton, NJ: Princeton University Press.

Macdonald, Sharon. 2012. "Presencing Europe's Pasts." In *A Companion to the Anthropology of Europe*, edited by Ulrich Kockel, Mairead Nic Craith and Jonas Frykman, 232–245. Chichester: Wiley-Blackwell.

Mains, Daniel. 2011. *Hope is Cut: Youth, Unemployment and the Future in Urban Ethiopia*. Philadelphia, PA: Temple University Press.

Mandel, Ruth. 2008. *Cosmopolitan Anxieties: Turkish Challenges to Citizenship and Belonging in Germany*. Durham: NC: Duke University Press.

Margomenou, Despina, and Faidra Papavasiliou. 2013. "Times of Crisis and Seeds of New Intimacies on a North Aegean Island: Activism, Alternative Exchange Networks, and Re-Imagined Communities." *Studies in Ethnicity and Nationalism* 13, no. 3: 523–529.

Markowitz, Fran. 2010. *Sarajevo: A Bosnian Kaleidoscope*. Champaign, IL: University of Illinois Press.

Marsh, Leslie L., and Hongmei Li. 2016. *The Middle Class in Emerging Societies: Consumers, Lifestyles and Markets*. New York: Routledge.

Matsaganis, Manos. 2014. "The Catastrophic Greek Crisis." *Current History* 113, no. 761: 110–116.

Matsaganis, Manos, and Chrysa Leventi. 2014. "The Distributional Impact of Austerity and the Recession in Southern Europe." *South European Society and Politics* 19, no. 3: 393–412.

Mauss, Marcel. 1967 [1925]. *The Gift*. Translated by Ian Cunnison. New York: Norton.

Mazower, Mark. 2006. *Salonica City of Ghosts: Christians, Muslims, and Jews 1430–1950*. New York: Random House.

Mazower, Mark. 2008. *Networks of Power in Modern Greece: Essays in Honor of John Campbell*. New York: Columbia University Press.

Mitsopoulos, Michael, and Theodore Pelagidis. 2012. *Understanding the Crisis in Greece: From Boom to Bust*. New York: Palgrave Macmillan.

Mouzelis, Nicos P. 1978. *Modern Greece: Facets of Underdevelopment*. New York: Holmes & Meier.

Muehlebach, Andrea. 2012. *The Moral Neoliberal: Welfare and Citizenship in Italy*. Chicago: University of Chicago Press.

Müller, Martin. 2015. "What Makes an Event a Mega-Event? Definitions and Sizes." *Leisure Studies* 34, no. 6: 627–642.

Narayan, Kirin. 1993. "How Native Is a 'Native' Anthropologist?" *American Anthropologist* 95, no. 3: 671–686.

Narotzky, Susana. 2012. "Europe in Crisis: Grassroots Economies and the Anthropological Turn." *Etnografica* 16, no. 3: 627–638.

Narotzky, Susana. 2016. "Between Inequality and Injustice: Dignity as a Motive for Mobilization During the Crisis." *History and Anthropology* 27, no. 1: 74–92.

Narotzky, Susana, and Niko Besnier. 2014. "Crisis, Value, and Hope: Rethinking the Economy." *Current Anthropology* 55, no. 9: 4–16.

Narotzky, Susana, and Victoria Goddard, eds. 2017. *Work and Livelihoods: History, Ethnography and Models in Times of Crisis*. New York: Routledge.

Neofotistos, Vasiliki. 2008. "'The Balkans' Other Within': Imaginings of the West in the Republic of Macedonia." *History and Anthropology* 19, no. 1: 17–36.

Newman, Katherine S. 1999 [1988]. *Falling From Grace: Downward Mobility in the Age of Affluence*. Berkeley: University of California Press.

Newman, Katherine S. 2012. *The Accordion Family: Boomerang Kids, Anxious Parents, and the Private Toll of Global Competition*. Boston: Beacon Press.

Newman, Katherine, and S. Aptekar. 2007. "'Sticking Around: Delayed Departure from the Parental Nest in Western Europe and Japan.'" In *The Price of Independence: The Economics of the Transition to Adulthood*, edited by S. Danziger and C. Rouse, 207–230. New York: Russell Sage Foundation Press.

Nishida, Hiroko. 2005. "Cultural Schema Theory." In *Theorizing About Intercultural Communication*, edited by William B. Gudykunst, 401–418. Sage Publications.

Oldenburg, Ray. 1999 [1989]. *The Great Good Place. Cafes, Coffee Shops, Community Centers, Beauty Parlors, General Stores, Bars, Hangouts, and How They Get You Through the Day*. St. Paul, MN: Paragon House.

Oliver-Smith, Anthony. 1996. "Anthropological Research on Hazards and Disasters." *Annual Review of Anthropology* 25: 303–328.

Oliver-Smith, Anthony, and Susanna Hoffman, eds. 1999. *The Angry Earth: Disasters in Anthropological Perspective*. New York: Routledge.

Ortner, Sherry. 2006. *Anthropology and Social Theory: Culture, Power, and the Acting Subject*. Durham, NC: Duke University Press.

Öztürk, Serdar. 2015. "Effects of Global Financial Crisis on Greek Economy: Causes of Present Economic and Political Loss of Prestige." *International Journal of Managerial Studies and Research* 3, no. 6: 26–35.

Pagden, Anthony, ed. 2002. *The Idea of Europe: From Antiquity to the European Union*. Washington, DC: Woodrow Wilson Center Press.

Panourgia, Neni. 2009. *Dangerous Citizens: The Greek Left and the Terror of the State*. New York: Fordham University Press.

Panourgia, Neni. 2017. "New Poor: The Being, the Phenomenon, and the Becoming in Greek Crisis." In *Critical Times in Greece: Anthropological Engagements with the Crisis*, edited by Dimitris Dalakoglou and Georgios Agelopoulos, 133–147. London: Routledge.

Papadaki, Marina, and Stefania Kalogeraki. 2017. "Social Support Actions as Forms of Building Community Resilience at the Onset of the Crisis in Urban Greece: The Case of Chania." *Partecipazione e conflitto* 10, no. 1: 193–220.

Papadimitriou, Lydia. 2016. "The Hindered Drive Toward Internationalization: Thessaloniki (International) Film Festival." *New Review of Film and Television Studies* 14, no. 1: 93–111.

Papataxiarchis, Evthymios. 2016. "Unwrapping Solidarity? Society Reborn in Austerity." *Social Anthropology* 24, no. 2: 205–210.

Pardo, Italo, ed. 2004. *Between Morality and Law: Corruption, Anthropology and Comparative Society*. London: Routledge.

Patico, Jennifer. 2008. *Consumption and Social Change in a Post-Soviet Middle Class*. Redwood City, CA: Stanford University Press.

Peebles, Gustav. 2010. "The Anthropology of Credit and Debt." *Annual Review of Anthropology* 39: 22540.

Pemble, John. 1987. *The Mediterranean Passion: Victorians and Edwardians in the South*. Oxford: Oxford University Press.

Perucca, Giovanni. 2014. "The Role of Territorial Capital in Local Economic Growth: Evidence from Italy." *European Planning Studies* 22(3): 537–562.

Petmesidou, Maria. 1991. "Statism, Social Policy and the Middle Classes in Greece." *Journal of European Social Policy* 1, no. 1: 31–48.

Pipyrou, Stavroula. 2014. "Cutting Bella Figura: Irony, Crisis, and Secondhand Clothes in South Italy." *American Ethnologist* 41, no. 3: 532–546.

Placas, Aimee. 2018. "Disrupted and Disrupting Consumption." In *Living Under Austerity: Greek Society in Crisis*, edited by Evdoxios Doxiadis and Aimee Placas, 321–346. New York: Berghahn Books.

Prothmann, Sebastian. 2019. "'Opportunistic Waiting': Tea and Young Men's Gathering in Pikine, Senegal." *City & Society* 31, no. 2: 1–19.

Quarantelli, E. L., and Russell R. Dynes. 1977. "Response to Social Crisis and Disaster." *Annual Review of Sociology* 3: 23–49.

Rakopoulos, Theodoros. 2014a. "Resonance of Solidarity: Meanings of a Local Concept in Anti-austerity Greece." *Journal of Modern Greek Studies* 32, no. 2: 313–337.

Rakopoulos, Theodoros. 2014b. "The Crisis Seen from Below, Within, and Against: From Solidarity Economy to Food Distribution Cooperatives in Greece." *Dialectical Anthropology* 38, no. 2: 189–207.

Rakopoulos, Theodoros. 2015. "Solidarity's Tensions: Informality, Sociality, and the Greek Crisis." *Social Analysis* 59, no. 3: 85–104.

Rakopoulos, Theodoros. 2016. "Solidarity: The Egalitarian Tensions of a Bridge-Concept." *Social Anthropology* 24, no. 2: 142–151.

Rakopoulos, Theodoros. 2017. *The Global Life of Austerity: Comparing Beyond Europe.* New York: Berghahn Books.

Ranci, C. 2014. *Social Vulnerability in European Cities: The Role of Local Welfare in Times of Crisis.* Basingstoke: Palgrave.

Ray, Paul H., and Sherry Ruth Anderson. 2000. *The Cultural Creatives: How 50 Million People are Changing the World.* New York: NY Harmony Books.

Richards, Greg. 2007. *Cultural Tourism: Global and Local Perspectives.* New York: The Haworth Hospitality Press.

Riessman, Catherine K. 1993. *Narrative Analysis.* Newbury Park, CA: Sage Publications.

Roitman, Janet. 2014. *Anti-Crisis.* Durham, NC: Duke University Press.

Roniger, Luis. 2004. "Review: Political Clientelism, Democracy, and Market Economy." *Comparative Politics* 36(3): 353–375. http://www.jstor.org/stable/4150135 Accessed: 08/23/17.

Rostow, Walt W. 1952. *The Process of Economic Growth.* New York, NY: W. W. Norton.

Rostow, Walt W. 1960. The Stages of Economic Growth: A Non-communist Manifesto. Cambridge, UK: Cambridge University Press.

Rozakou, Katerina. 2016a. "Crafting the Volunteer: Voluntary Associations and the Reformation of Sociality." *Journal of Modern Greek Studies* 34, no. 1: 79–102.

Rozakou, Katerina. 2016b. "Socialites of Solidarity: Revising the Gift Taboo in Times of Crisis." *Social Anthropology* 24, no. 2: 185–199.

Ruprecht, Louis A. Jr. 2016. "The Agony of Inclusion: Historical Greece and European Myths." *Arion* 24, no. 1: 65–85.

Ruprecht, Louis A. Jr. 2018. "Who Owes What to Whom? Some Classical Reflections on Debt, Greek and Otherwise." *Arion* 26, no. 1: 165–194.

Rutherford Jonathan, and Sally Davison, eds. 2012. *The Neoliberal Crisis.* London: Lawrence and Winshart.

Sabaté, Irene. 2016. "The Spanish Mortgage Crisis and the Reemergence of Moral Economies in Uncertain Times." *History and Anthropology* 26, no. 1: 107–120.

Sakellaropoulos, Spyros. 2010. "The Recent Economic Crisis in Greece and the Strategy of Capital." *Journal of Modern Greek Studies* 28, no. 2: 321–348.

Sakwa, Richard. 2015. "Liminality and Postcommunism: The Twenty-First Century as Subject of History." In *Breaking Boundaries: Varieties of Liminality*, edited by Agnes Horvath, Bjorn Thoassen, and Harald Wydra, 205–225. New York: Berghahn Books.

Sawyer, Keith. 2001. "Emergence in Sociology: Contemporary Philosophy of Mind and Some Implications for Sociological Theory." *American Journal of Sociology* 107(3): 551–585.

Schuller, Mark. 2009. "Gluing Globalization: NGOs as intermediaries in Haiti." *Political and Legal Anthropology Review* 32(1): 84–104.

Shevchenko, Olga. 2009. *Crisis and the Everyday in Postsocialist Moscow.* Bloomington: Indiana University Press.

Shore, Chris. 2000. *Building Europe: The Cultural Politics of European Integration.* London: Routledge.

Shore, Chris, and Susan Wright. 1997. *Anthropology of Policy: Critical Perspectives on Governance and Power.* New York: Routledge.

Simou, Effie, and Eleni Koutsogeorgou. 2014. "Effects of the Economic Crisis on Health and Healthcare in Greece in the Literature from 2009 to 2013: A Systematic Review." *Health Policy* 115, no. 2-3: 111–119.

Smith, Andrew. 2012. *Events and Urban Regeneration: The Strategic Use of Events to Revitalize Cities.* New York: Routledge.

Spyridakis, Manos. 2013. *The Liminal Worker: An Ethnography of Work, Unemployment and Precariousness in Contemporary Greece.* Burlington, VT: Ashgate Publishing Company.

Stanley, Jason. 2018. *How Fascism Works: The Politics of Us and Them.* New York: Random House.

Steger, M. B., and R. K. Roy. 2010. *Neoliberalism: A Very Short Introduction.* Oxford: Oxford University Press.

Stewart, Charles. 2014. *Colonizing the Greek Mind? The Reception of Western Psychotherapeutics in Greece.* Athens: The American College of Greece.

Stout, Noelle. 2019. *Dispossessed: How Predatory Bureaucracy Foreclosed on the American Middle Class.* Berkeley, CA: University of California Press.

Strauss, Claudia, and Naomi Quinn. 2001 [1997]. *A Cognitive Theory of Cultural Meaning.* New York: Cambridge University Press.

Sutton, David. 1998. *Memories Cast in Stone: The Relevance of the Past in Everyday Life.* London: Routledge.

Swyngedouw, Erik. 2008. "The Cities on the Edge: Resettlement of the City in the 21st Century." In *Thessaloniki on the Edge: The City as a Process of Changes,* edited by G. Kafkalas, L. Labrianidis, and N. Papamihos, 69–94. Athens: Kritiki Publishers.

Theodossopoulos, Dimitrios. 2013. "Infuriated with the Infuriated? Blaming Tactics and Discontent about the Greek Financial Crisis." *Current Anthropology* 54, no. 2: 200–221.

Theodossopoulos, Dimitrios. 2014. "The Ambivalence of Anti-Austerity Indignation in Greece: Resistance, Hegemony and Complicity." *History and Anthropology* 25, no. 4: 488–506.

Thomassen, Bjorn. 2009. "The Uses of Liminality." *International Political Anthropology* 2, no. 1: 5–27.

Thomassen, Bjørn. 2015. "Thinking with Liminality: To the Boundaries of an Anthropological Concept." In *Breaking Boundaries: Varieties of Liminality,* edited by Agnes Horvath, Bjorn Thomassen and Harald Wydra, 39–58. New York: Berghahn Books.

Toby, Lee K. 2012. "Festival, City, State: Cultural Citizenship at the Thessaloniki Film Festival." In *Coming Soon to a Festival Near You: Programming Film Festivals,* edited by Jeffrey Ruoff, 1–16. St. Andrews, Scotland: St. Andrews Film Studies.

Triandafyllidou, Anna, and Ruby Gropas. 2014. "Voting with their Feed: Highly Skilled Emigrants from Southern Europe." *American Behavioral Scientist* 58, no. 12: 1614–1633.

Triandafyllidou, Anna, Ruby Gropas, and Hara Kouki, eds. 2013. *The Greek Crisis and European Modernity.* Basingstoke: Palgrave Macmillan.

Turner, Edith. 2012. *Communitas: The Anthropology of Collective Joy.* New York: Palgrave Macmillan.

Turner, Victor W. 1995 [1969]. *The Ritual Process. Structure and Anti-Structure.* Ithaca, NY: Cornell University Press.

Tzanelli, Rodanthi. 2004. "Giving Gifts (and then Taking them Back): Identity, Reciprocity and Symbolic Power in the Context of Athens 2004." *Journal of Cultural Research* 8, no. 4: 425–446.

Tzanelli, Rodanthi. 2011. "Domesticating the Touristic Gate in Thessaloniki's Prigipos." *Ethnography* 13, no. 3: 278–305.

Tzanelli, Rodanthi. 2012. "Domesticating Sweet Sadness: Thessaloniki's Glykà as a Travel Narrative." *Cultural Studies-Critical Methodologies* 12, no. 2: 159–172.

Tzanelli, Rodanthi. 2016. "Tourism in the European Economic Crisis: Mediatized Worldmaking and New Tourist Imaginaries in Greece." *Tourist Studies* 16, no. 3: 296–314.

Vacalopoulos, Apostolos, E. 1972. *A History of Thessaloniki.* Translated by T. F. Carney. Thessaloniki, Greece: Institute for Balkan Studies.

Vaiou, Dina, and Ares Kalandides. 2017. "Practices of Solidarity in Athens. Reconfigurations of Public Space and Urban Citizenship." *Citizenship Studies* 21, no. 4: 440–454.

Walker, Jeremy, and Melinda Cooper. 2011. "Geneologies of Resilience: From Systems Ecology to the Political Economy of Crisis Adaptation." *Security Dialogue* 42, no. 2: 143–160.

Wallerstein, Immanuel. 2004. "The Modern World Systems in Crisis: Bifurcation, Chaos and Choices." In *World-Systems Analysis*, 76–90. Durham, NC: Duke University Press.

Wallerstein, Immanuel, and Charles Lemert, and Carlos Antonio Aguirre Rojas. 2013. *Uncertain Worlds: World Systems Analysis in Changing Times.* Boulder, CO: Paradigm Publishers.

Werbner, Pnina. 2006. "Vernacular Cosmopolitanism." *Theory, Culture and Society* 23, no. 2–3: 496–498.

Wolf, Eric R. 2010 [1982]. *Europe and the People without History.* Berkeley: University of California Press.

Woodhouse, C. M. 1977 [1968]. *Modern Greece: A Short History.* London: Faber and Faber.

Zaharopoulos, Thimios, and Manny E. Paraschos. 1993. *Mass Media in Greece: Power, Politics, and Privatization.* Westport, CT: Praeger.

Zambarloukou, Stella. 2015. "Greece After the Crisis: Still a South European Welfare Model?" *European Societies* 17, no. 5: 653–673.

Zhang, Li. 2010. *In Search of Paradise: Middle-Class Living in a Chinese Metropolis.* Ithaca, NY: Cornell University Press.

Zournazi, Mary, ed. 2002. *Hope: New Philosophies of Change.* New York, NY: Routledge.

INDEX

....

Figures are indicated by *f* and maps by *m*, respectively, following the page number.